Step-by-Step

COVER LETTERS

Build an Cover Letter in 10 Easy
Steps Using Personal Branding

Evelyn U. Salvador

Certified Resume Writer and Career Coach

Step-by-Step Cover Letters

© 2011 by Evelyn U. Salvador

Published by JIST Works, an imprint of JIST Publishing
7321 Shadeland Station, Suite 200
Indianapolis, IN 46256-3923
Phone: 800-648-JIST   Fax: 877-454-7839   E-mail: info@jist.com

Visit our Web site at **www.jist.com** for information on JIST, tables of contents, sample pages, and ordering instructions for our many products!

Quantity discounts are available for JIST books. Please call our Sales Department at 800-648-5478 for a free catalog and more information.

Trade Product Manager: Lori Cates Hand
Development Editor: Heather Stith
Cover Designer: Aleata Halbig
Page Layout: Toi Davis
Proofreaders: Laura Bowman, Jeanne Clark
Indexer: Kelly D. Henthorne

Printed in the United States of America
15 14 13 12 11 10   9 8 7 6 5 4 3 2 1

Library of Congress Cataloging-in-Publication Data

Salvador, Evelyn U., 1952-
   Step-by-step cover letters : build a cover letter in 10 easy steps using personal branding / Evelyn U. Salvador.
         p. cm.
   Includes index.
ISBN 978-1-59357-780-3 (bound-in cd-rom : alk. paper)
 1. Cover letters. I. Title.
   HF5383.S247 2011
   650.14'2--dc22
                                        2010027700

We have been careful to provide accurate information in this book, but it is possible that errors and omissions have been introduced. Please consider this in making any career plans or other important decisions. Trust your own judgment above all else and in all things.

Trademarks: All brand names and product names used in this book are trade names, service marks, trademarks, or registered trademarks of their respective owners.

ISBN 978-1-59357-780-3

About This Book

My goal in this book is to give you precisely what you need to write a top-notch, high-impact, marketing-savvy, persuasive, and compelling cover letter so you don't have to wade through tons of books and make an already daunting task more complex.

My mission is to help you catapult your career via a simple cover letter–building process so that you can achieve the highest-level result possible by writing your cover letter yourself. My objective is to impart to you the methods, techniques, and trade secrets I and other professional resume writers have successfully used in our private practices to help clients advance their careers and to coach you as you complete each step.

Step-by-Step Cover Letters, coupled with *Step-by-Step Resumes,* is everything you need to get your foot in the door of your prospective employers and be part of the top 2 percent of job candidates considered for positions. (If you haven't already purchased the *Step-by-Step Resumes* book, you can purchase it from the same place you purchased this book.)

The amount of effort you put into preparing your cover letter is commensurate with the level of success you will achieve when you send it out along with your resume. The greater the effort, the greater the interview results, and the more satisfied you can be with the type of job you land and, ultimately, your lifestyle. So pay particular attention as you review each step to make your cover letter the best it can possibly be! The end result will show prospective employers why you are the best candidate for the job.

As resume writers and career coaches, my colleagues and I take every bit of information from our clients to capitalize on their strengths and competitive edge. We weigh every word in the cover letter before we consider it complete. So to get the most out of this process, take your time with each step to be sure you have left no stone unturned in making yourself shine.

All you need to do is follow each step carefully to develop your compelling cover letter. And when you're reading your final draft, don't be surprised if you say, "Wow, I'd hire me!" as clients of professional resume writers often do.

Let's get started on your road to success by developing your winning cover letter!

Acknowledgements

I dedicate this book to my husband and my family who have provided support and encouragement along the way and a push when I needed it. I also acknowledge the professional resume writing and career coaching organizations that help me and other professionals keep on top of our skills and changing career conditions. They are the National Resume Writers' Association (www.thenrwa.com)—for which I have served as East Coast regional representative and advertising and public relations chairperson—Career Management Alliance (www.careermanagementalliance.com), and Career Directors International (www.careerdirectors.com).

If you need additional help with any of your career endeavors—be it personal branding, resume or cover letter writing, online identity building, social networking profile development, web resume development, job board posting, personal branding, career transition coaching, reference checking, portfolio development, or interview training—please visit my Total Career Management Center at www.careerimagebuilders.com. And by all means, feel free to contact me at any time at CareerCatapult@aol.com or (631) 698-7777.

Contents

INTRODUCTION: HOW TO USE THIS BOOK ix

STEP 1: UNDERSTAND YOUR PERSONAL BRAND 1

Cover Letters and Your Personal Brand 2

Business Branding Defined 2

Personal Branding Defined 3

The Benefits of Personal Branding 4

A Personal Branding Epiphany 4

    Multiple Talents, One Brand 4

    The Business of Branding 5

Identify Your Personal Brand 5

The Five Critical Components of Personal Branding 7

Target Potential Employers' Needs 7

    Apply Maslow's Hierarchy of Needs 8

    Determine an Employer's Needs 10

    Base Your Marketing Strategy on Your Prospective Employer's Achilles' Heel 11

    Satisfy Others' Needs to Get What You Want 12

Developing Your Personal Branding Campaign 12

Building Your Personal Brand 13

STEP 2: DEVELOP YOUR UNIQUE PERSONAL BRAND MESSAGE 15

Keep the Five Critical Components of Personal Branding in Mind 16

Assess Your Goals and the Purpose of Your Cover Letter..............................19

Identify Your Assets/Features 20

    Determine Your Personal Attributes and Characteristics 20

    Determine Your Transferable Skills and Areas of Expertise 23

    List Your Degrees, Licenses, and Certifications 25

    List Any Other Acquired Knowledge or Related Skills 25

Target Your Assets and Features to Prospective Employers 25

    Research and Identify Employers' Requirements 26

    Match Your Assets and Features to Prospective Employers' Requirements 28

    Identify Matching Achievements That Prove Your Expertise 30

Document the Benefits You Offer to Employers 32

    Find Out Employers' Needs and Challenges 32

    Determine How Your Assets Help Employers 34

Determine Your Competitive Edge 36

Develop Your Value Proposition 37

Uncover Your Return on Investment (ROI) to Prospective Employers 39

Create and Edit Your Brand Message 40

    Determine the Best Strategy to Convey Your Brand 42

    Create Your Final Brand Message 44

STEP 3: WRITE A COMPELLING FIRST PARAGRAPH 47

Understand the Purpose of the First Paragraph 48

Determine How to Use Your Personal Brand Message 48

Draw the Reader In 52

Include the Position Particulars 53

Make the Reader Want to Read Further by Introducing Your Areas of Expertise 53

Select a First Paragraph Foundation 54

Write and Finalize Your First Paragraph 63

STEP 4: STATE YOUR QUALIFICATIONS AND BENEFITS 65

A Winning Cover Letter Formula 66

Develop Your Second Paragraph 66

    List the Job Requirements and Your Matching Qualifications 68

    State the Benefits of Your Qualifications 70

    Identify and Include the Value Proposition of Your Benefits 71

    State Your Return on Investment (ROI) 72

    Include Your Competitive Edge 73

Review Second Paragraph Foundations and Examples 74

Finalize Your Second Cover Letter Paragraph 82

STEP 5: SUMMARIZE YOUR KEY ACCOMPLISHMENTS 85

Select Achievements to Validate Your Skill Statements 86

Summarize Your Achievements in Concise Statements 87

Review Examples and Select a Third Paragraph Foundation 87

Write Your Third Paragraph 98

STEP 6: PERSONALIZE YOUR MESSAGE 99

Determine Whether to Include a Fourth Paragraph 100

State Why You Want This Job 100

Address Industry or Company Issues or Needs 102

Tell a Compelling Story 104

Review Fourth Paragraph Foundations 104

Write Your Fourth Paragraph 107

STEP 7: CLOSE WITH A STATEMENT OF INTEREST AND A CALL TO ACTION 109

State Your Interest 110

Include Your Call to Action 110

Review and Choose a Closing Paragraph Foundation 111

Write Your Last Cover Letter Paragraph 116

Close Your Cover Letter 117

Your Complimentary Close.. *117*

Your Signature *117*

Your Typed Name *118*

STEP 8: COMPLETE YOUR COVER LETTER DRAFT 119

Pull Your Cover Letter Together... 120

Ensure Your Cover Letter Contains the Five Critical Components of
Your Personal Brand 121

Sprinkle Your Cover Letter with Industry-Specific Keywords 121

Industry-Specific Keywords by Profession *121*

Keyword-Rich Paragraph Examples *128*

Make Your Cover Letter the Best It Can Be 129

STEP 9: FORMAT AND DESIGN YOUR COVER LETTER.....131

Follow the Cover Letter Formatting Guidelines... 132

Select a Professional Letterhead Design or Create One of Your Own 133

Add Brand Identification Elements.. 136

Add a Slogan or Tagline *136*

Add Testimonials.. *136*

Add a Mission Statement *137*

Create an Email Version of Your Cover Letter.. 138

Send It Out!.. 138

STEP 10: REVIEW COMPLETE COVER LETTER FOUNDATIONS AND SAMPLES 139

Complete Personally Branded Cover Letters and Foundations............................ 140

Situational Cover Letter Foundations and Samples.. 142

Profession-Specific Cover Letter Foundations 204

Other Personally Branded Cover Letter Samples.. 216

INDEX OF CONTRIBUTORS 222

INDEX 223

Introduction

Step-by-Step Cover Letters contains everything you need to write your cover letter like a professional resume writer—one step at a time. Each step corresponds with a part of the cover letter–writing process or a cover letter paragraph and includes simple, easy-to-follow instructions and foundation worksheets. All you need to do is fill in the blanks and select applicable options, and then move on to the next step to complete everything from your opening to your closing paragraphs.

Step-by-Step Cover Letters is meant to be used as a workbook; so please delve right into the worksheets, and don't hesitate to write in the book (unless, of course, you borrowed it from the library or a friend). Or you can pop the accompanying CD into your computer to develop your unique personal brand, complete the various cover letter paragraphs, or use the full cover letter foundations to build your cover letter.

Completing this process thoroughly will provide you with an extremely professional cover letter that can ensure your accompanying resume is read and significantly increase your odds of getting an interview. This process also aids you in preparing for interviews as it provides the steps to develop your personal brand—*the single most critical process to get ahead in today's world of work.* You will be getting the inside knowledge and expertise of professional resume writers and personal branding strategists to use to your advantage.

If you don't think you have the writing skills, achievements, or confidence to write an effective cover letter, don't worry. The cover letter–writing process described in this book enables you to incorporate cutting-edge professional cover letter strategies without having to be a resume and cover letter expert. And the provided foundations take all the work out of this process!

This cover letter–writing process is easily adapted to each profession and precisely customized to each individual, whether you are a file clerk or a chief executive officer. Everyone who completes the 10-step process— *no matter how similar their positions are to each other*—will end up with a unique cover letter.

WHY COVER LETTERS ARE IMPORTANT

The main purpose of your cover letter is to whet the appetite of your prospective employers so that they want to learn more about you and read your resume. To do this, your cover letter must contain and convey your personal brand message so that hiring managers are compelled to contact you. (You will learn how to develop and write your brand message containing your value proposition and return on investment to your prospective employers in Step 2.) If written well, the cover letter alone can compel hiring managers to call you in for an interview.

What Your Cover Letter Isn't and What It Is

What it isn't: Your cover letter is not just a letter to accompany your resume. For that purpose, you would be better off with no cover letter at all. It is not a letter that replicates the information contained in your resume. If the cover letter is boring or basic, five out of seven human resource professionals will not even read it. So it should not be generic, or routine, or lackluster.

What it is: Your cover letter is your personal introduction to a prospective employer when you can't meet in person. As such, it's the employer's first impression of you. So make it count! Be sure it is persuasive, compelling, and impactful and sells you ahead of your competition, so that you can obtain the position you seek. It should contain your personal brand message with eye-opening statements that make a hiring manager want to read your resume, get to know you further, and even call you in for an interview based on the cover letter itself. Your cover letter should contain the "wow" factor.

What Makes a Successful Cover Letter

A successful cover letter does a number of things:

- ✔ Entices the reader to read your resume.
- ✔ Provides a human touch so that the reader can get a feel for the person behind the resume.
- ✔ Summarizes your major achievements in brief statements that make an impact, including only bottom-line information to whet prospective employers' appetites to know more about how you might be able to do the same for them.
- ✔ Shows you will be an asset to prospective employers and will be able to improve their bottom line or otherwise help their businesses grow and/or meet their challenges.
- ✔ Compels employers to call you in for an interview. Well-written cover letters might, in fact, do this before the resume is even read!

What to Do and What Not to Do in a Cover Letter

Don't:

- ✔ Copy generic statements that are cliché.
- ✔ Bore your reader with job description information they are already aware of.
- ✔ Replicate the information contained in your resume. (Don't duplicate, summarize.)
- ✔ Send out broadcast cover letters if you can help it (that is, take the time to find out to whom the letter should be sent by checking the Internet or calling the company, if known).

Do:

- ✔ Write compelling, marketing-savvy statements that make readers take notice.
- ✔ Back up your outlandish, head-turning statements with achievement facts.
- ✔ Make promises you can keep.
- ✔ Determine what your possible return on investment is to prospective employers if they were to hire you.
- ✔ Make statements that show how you can outcompete your peers.
- ✔ Conduct company research so that you can obtain the name, title, and company name and address of your targeted employers and personally address and date each of your nonbroadcast cover letters.
- ✔ Show how you are a match for a position opening by including all of the requirements in the original job posting and noting your expertise and qualifications in these areas.

What a Compelling Cover Letter Contains

A compelling cover letter includes the following:

- ✔ Your personal brand, which is the benefits of hiring you, your value proposition to your prospective employers, and their return on investment

✔ An explanation of how you can meet and exceed your prospective employer's needs and how your qualifications match the open position

✔ Marketing-savvy, persuasive statements that make hiring managers want to meet with you (and read your resume)

✔ Information about how you can help prospective employers reach their goals

✔ Industry-specific keywords

How to Make Your Cover Letter Really Work

To write a cover letter that knocks an employer's socks off, you need to

✔ Make it different and unique.

✔ Provide specific ways you might be able to help the prospective employer.

✔ Tell an interesting, compelling story that makes employers want to read further.

✔ Be sure it contains the "wow" factor.

✔ Persuade employers that you are the best candidate for the position!

WHAT ARE THE 10 STEPS?

The 10 steps in this book will guide you in developing a winning cover letter:

Step 1: Understand Your Personal Brand

Step 2: Develop Your Unique Personal Brand Message

Step 3: Write a Compelling First Paragraph

Step 4: State Your Qualifications and Benefits

Step 5: Summarize Your Key Accomplishments

Step 6: Personalize Your Message

Step 7: Close with a Statement of Interest and a Call to Action

Step 8: Complete Your Cover Letter Draft

Step 9: Format and Design Your Cover Letter

Step 10: Review Complete Cover Letter Foundations and Samples

The Benefits of Completing This 10-Step Process

The information and guidelines in this book have helped job seekers

✔ Increase their interview odds

✔ Heighten their confidence level

✔ Gain renewed enthusiasm for the job search

✔ Feel empowered in the interview stage

✔ Land the position they seek sooner

✔ Obtain higher salaries

How to Use the Worksheets in This Book

Steps 3–7 in the book each cover a cover letter paragraph and contain numerous foundations from which to select a paragraph most suitable to you and your profession. Simply review the options and samples, choose an applicable one, select options, and fill in the blanks with your own unique information. It is recommended that you try several of the foundations in each step and select the one that makes the most impact for your field.

Step 10 has cover letter foundations and samples you can use to develop your own cover letter. When you complete all 10 steps, you will have all of the written information you need to finalize your cover letter, so you can sign it and send it off (accompanied with your resume, of course)!

Why This 10-Step Process Works

The original cover letters from which the foundations contained in this book were obtained were painstakingly written by professional resume writers (me and other writers) for their clients. I have created foundations using the general language and included fill-in-the-blank options where you can insert your own unique, profession-specific information to write your own cover letter.

 note Because all of the cover letter foundations in this book are equally as effective, you should be fine with whichever one you select based on what you feel is your own best fit.

These foundations are tried-and-true methods that work so you don't have to reinvent the wheel and start from scratch. Your cover letter will be completed in no time, so you can go on with your important job search tasks and not get hung up on writing.

This book contains cover letter templates that absolutely anyone can use as a foundation to prepare a cover letter—*no matter what the profession.* However, do not overlook any other major compelling information that you can think of. If you feel you have additional important information to include that hiring managers should know about you, and you do not see it in a specific section of the book, work it into your cover letter. This information could include a particular reason why you are drawn to the position, what event prompted you to enter the profession, why you would like to work for that particular firm, how a similar job you had precisely matches what the employer seeks, or the like.

HOW TO WRITE YOUR COVER LETTER

Your cover letter should be one page with approximately four to six paragraphs. The first few sentences should entice the reader with your general qualifications right up front (a benefit-driven statement will have the most impact), indicate what type of position you are applying for, and explain why you would be an asset to the firm. Adding your value proposition right up front is also recommended.

 **note** If there is a compelling reason why your cover letter needs to be longer than one page, try not to exceed one-and-a-half pages. You don't want to lose your readers' interest!

The middle paragraphs substantiate why you are a qualified applicant for this particular position and summarize some heavy-hitter achievements you have already accomplished as proof.

The last paragraph states your call to action, what you plan to do next or want the reader to do. For example, you might state that you will follow up in a week or request that the hiring manager call you. You should also thank the reader for his or her consideration.

The Successful Cover Letter Success Quotient

The product = You

Your target market = Your prospective employers

Your features/assets = Your skills, attributes, experience, education, achievements, and other qualifications

Your benefits = What will sell you to hiring managers

Your value proposition = The value your benefits offer

Your return on investment = The figurative amount of profit your prospective employer can expect to generate from hiring you

WHAT ABOUT YOUR RESUME?

If you haven't already completed your resume and you would like to use the same simple, easy-to-follow process as this *Step-by-Step Cover Letters* book contains, just go back to the store or website where you purchased this book and ask for its companion book, *Step-by-Step Resumes*, Second Edition: *Build an Outstanding Resume in 10 Easy Steps!* It's the easiest resume writing book on the market and explains exactly how to prepare your resume with concise instructions every step of the way. And you don't need a writing degree or to be a certified resume writer to create an outstanding resume that garners interviews.

HOW TO INSTALL AND USE THE ACCOMPANYING CD

The CD at the back of this book will save you a lot of typing, and you can develop your cover letter systematically by selecting and using the various sample foundations for each paragraph or the full cover letter foundations.

Installing the CD

Put the CD in your computer's CD-ROM drive and open the window for the drive. You will see folders for the various cover letter foundations, from your opening paragraph to your closing paragraph and the various paragraphs in between, as well as full cover letter foundations you can use to prepare your cover letter, including situational-type cover letter foundations as well as profession-specific ones.

Using the Cover Letter Foundations

The CD contains a set of paragraph foundations for writing your various cover letter paragraphs as well as a set of complete cover letter foundations. You can either work within the various paragraphs as provided in steps within this book or skip right to the numerous cover letter foundations and develop your cover letter right within a selected foundation, or a mixture of both.

Access these files by opening the appropriate folder. The paragraph foundations are sectioned by your first (opening), second, third, fourth, and fifth (closing) paragraphs as you see in the book. The complete cover letter foundations include both situational cover letter foundations and profession-specific cover letter foundations.

step 1

Understand Your Personal Brand

- Cover Letters and Your Personal Brand
- Business Branding Defined
- Personal Branding Defined
- The Benefits of Personal Branding
- A Personal Branding Epiphany
  - Multiple Talents, One Brand
  - The Business of Branding
- Identify Your Personal Brand
- The Five Critical Components of Personal Branding
- Target Potential Employers' Needs
  - Apply Maslow's Hierarchy of Needs
  - Determine an Employer's Needs
  - Base Your Marketing Strategy on Your Prospective Employer's Achilles' Heel
  - Satisfy Others' Needs to Get What You Want
- Develop Your Personal Branding Campaign
- Build Your Personal Brand

Material in this step is copyrighted by Creative Image Builders.

COVER LETTERS AND YOUR PERSONAL BRAND

Personal branding is critical in today's world of work. Understand branding and you will be in the top 2 percent of job candidates applying for positions. Ignore it, and you will be in the other 98 percent of the general public who do not know what this term means and, as a result, have not capitalized on their personal brands. Knowing your personal brand, developing it, and using it is a trade secret that will greatly increase your odds of getting hired. Incorporating your personal brand in your cover letter will help you achieve success because employers will seek *you* out!

This first step in the cover letter writing process begins with knowing what personal branding is and what it can accomplish. The next part of the step is identifying and developing your personal brand message so that you can use it to grab prospective employers' attention in your cover letter.

BUSINESS BRANDING DEFINED

Dating back to 2700 BCE, *branding* referred to the process of making a distinctive, permanent ownership mark on an animal (by way of a hot iron) for the purpose of identification. This process was used to deter theft and to find lost or stolen animals. To be effective, a good livestock brand was and still is one that is distinctive, simple, and readily recognized.

Much like livestock branding, a goal of branding in business is to create a brand that is distinctive and can be easily identified and recognized by others. Of course, modern branding for business has expanded beyond its livestock origins. Today, business branding is essential to achieve business success and growth.

According to advertising executive David Ogilvy, "The Father of Branding", business branding is

> The intangible sum of a product's attributes: its name, packaging, and price, its history, its reputation, and the way it is advertised…Successful advertising for any product is based on information about its consumer.

Business branding is also…

> "…the process of creating a unique, positive, and recognizable identity for a product or service" (Sign Kraft, signkraft.biz/).
>
> "…a promise of the value of a product…that the product is better than all the competing products… The combination of tangible and intangible characteristics that make a brand unique" (Randall S. Hansen, Ph.D.).
>
> "…the process by which a commodity in the marketplace is known primarily for the image it projects rather than any actual quality" (Center for Media Literacy, www.medialit.org).
>
> "…a value or core set of values that allow your offer to be identified in the marketplace" (Edinburgh Napier University, staff.napier.ac.uk).
>
> "…the actions of gaining a favored view on the part of consumers for a product, service, organization, or experience" (SignIndustry.com).

In business branding, organizations market themselves to customers and investors through self-promotional materials and corporate identity pieces. In personal branding, you present yourself to the prospective employers in your field with marketing materials *(your resume, cover letter, web resume or online career portfolio, thank you letters, letterhead, business cards, and/or other promotional materials)* that define your competitive edge in your industry through content and presentation.

Personal branding will help you to develop your niche in your market, build name recognition, and set you apart from other job seekers. Just as business branding is essential to achieve business success and growth, personal branding is critical to catapult and manage your career.

PERSONAL BRANDING DEFINED

There is no one definition for personal branding. My definition is a derivative of many:

> Personal branding is an essential career and reputation management marketing tool that creates a successful, credible identity so that hiring managers who view your brand know your value proposition and your return on their investment and seek you out.

Personal branding is also…

> "…the process whereby people and their careers are marked as brands. The concept suggests that success comes from self-packaging" (Wikipedia).

> "…a revolution in career management and an essential tool for thinking in the new world of work…being your best, authentic self and standing out from your peers so you can achieve your goals. What makes you unique makes you successful" (William Arruda).

> "…the art of articulating and communicating your skills, personality, and values so that others seek you to help them solve a problem" (Dan Schawbel).

> "…the embodiment of your values, vision, purpose, goals, and passions…to enhance and enrich your career success. The message you communicate in speech, writing, online presence, and appearance. Your fingerprint, your DNA. No one else has it or can successfully imitate it" (Valerie and Company, valerieandcompany.com).

> "…the process by which individuals…differentiate themselves…by identifying and articulating their unique value proposition…and then leveraging it across platforms with a consistent message and image to…enhance their recognition as experts in their field, establish reputation and credibility, advance their careers, and build self-confidence" (personalbrandingwiki.pbwiki.com).

As Tom Peters puts it, "We are CEOs of our own companies: Me, Inc. To be in business today, our most important job is to be head marketer for the brand called You."

Personal branding is essential to achieve career success and personal growth. Because it is a relatively new concept, people struggle to identify with it and therefore have difficulty applying this concept to themselves.

 tip When the solution to the challenge of meeting your target audience's needs is strategically developed and executed through a high value proposition and return on investment, that's what successful branding is all about.

There are two reasons for this difficulty. One, people are reluctant to think of themselves as a product with features and benefits. Two, many people are not used to comparing themselves to others in terms of what they do better than the next person. As a result, people tend to underestimate what they are worth.

Whether you are consciously aware of it or not, you already have a brand—it is your authentic, unique self. By defining and developing it in writing, including it in your cover letter, backing it up in your resume through achievements, presenting it online, and managing it, you convey your brand—*your perceived value*—to others. A well-defined brand is sought after and brings opportunities your way.

tip Defining your own unique qualities and talents can be difficult. It is always easier for another person to do this for you. Ask a close friend or relative or—better—a professional skilled in personal branding to help you with this task.

THE BENEFITS OF PERSONAL BRANDING

Personal branding can do several things for you:

- ✔ Your cover letter and resume, if branded properly, will instantly and significantly help you stand out from the crowd.

- ✔ Your cover letter will invite readers in and make them want to read your resume and call you in for an interview.

- ✔ Having a personal brand will help you sell yourself to prospective employers and increase your earning potential.

- ✔ Employers will immediately know what position you are seeking and what distinguishes you from the competition.

- ✔ Personal branding will help make you known in your industry. It helps to establish you as an expert in your own professional niche and build a solid reputation in your field.

- ✔ If done correctly, branding will compel employers to seek you out! When you brand yourself, you make it clear to employers that you can help them solve their problems, meet their challenges, increase their bottom line, or otherwise contribute to their firm in a way no one else can or will.

- ✔ You will get many more calls for interviews, take less time to secure a position, and have a much higher probability of receiving the position and salary you want. Applying your personal brand during an interview and subsequent job offer helps you negotiate a higher salary because it emphasizes the value of what you have to offer.

The ultimate benefit of personal branding is that once you know your own unique brand inside and out, it is a revelation that empowers you with confidence to go ahead and fulfill your goals!

A PERSONAL BRANDING EPIPHANY

Once your personal brand is defined, you will forever be changed. The best way to illustrate this change is to share a personal branding epiphany story. This one is mine.

That moment of sudden revelation came to me while I was developing my web portfolio (at EvelynSalvador .com). When writing and designing the content for my site, I knew the time had come for me to define my personal brand for myself just as I had helped my clients define their brands for themselves over the years. Yet I found that it was much easier to help others identify their brands than it was to identify my own. Once I established what my personal brand was, however, I felt more focused and empowered and sure of the high value proposition and return on investment that my competitive edge was carrying to my target audience. At that moment, the light bulb went on, and my life changed forever. It was my own catharsis.

Multiple Talents, One Brand

As a creative person, I work in many arenas, each of which brings in revenue. These arenas include graphic design, copywriting, resume writing, career coaching, website and web resume development, book authoring, photography, and illustration.

Doing all of these things, I had toyed with many different ways of how to present what I had to offer clients in my slogan, on my stationery, in my business literature, in my sales pitch, and on my website. I struggled for years to determine how to pull it all together as one brand. I could only see several.

The closest I came to tying all of my different talents (or *assets*) into one brand was when I created my slogan back in 1990: "Writing and designing effective self-promotions for businesses and individuals." Yet I still had difficulty determining what to put on my letterhead and business card. Corporate clients, for example, were not interested in knowing that I was a certified resume writer. And including creative director/graphic designer on my business card made it appear to resume clients that I did not specialize in resume writing.

When I created my various websites, I found myself having to make a choice. I had to come up with *one* online identity—the brand called "Evelyn Salvador." And I had to come up with a brand that did not turn away other business that I was highly capable of conducting, especially in this economy.

The Business of Branding

When I took a hard look at everything I do, I realized I was in the business of branding across the board: business branding for companies and personal branding for individuals. Everything I did revolved around this concept. All of my assets (including my creativity, organizational skills, marketing savvy, and business know-how) worked together so that I could strategize, market, design, and write the ideas I conceived all under one roof, without having to outsource. I could offer all of my different services to clients because they really were one brand, the Evelyn Salvador brand.

I captured this brand in a new job title, personal and business branding strategist and marketer, and a new slogan/tagline, "Championing Your Success." Once I defined my brand, I felt like I received a promotion. I was more aware of what my assets were, how they worked together, how my benefits helped my target audience, and what my highly competitive edge over others in my field was. I could offer, through my value proposition, a high return on investment to those who procured my services. In fact, once my brand was defined, I felt that it made no sense for people to go elsewhere to develop their brand—I had everything they needed. And this belief system was what gave me the confidence to sell myself.

When I told my husband about my personal branding epiphany, he asked me if I recalled the illustration I drew for him when we dated. I didn't. At the time, he was an architect/project manager for the bank where we both worked. As a gift, I created a pen and ink and color wash collage for him of various elements that were a part of his professional life, including a blueprint strewn across a drawing table and topped with a T-square, a compass, and the green Kool cigarettes he smoked back then. He explained that I created his brand. I then recalled that I did similar illustrations for my mother, who was a seamstress; my dad, who was a tool-and-die engineer; and my sister, who is in pharmaceuticals.

Through these illustrations, I was defining others' personal brands several decades before personal branding was an established concept and long before my ad agency days when I first learned about business branding. What did this mean? Was it an innate sense? The only thing I knew for sure was that branding was something I loved to do and did well.

 tip Your ultimate career and personal life satisfaction can only be achieved when you strive for your passion. Developing your personal brand message around that passion will make it happen for you!

This is the catharsis or epiphany that happens when you identify your personal brand. When you discover what your unique assets are and how your industry needs them, you know the value of what you have to offer. You feel it. You believe in it. And you can sell it better than anyone else.

IDENTIFY YOUR PERSONAL BRAND

Can you answer any of the questions in the following exercise in 10 seconds or less?

PERSONAL BRAND EXERCISE

Use the blank lines to jot down what comes to mind when you hear these questions:

What do you do? _____

_____

What can you tell me about yourself? _____

_____

What does your work entail? _____

_____

What makes you unique? _____

_____

If you find this exercise difficult, welcome to 98 percent of the general public! All too often when someone asks us, "What do you do?" (or any of the preceding questions), we stammer a bit to get something out. Most people respond with something quite generic like the following:

> I work in marketing, develop products, and launch new brands.

By changing your response to such questions to a personal brand message, you can achieve a much different result:

> As a marketing specialist, I develop and launch innovative new products and brands for new untapped target markets of forward-thinking companies so they can dramatically increase their revenues through my visionary creativity.

This type of thorough, compelling, and high-impact statement makes others who require your expertise or services want to reach out to you. It sells you as an expert in your own unique expertise niche.

Try answering the previous questions again by filling in the following worksheet. This time, be sure you do so with a compelling message that makes someone want to get to know you and hire your talents because you have something to offer that they believe no one else can do as well.

PERSONAL BRAND MESSAGE FIRST DRAFT

Write a sentence or two that explains what your work entails and what makes you unique in your profession. If this exercise is difficult, not to worry, you will be taken step by step through the process of developing your personal brand message in Step 2.

_____

_____

_____

_____

_____

_____

Step 1

THE FIVE CRITICAL COMPONENTS OF PERSONAL BRANDING

Personal branding (or *any* branding) has five critical components. Each of these components is critical to developing your personal brand message that you will be including in your cover letter (and each will be discussed and developed in detail via a worksheet process in Step 2):

- ✔ **Assets/features:** These are the qualities, attributes, skills, and/or know-how you possess that can be valuable or useful to a prospective employer.

- ✔ **Benefits:** These are the ways in which your features help employers. Benefits might include assistance, profit, or other type of advantage or contribution to the employer's mission and objectives.

- ✔ **Competitive edge:** This is a clear advantage that you have over the competition by way of certain unique strengths or aspects of you that make you stand out from others in your profession. It is your individual "marketing mix" of assets and benefits that others may not possess.

- ✔ **Value proposition:** The total worth of all of the benefits you can offer an employer in exchange for salary by way of promised deliverables backed by matching achievements. (Obviously, employers want the value of all the benefits you offer to be higher than the cost of paying you.)

- ✔ **Return on investment (ROI):** A measurement of your contributions (expected future value) to an employer. You can get this number by dividing the amount of money you have saved or earned (or a similar measurement appropriate to your field) for your employers by the cost of hiring you. (Naturally, prospective employers want this number to be high.)

Unearthing the numbers attached to what you do can take some digging. I had a client who initially claimed he had no achievements whatsoever in his job. "I just paint cars, and that's it," he told me. After asking him very specific questions, I learned that he saved his firm $350,000 a year because he eliminated the need for a prime coat. This number included labor savings and reduced paint costs. When I took that $350,000 and divided it by his $35,000 salary, his return on investment to a prospective employer equated to 1,000 percent! A return on investment such as this makes a prospective employer say, "Wow!" And that "wow" factor is what you need to include in your cover letter to make you stand out amongst your competition.

The way to hit the mark in identifying your personal brand is to first determine all of your assets (your features) and then develop the benefits your features have to your target market (your prospective employer). Add a strong value proposition and a high return on investment, and you've got yourself your own unique personal brand that will help you succeed!

TARGET POTENTIAL EMPLOYERS' NEEDS

Writing your cover letter is all about selling yourself to meet the most direct needs of your prospective employer audience by way of your features, benefits, competitive edge, value proposition, and return on investment.

Understanding and uncovering an employer's needs and then finding a way to match those needs is the key to success. Developing a personal brand with a high value proposition and return on investment around those needs through compelling benefits will satisfy the needs of both you and your future employer. The employer gains a valuable employee, and you get the job you want.

How do you find out what an employer needs? You use a strategy that has stuck with me since my college days as a marketing student. You use Maslow's hierarchy of needs.

Apply Maslow's Hierarchy of Needs

Abraham Maslow had a theory back in 1943 that described human motivation as a means by which people make choices based on meeting their most direct needs. That theory is significant today in marketing as it pertains to selling products and services. In the case of personal branding, it is a critical component of selling yourself to hiring managers. When you meet a person's or organization's greatest needs, he/she/it will take the bait and "buy" or say, "You're hired."

In terms of marketing, Maslow's hierarchy of needs works on the premise that you can more readily sell to members of your target audience by showing them how your product (in this case, you) meets their level of need (by way of its features, benefits, competitive edge, value proposition, and return on investment). If you do this, they will find the value of what you have to offer significant and will want to make a spontaneous buy. That's why it is important to determine your target audience's greatest needs and to work toward meeting them.

In terms of a job search, if you hit the mark in meeting prospective employers' most direct needs and challenges, and they find that the cost to hire you is nominal in comparison with the value the company will derive from hiring you (such as increasing sales or profitability, decreasing costs, elevating productivity, streamlining operations, and so on), they will pick up the phone to want to meet you and call you in for an interview. The stronger your case (that is, the more benefits and higher return on investment you have to offer), the better your odds of securing the position.

Maslow grouped human needs into different levels. This grouping is typically shown as a pyramid, with the base being basic human needs, such as food and water, and the top being needs such as creativity (see Figure 1.1). In Maslow's theory, people have to satisfy the needs at the lower levels before they can move on to the higher levels.

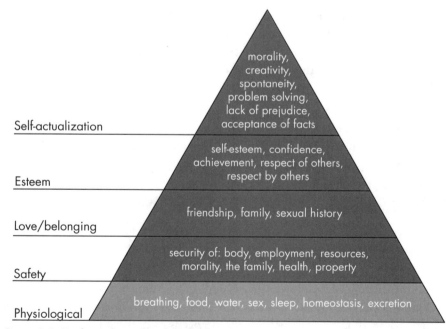

Figure 1.1: Maslow's hierarchy of needs.

These levels of individual needs correspond to the levels of needs of different employers (see Figure 1.2). And like individuals, employers are at different levels on the pyramid at any given time. To sell yourself to a prospective employer, you need to meet the particular level of need that the particular employer has at that moment in time. When you match your features and benefits with the correct level of employer need, you will be more apt to receive interviews and a job quickly.

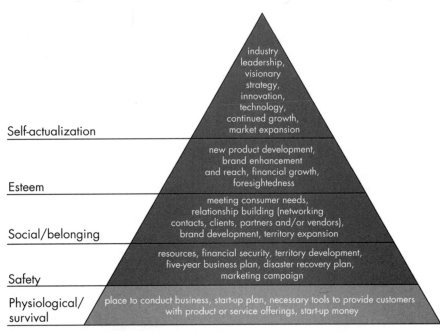

Self-actualization

industry leadership, visionary strategy, innovation, technology, continued growth, market expansion

Esteem

new product development, brand enhancement and reach, financial growth, foresightedness

Social/belonging

meeting consumer needs, relationship building (networking contacts, clients, partners and/or vendors), brand development, territory expansion

Safety

resources, financial security, territory development, five-year business plan, disaster recovery plan, marketing campaign

Physiological/ survival

place to conduct business, start-up plan, necessary tools to provide customers with product or service offerings, start-up money

Figure 1.2: Employer-based hierarchy of needs.

Starting with the most basic level of needs, the following descriptions explain how you might position yourself to meet an employer's level of need:

✔ **Physiological/survival needs:** People need food, water, sleep, and shelter. If these basic needs are not met, people cannot survive. In terms of a business, survival needs include a place to conduct business and the necessary tools to provide consumers with what the business wishes to offer. Without these things, the business cannot get to the next level of the pyramid or grow.

So, if you are a job seeker wishing to obtain a position with a company who is at this basic level, you would have to offer the prospective employer features and benefits that fulfill its basic needs, such as business start-up skills, experience, and/or knowledge. If the business were, for example, a website development firm, it would need someone experienced in building websites to satisfy its clients. Without that expertise, it could not fulfill its clients' needs or make money.

✔ **Safety needs:** These requirements must be met in order for people to feel safe. They include personal and financial security, health and well-being, and a safe environment.

An organization requires resources to fulfill its safety needs. A human resources specialist, for example, can help them fulfill their staffing needs. A business plan and/or disaster recovery plan, for example, can help fulfill a firm's safety net need, so a management consultant or a business plan specialist can target that particular need if it has not yet been met. If securing property is an issue for a firm, a land acquisition specialist can help fulfill that need. An accountant can perhaps fill the financial security need of a floundering firm going through economic turmoil.

✔ **Social (love/belonging) needs:** These are the third tier in the pyramid and involve emotionally based relationships in general and having a supportive and communicative environment in which to thrive. People need to feel/have a sense of belonging and acceptance from small and/or large connections. In organizations, these relationships can include partners, vendors, networking contacts, and, of course, clients.

New business development managers, for example, can fulfill a firm's relationship-building needs. Marketing specialists can grow territories, reaching into untapped markets, if the business's need is to strengthen its brand in the marketplace, for example.

✔ **Esteem needs:** This level includes the need for respect, belonging, strength, competence, recognition, mastery, and independence. Imbalances can result in low self-esteem or inferiority. For a business, a weak brand or market position could indicate this level of need. Organizations at this level seek fame or glory to improve their view of themselves and depend upon others to meet/fulfill this need for them. Branding strategists, marketing specialists, and public relations experts can help fulfill a firm's esteem needs.

✔ **Self-actualization needs:** Self-actualization is at the top of the pyramid and can be realized only after all other lower needs are met. In Maslow's book *Motivation and Personality* (Harper and Row, 1954), he describes this need as "the desire to become more and more what one is, to become everything that one is capable of becoming."

> **note**
> There are various stages of self-actualization (and each level of needs for that matter). Self-actualization is a continual process where the challenge to be the best is only met through knowledge, innovation, technology, and growth.

Firms that have self-actualized might include Fortune 100 or 500 firms. Apple, for example, is at the beginning of its self-actualization stage. An early innovator in the personal computer industry, Apple was surpassed in business sales by other technology companies. Now, due to additional technology and innovation such as iPods, iTouches, iPads, and iMacs, Apple is gaining market share. I believe it is becoming more self-actualized as the general public respects its innovation and technology and starts to see Apple as the leader once again.

To sell to a prospective employer that is at the self-actualization level, a job seeker could address innovative, visionary strategy and the ability to meet the growing technology needs of its targeted consumer market, for example.

Determine an Employer's Needs

So how do you determine a prospective employer's level of need? And how do you know exactly what features and benefits you have that can target their needs?

In that marketing class I took way back when, I learned a quick and dirty way to determine a target audience's (in this case, a prospective employer's) most direct needs:

1. Make a list of the employer's needs.

2. As you list each need, ask, "How does that help?"

3. Continue asking and answering that question until there is no other answer to it. It is then that you've found the greatest need to satisfy and to use to sell your value proposition and return on investment to your audience.

That greatest need should be met with your most significant matching benefit(s). When you state how you can fulfill that need through the use of your assets and benefits and your own unique competitive edge, you can develop your value proposition and return on investment to your prospective employer. (Step 2 details this process.)

Say you are a marketing specialist wanting to sell yourself to a prospective employer that is at the esteem needs level. You'll want to help it fulfill its need for recognition as well as improve the public's view of the employer's products, services, and/or brand(s). You should make an initial list of your assets (or features) that can help the employer. Here is the process for just one of your features, that is, the fact that you develop marketing campaigns.

I develop strategic, innovative marketing campaigns. (This is your feature.)

How does that help the prospective employer?

> My campaigns meet my employer's target audience's direct needs. (This is your benefit.)

How does that help the prospective employer?

> It puts the employer a cut above its competition in the marketplace and increases its market share. (This is your competitive edge.)

How does that help the prospective employer?

> It can sell more products or services. (This is your value proposition.)

How does that help the prospective employer?

> Its sales and profits will increase. (This is your return on investment.)

If you were to put the above exchange into a personally branded statement, it would look something like the following:

> I develop strategic, innovative marketing campaigns (your feature) that meet my employer's target audience's direct needs (your benefit), thereby putting my employer ahead of its competition (your competitive edge), increasing its market share, and helping it to sell more products and services (your value proposition), which results in increased profits (your return on investment).

In a cover letter, you need to prove your brand statement by describing your achievements at current or prior employers that have, indeed, resulted in increased sales and profits. These achievement statements should include dollar amounts and percentages whenever possible. Step 5 explains how to write this part of your cover letter.

Base Your Marketing Strategy on Your Prospective Employer's Achilles' Heel

Try to find your prospective employer's most vulnerable area, a weak spot that you can help strengthen through your own unique talents or assets. You can figure out this weak spot by working in the field and knowing what pitfalls a firm can get into (for example) and/or by learning more about the organizations you apply to. A good place to start is by Googling job descriptions for your position title and reviewing what various organizations seek. Take a look at their job applicant "wish lists" and where the job postings state "helpful but not required," for example. Know that most applicants do not have all of the experience prospective employers request. Compare job descriptions to your own experience and background; see where you excel. Check the websites of individual organizations you want to work for to see what jobs they offer and what their missions are to determine how you may be of help in reaching their goals.

My many years as a branding expert have taught me that when you offer a benefit that matches a person's (or organization's) vulnerability, you are more apt to cause that person to stop, take notice, and listen to what you have to say. By offering to strengthen an area of weakness by increasing sales or profits, elevating productivity, cutting costs, streamlining operations, or otherwise helping to contribute to your prospective employer's mission or bottom line, you are more than just meeting a need, you are fulfilling a requirement that will help your prospective employer come out way ahead of the game. It's a win/win for both you and the employer.

Satisfy Others' Needs to Get What You Want

My experience has shown me that anyone who is requesting something from someone should do so by first showing a benefit to that person (or organization). If the benefit you're offering also has a high return on investment (ROI), the person is more likely to agree to your request.

This strategy works in many kinds of situations with all kinds of people: hiring managers, venture capital firms, family, friends, strangers—anyone. It works if you are seeking a new job, looking to be promoted on your current job, or wanting to capitalize on any type of opportunity.

I've even taught my children early on that the best way to achieve absolutely anything in life is to first determine how you can meet the needs of the person or entity from whom you wish to gain something. If they remember nothing else, this strategy will get them far in life.

For example, whenever my kids ask for permission to go somewhere or for me to take them somewhere, I always have to ask: "Did you do your homework? Have you completed your chores? Do I know this person? Where will you be? Will there be parents there? Will you get a ride home?" and so on. As a parent of several kids who works from home, I find that this exchange can get pretty repetitive, tedious, and time-consuming, especially if I am in the middle of work.

My kids know that they are more apt to receive a "yes" to their requests if they first meet all my needs. So they have learned to say, "I've completed my homework and chores and would like to go to so-and-so's. Here's the number and address." Or, "When you drop off (my sister or brother) at such-and-such time, do you mind bringing me to (the mall, my friend's house, a party, other)? I have a ride home, so you won't have to stop work to get me." When they come to me prepared with answers to all my questions, I am more inclined to agree with what they want because they are meeting my needs.

The same holds true for prospective employers. If what you have to offer matches what they need and you provide a value proposition they can't refuse, you win!

DEVELOP YOUR PERSONAL BRANDING CAMPAIGN

Personal branding (also called *career branding* and *self-branding*) is about building a name for yourself based on what you have achieved and what differentiates you from others. It essentially is your reputation. Job seekers and all career-minded individuals need to define their personal brand in order to achieve their ultimate career success. And once they've defined it, they need to spread the word in as many ways as possible.

To successfully brand yourself, you must complete the following process (which is detailed in Step 2):

1. Identify all of your most significant assets (your features).
2. Determine how your features help you solve problems within your field (your benefits).
3. Focus this message on what you stand for (your value proposition).
4. Determine what your return on investment is to your prospective employers.
5. Establish and define what your personal brand identity is by writing your personal brand message.
6. Repeatedly get the word out to others.

A well-strategized, well-created, and well-executed personal branding campaign creates a consistent, strong message to prospective employers as to your perceived value. All of your career communications must be branded and differentiated from your competition to attract job opportunities, maximize your salary potential, and achieve career success.

Your online identity message must be positive and consistent. Everything you write, say, and present (your words, tone, and attitude) must be consistent with your personal brand message. Doing otherwise will create confusion and hinder your brand. Repetition is key in marketing your brand in your email messages, your blogs, your social networking profiles, and your Web presence. Integrating your brand message into all of your online communications will help you to create a positive and consistent online identity.

BUILD YOUR PERSONAL BRAND

Establishing and building your career brand is essential for your career success. Brand management plays a strategic role in your career management. Managing your brand much the same way a firm manages a brand is your key to success. And applying marketing techniques to help brand you in your career allows you to manage it successfully.

> **note** *Step-by-Step Cover Letters* explores various ways to verbally brand yourself by defining your brand message and using it successfully in your cover letter. There are additional ways to verbally brand yourself, such as developing a mission statement as a way to show your prospective employers you are serious about your career and including success stories and/or case studies in your resume package. These additional methods are all covered in my companion book, *Step-by-Step Resumes*, which should be used in conjunction with this book to fully explore all possibilities and make your resume package the best it can be. *Step-by-Step Resumes* also covers visual branding through resume design, occupational icons, graphic elements, color, charts and graphs, work samples, and other methods.

Following are techniques you can use to build and strengthen your career brand and become the best you can be:

✔ **Become an expert in your field.** Establishing yourself as an expert in your field is one of the most essential ways to brand yourself. It builds credibility and demonstrates your achievements and proven abilities through various venues, such as by writing articles published in trade journals, giving speeches at conferences and conventions, being quoted by the news media, and the like.

✔ **Gain more knowledge, education, and experience.** No matter how much you already know, you can always learn more. First, determine what you want your brand to stand for. Then decide what you need to learn, and develop a strategy to accomplish that. To enhance your personal career brand, further your education if you haven't already completed the degrees, licenses, or certifications needed in your field, or earn those that put you at the top.

✔ **If you are currently employed, seek additional opportunities that can enhance your brand.** To help build your brand while on your existing job, see whether you can become involved in new and challenging assignments, projects, or opportunities that can further enhance your expertise and add some additional achievements under your belt, especially ones that can provide some notoriety to your online presence.

✔ **Maintain an up-to-date record of all of your accomplishments.** Extract information from your performance evaluations. Reference letters, sales reports, customer comments, and the like. Make and keep copies for yourself, and maintain a complete list of your own. Be sure to compile quantifying numbers and percentages wherever possible.

✔ **Create an outstanding resume and cover letter.** Certified resume writers are skilled in helping people identify and document the qualifications, transferable skills, key accomplishments, attributes, and training that they have achieved throughout their careers and crafting print marketing tools. With this book, you can create an outstanding cover letter by yourself. (My companion book, *Step-by-Step Resumes,* explains how to build that same kind of resume.)

✔ **Develop your elevator pitch.** Once you've developed your personal brand message (Step 2 shows you how), you can create your elevator pitch. Think in terms of how much you can actually say during floor stops on an elevator. It shouldn't be any longer. Edit your brand message down to its most condensed format without losing content.

✔ **Network and promote yourself all the time.** Every time you meet someone new, use your elevator pitch and inform the person about what you do. You should learn and memorize your elevator pitch so it flows off your tongue effortlessly, confidently, and compellingly.

✔ **Join LinkedIn, Twitter, Facebook, and/or other social networking platforms.** With 50 million members and growing exponentially, LinkedIn is the social network of choice for human resource professionals and all career-minded individuals. Currently 88 percent of hiring managers view candidates' online identities before calling them for an interview or making a job offer. Request membership in like-minded groups and share your expertise in blogs and forums of interest to you. Be sure your brand message is consistent in all of your communications. (For more information on building your social networking profile and online identity, go to CareerImageBuilders.com.)

✔ **Become the "go to" person in person and online.** Reach out to members in your professional community and offer assistance when someone seeks help that you can provide. Your brand will become known and you will be the one others come to for expertise in your field.

✔ **Build ongoing relationships in person and online.** Request information interviews from companies in your field of interest. Grow your online network in social networking forums.

✔ **Reinforce your brand repetitively.** Perform your personal brand all the time—in your actions, in your words, in the way you dress, and in your demeanor. Display it in person, in your marketing materials, in your resume, in interviews, during online social networking, within the content of your email messages, and in your Web resume. The more ways you showcase and the more times you repeat your brand, the stronger it becomes. When you start to meet people who already know who you are, you know your brand is becoming successful.

✔ **Monitor your online presence.** When conducting a Google search of yourself (your name in quotes), review all of the entries that come up. The goal is to have your online presence be on target with your brand. If you come across an entry that is not on brand and/or might be viewed negatively, contact the site's webmaster to ask that the information be removed or corrected.

✔ **Create a web resume or online portfolio.** In today's world of work, your brand must have a strong, positive online presence. One way to build this presence is to create a web resume or online career portfolio. These can include items such as your resume, a mission statement, a personalized logo, articles you have written or have been quoted in and their links, transcripts of speeches you have performed, testimonials and endorsements, work samples, awards, honors, and more. (An experienced branding strategist and marketer can help you put these together. To find out more, go to CareerImageBuilders.com and click on Web Resumes.)

✔ **Redefine and strengthen your brand as it evolves.** As CEO and founder of Me, Inc. (as Tom Peters calls it), the more you do to cultivate and grow your brand, the more successful you'll become in your career and in life, and the more satisfied you will be!

step 2

Develop Your Unique Personal Brand Message

- Keep the Five Critical Components of Personal Branding in Mind
- Assess Your Goals and the Purpose of Your Cover Letter
- Identify Your Assets/Features
  - Determine Your Personal Attributes and Characteristics
  - Determine Your Transferable Skills and Areas of Expertise
  - List Your Degrees, Licenses, and Certifications
  - List Any Other Acquired Knowledge or Related Skills
- Target Your Assets and Features to Prospective Employers
  - Research and Identify Employers' Requirements
  - Match Your Assets and Features to Prospective Employers' Requirements
  - Identify Matching Achievements That Prove Your Expertise
- Document the Benefits You Offer to Employers
  - Find Out Employers' Needs and Challenges
  - Determine How Your Assets Help Employers
- Determine Your Competitive Edge
- Develop Your Value Proposition
- Uncover Your Return on Investment (ROI) to Prospective Employers
- Create and Edit Your Brand Message
  - Determine the Best Strategy to Convey Your Brand
  - Develop Your Slogan/Tagline
  - Create Your Final Brand Message

Evelyn Salvador's personal branding process is copyright 2008–2010, Creative Image Builders.com.

KEEP THE FIVE CRITICAL COMPONENTS OF PERSONAL BRANDING IN MIND

In this step, you will develop your personal brand message. Once you identify and define this message, you will convert it into one or several paragraphs in your cover letter in the next steps in this book.

tip If you start to find that completing the exercises is becoming tedious, just step away from it for a bit and come back to it with a fresh mind when you are ready. Do not skip this step—it is too important to your career!

This step is the most thought provoking and time consuming in the book. It will require some soul searching and will get you thinking, but that's what developing your personal brand is all about. Once you know your personal brand, you will use it throughout all of your networking communications as well as in your cover letter, and it will help you get the job you seek. When you complete this step, the remainder of the book is free sailing.

Throughout this entire *Step-by-Step Cover Letters* process, keep in mind the five critical components your personal brand and cover letter message must convey:

- ✔ Assets/features
- ✔ Benefits
- ✔ Competitive edge
- ✔ Value proposition
- ✔ Return on investment (ROI)

Remember, these five components are what will put you in the top 2 percent of candidates considered for positions. Keep them in mind as well when you network, job search, interview, and absolutely anywhere else you discuss what you do. It's what will set you apart from your competition, give you a winning edge, make you the expert that you are in your own unique niche, and compel hiring managers to contact you. It is important that you remember each of these components during this exercise, and most importantly, in your life.

THE FIVE CRITICAL COMPONENTS OF PERSONAL BRANDING

This exercise is simple, but completing it will help you remember the importance of the five critical components of personal branding. You will need to keep these components in mind throughout Step 2. Define the components in your own words in the space provided. If you need help, just go back to Step 1.

Assets/features:

_____

_____

Benefits:

_____

_____

Competitive edge:

_____

_____

Value proposition:

_____

_____

Return on investment:

_____

_____

Before you get into the in-depth process of developing your brand, take a stab at defining your personal branding components. If you find it difficult to do at this stage, just complete what is easy for you now, and move on to the next section of this step.

YOUR OWN PERSONAL BRANDING COMPONENTS

List what you believe are your assets/features, benefits, value proposition, competitive edge, and/or return on investment to prospective employers. Just brainstorm and write what you can think of off the top of your head. You will be defining and refining each of these components later in this step.

Assets/features:

_____

_____

Benefits:

_____

_____

Competitive edge:

_____

_____

Value proposition:

_____

_____

Return on investment:

_____

_____

Now, let's get into developing each of these areas so that you have a full understanding of what you have to offer and can develop your own unique personal brand message to use in your cover letter.

ASSESS YOUR GOALS AND THE PURPOSE OF YOUR COVER LETTER

The general purpose of a cover letter is to help you land an interview so that you can get a job. But in order for you to achieve this purpose, you have to have a clear career goal in mind. Specifically, what kind of job are you seeking? Complete the following worksheet to define your current career goals.

DREAM JOB DESCRIPTION

Use the prompts below to describe your dream job, bar none. Think about what would make you happy.

Which job titles appeal to you? List several that you are interested in pursuing.

_____

_____

What sort of tasks would you most like to do?

_____

_____

_____

_____

Which job functions would you not want to do?

_____

_____

What kind of organization would you like to work for? What industry is it in and what size is it? Where is it?

_____

_____

_____

_____

What kind of work environment is ideal for you? Is your dream job a desk job or one in the field?

_____

_____

Whom do you work with? Is your dream job a position where you work with others or where you work independently?

_____

_____

What is your ideal work schedule? What hours would you work? Would you like to travel or telecommute?

_____

_____

_____

Step 2

Keep these overall career goals in mind as you craft your cover letter and and later when you respond to job openings. Use them as a guideline to define the purpose of your cover letter by filling in the blanks of the following worksheet. Note that this statement should not be used in your cover letter!

COVER LETTER PURPOSE

The purpose of my cover letter is to obtain a job as a _____ [ideal job title] where I can _____ and _____ [favorite work tasks] for an organization that _____ and _____ [most important work conditions].

IDENTIFY YOUR ASSETS/FEATURES

An important part of selling any product is to highlight its features. These are the things that make the product valuable to a buyer. In the case of a cover letter, you are the product, and the prospective employer is the buyer. Your features are your assets.

Everyone has unique assets. These personal traits, competencies, and qualifications can include anything about you that might be valuable to an employer:

✔ Personal attributes/characteristics

✔ Transferable skills and areas of expertise

✔ Degrees, licenses, and certifications

✔ Any other acquired knowledge, expertise, or related skills

To ensure that you leave no stone unturned in finding all of your features, I have included worksheets in the following sections for your input on all of these types of assets. Being so thorough takes time, but it also is thought provoking. In addition, you need a complete picture of your assets in order to develop your benefits.

Determine Your Personal Attributes and Characteristics

In terms of careers, a *personal attribute* is a quality that helps you on the job or in your profession. A *characteristic* is something that helps to describe or identify you. When I ask clients what their attributes are, they typically can come up with only a few, or they find it difficult to determine any at all. To make this process easier for you, I've included a complete listing of attributes or characteristics that are helpful to career-minded individuals. Certain attributes are important to certain careers. So think in terms of those attributes that help you on the job.

PERSONAL ATTRIBUTES AND CHARACTERISTICS

Check all of the personal attributes and characteristics you feel come closest to who you are and that help you in your profession. Items in bold are important attributes for all management professionals.

Step 2

- **Able to develop loyalty in staff**
- Able to help others solve problems
- Able to overcome adversity
- **Able to overcome barriers and obstacles**
- Able to show good judgment
- Able to show initiative
- Able to streamline operations
- Accepting
- Accessible
- Accommodating
- Accountable
- Accurate
- **Action-driven leader**
- Active
- Adaptable
- Adventurous
- Advocate
- Aesthetically inclined
- Agile
- Alert
- Ambitious
- Analytical
- **Approachable**
- Articulate
- Artistic
- Assertive
- Astute
- Attentive
- Authoritative
- Autonomous
- Balanced
- Budget conscious
- Calm
- **Candid**
- Caring
- Cautious
- Challenge seeker
- Chameleon-like
- Cheerful
- Child focused
- Client focused
- Client service-oriented
- Collaborative
- Comfortable with ambiguity
- **Commanding**
- Committed

- Communicative
- Community-oriented
- Compassionate
- Competitive
- **Composed**
- Comprehensive
- Computer literate
- **Conceptualizer**
- Conciliatory
- Concise
- Confident
- **Conflict manager**
- Congenial
- Connected
- Conscientious
- Considerate
- Consistent
- Convincing
- Cooperative
- Coordinator
- Courteous
- Crafty
- Creative
- Credible
- Critical thinker
- Cultivator
- Curious
- Customer service-oriented
- Deadline conscious
- Decisive
- Dedicated
- Degreed
- Delegator
- Dependable
- Detail oriented
- Devoted
- Diligent
- Diplomatic
- Director
- Disciplined
- Discreet
- Diversity manager
- Down-to-earth
- Driven
- Dynamic
- Easy to get along with
- Easygoing
- Economical
- Educated
- Effective
- Efficient

- Empathetic
- Empowered
- Empowering
- Encouraging
- Energetic
- Engaging
- Entertaining
- Enthusiastic
- Entrepreneurial
- **Ethical**
- Expeditor
- Experienced
- Expert
- Expressive
- Facilitator
- Fair
- Flexible
- Focused
- Follow-up oriented
- Forward-thinking
- Friendly
- Future-oriented
- Generous
- Genuine
- Globally focused
- Goal driven
- Good at working under pressure
- Good listener
- Hardworking
- Health-conscious
- Healthy perspective
- Helpful
- Honest
- Humanistic
- Humorous
- Imaginative
- Impartial
- Implementer
- Inclusive
- Independent
- Influencer
- Initiator
- **Innovative**
- Inquisitive
- Insightful
- **Inspiring**
- Instructor
- **Integral**
- Intelligent
- International
- Intuitive

- Inventive
- Investigative
- Kind
- Leader
- Learning oriented
- Levelheaded
- Likable
- Logical thinker
- Loyal
- Mechanical
- Mediator
- **Mentor**
- Methodical
- Meticulous
- **Morale builder**
- Motivated
- Motivator
- Multiskilled
- Multitalented
- Multitasker
- Negotiator
- Nonjudgmental
- **Nonthreatening**
- Nurturing
- Objective
- Observant
- Open
- Opportunistic
- Optimistic
- Organized
- Original
- Outcome focused
- Outgoing
- **Outside-the-box thinker**
- Passionate
- Patient
- People oriented
- Perceptive
- Persevering
- Persistent
- Personable
- Persuasive
- Philanthropic
- Physical
- **Planner**
- Pleasant
- Politician
- Positive
- Practical
- Precise
- Presenter

(continued)

PERSONAL ATTRIBUTES AND CHARACTERISTICS *(continued)*

Step 2

- Priority setter
- Proactive
- Problem solver
- Process oriented
- Productive
- Professional
- **Profitability conscious**
- Project oriented
- Prolific
- Promoter
- Protector
- Punctual/prompt
- Quality conscious
- Quick learner
- Rapport builder
- Realistic
- Reasonable
- Recruiter
- Refined
- Reflective
- **Relationship builder**
- Reliable

- Resilient
- Resourceful
- Respected
- Respectful
- Responsible
- Responsive
- Results oriented
- **Revenue growth oriented**
- **Risk taker**
- Role model
- Safety conscious
- Savvy
- Security conscious
- Self-confident
- Self-directed
- Self-disciplined
- Self-motivated
- Self-reliant
- Self-starter
- Sense of humor
- Sensible

- Sensitive to others
- Service oriented
- Sincere
- **Skilled at employee retention**
- Skilled interpersonally
- Sociable
- **Sound decision maker**
- Spiritual
- Stable
- **Straightforward**
- **Strategic**
- Streamline operations
- Success driven
- Successful
- Supportive
- Systematic
- Tactful
- **Tactical action plan developer**
- Task oriented
- **Team builder**

- Team oriented
- Team player
- Technical
- Thorough
- Thoughtful
- Time manager
- Tolerant
- Trendsetter
- Troubleshooter
- Trusting
- Trustworthy
- Understanding
- Versatile
- Visionary
- Vital
- Warm
- Well rounded
- Willing to learn
- Willing to try new things
- Wise
- Witty
- Youthful

Determine Your Transferable Skills and Areas of Expertise

Everybody has *transferable skills* they have garnered throughout the years in their profession or position and even in life. These skills are useful in many jobs. *Areas of expertise* are knowledge and skills that you have gained in a particular field (profession-specific areas of expertise) or in various functions (function-specific

> **note** You will be playing up these skills to develop your brand niche. Determining your niche does not mean you have to be an expert in all areas of your job, you can just focus on the functions you excel in to develop your niche of expertise.

areas of expertise) within your chosen industry. All of these skills can be summed up in *keywords* that are specific to your industry. In your cover letter, it's important to include keywords that both describe your skills and are related to the position you are seeking.

In the following examples, the keyword in bold is the profession-specific area of expertise, and the other keywords indicate function-specific areas of expertise:

✔ **Marketing:** Internet marketing, demographic studies, competitive surveys, product launches, pricing analysis, brand management, PowerPoint presentations

✔ **Teaching:** Lesson plan development, thematic units creation, classroom management, self-esteem building, technology integration, special education inclusion, cooperative learning

✔ **Accounting:** General ledger, accounts receivable, accounts payable, tax return preparation, bank reconciliations, year-end closings

✔ **Project Management:** Building plan reviews, on-site construction management, trades coordination, contractor negotiations, punch lists completion

To find keywords for your transferable skills and areas of expertise, look at your resume, job descriptions that match your position title, job postings on job boards, classified ads, performance evaluations, and so on. You can consolidate all of these keywords on the following worksheet.

> **note** The *Step-by-Step Resumes* book lists hundreds of keywords for skills in specific areas of expertise.

Step 2

TRANSFERABLE SKILLS

List all of your transferable skills:

_____   _____   _____
_____   _____   _____
_____   _____   _____
_____   _____   _____
_____   _____   _____
_____   _____   _____
_____   _____   _____

AREAS OF EXPERTISE

List your areas of expertise:

_____   _____   _____
_____   _____   _____
_____   _____   _____
_____   _____   _____
_____   _____   _____
_____   _____   _____

List Your Degrees, Licenses, and Certifications

Continue compiling your assets and features by noting all of your degrees, licenses, and certifications. For example, if you work as a nurse, your assets in this area may include one of the following:

✔ Bachelor's degree in nursing

✔ Registered Nurse

✔ Licensed Practical Nurse

DEGREES, LICENSES, AND CERTIFICATIONS

List any degrees, licenses, and/or certifications you have attained on the following lines:

_____

_____

_____

_____

List Any Other Acquired Knowledge or Related Skills

In the following worksheet, list any other acquired knowledge or related skills that might be important to your profession. These skills may have been garnered from other professions, your personal life, volunteer positions, internships, seminars, professional associations, and so on.

OTHER ACQUIRED KNOWLEDGE OR RELATED SKILLS

List any other related skills you have here:

_____

_____

_____

_____

You have now completed one-third of the process of building your personal brand. If you can hang on through the rest of this chapter, I promise the rest of the book will just fly by. If you need to, take a break and come back with a refreshed mind to continue.

TARGET YOUR ASSETS AND FEATURES TO PROSPECTIVE EMPLOYERS

To position yourself as a perfect match for prospective employers, you must show how you can meet or exceed their requirements through your assets and achievements. This process will help you understand the components of your brand better and will give you more compelling information for your cover letter.

Research and Identify Employers' Requirements

Before you can be sure that your assets/features meet the requirements of prospective employers, you must first know exactly what those requirements are. With Internet access, that is easy to do: Just enter the words *job description* followed by your preferred job title(s), all within quotation marks, in your favorite Internet search engine. Scroll through random or specific job descriptions that come closest to the position(s) you seek. It doesn't matter whether the positions are local or you would otherwise apply for them. This step is for informational purposes only. Read at least three.

tip — If you are a form hater, you can either print out the job descriptions you find and write your qualifications next to each requirement listed or copy and paste them into the Prospective Employer's Requirements form on the CD. Then skip to the next section.

For each type of position sought, use the following form (the CD at the back of the book has it as a file) to combine all the descriptions you read for a certain job title into one list of the important requirements prospective employers most often state.

The following sample shows the information gathered for a social worker position.

Position title: clinical social worker, professional counselor

Required number of years of experience: 5 years preferred

Education requirement, if any: Bachelor's degree

Licenses or certifications required: LBSW (Licensed Social Worker)

Job summary: Planning, implementing, and evaluating programs and services in the social services department in accordance with federal, state, and local standards and established procedures to ensure that the medically related emotional and social needs of patients are met.

Job functions/main activities:
1. Work with residents and their families to achieve optimal outcomes.
2. Meet with medical and nursing staff in planning social services.
3. Develop working relationships with colleagues and other agencies.
4. Receive, transmit, store, retrieve, and manage information in line with good practice and departmental policy and procedure.

Required knowledge:
1. Risk assessment of parents, critical analysis, and decision-making
2. Relevant legislation and appropriate court procedures

Practical skills required:
1. Able to organize and prioritize many tasks effectively.
2. Able to react to emergency situations appropriately when required.
3. Ability to communicate effectively in all formats.

Personal qualities and attributes:
1. Have an enormous amount of patience and compassion.
2. Believe in teamwork and care about what you do every day.
3. Must be a skilled communicator, director, and motivator.

PROSPECTIVE EMPLOYER'S REQUIREMENTS

Position title: _____

Required number of years of experience: _____

Education requirement, if any: _____

Licenses or certifications required: _____

Job summary: _____

_____

_____

_____

_____

Job functions/main activities:

1. _____

2. _____

3. _____

4. _____

5. _____

6. _____

7. _____

8. _____

Required knowledge:

1. _____

2. _____

3. _____

4. _____

Practical skills required:

1. _____

2. _____

3. _____

4. _____

Personal qualities and attributes:

1. _____

2. _____

3. _____

4. _____

Other requirements:_____

Step 2

> **note** You don't have to match all requirements exactly. Know that a prospective employer's wish list may include more requirements than are generally accepted. You may meet or exceed these requirements in different ways, as in the first and second examples in the following table.

Match Your Assets and Features to Prospective Employers' Requirements

The next part of this process is to take the list of the requirements you gathered from job postings and position descriptions and address all the ways you can meet these requirements by using the lists of features you made in the previous section. The following table shows an example of a job seeker who is targeting a social worker position.

Position Requirement	How Met
Minimum of a bachelor's degree in psychology	Master of Social Work degree.
5 years of social work experience	7 years of experience in the field (4 as a social worker, 3 as a therapist).
Ability to handle a large caseload, providing counseling, advocacy, and linkage services	Have handled caseloads from 5 to 35 in various types of facilities, providing counseling, advocacy, linkage, and outreach services, as well as developing psychosocial evaluations and individualized treatment plans and keeping up-to-date progress notes.
Ability to communicate with all types of people and cultures	Bilingual Spanish-English. Worked with adolescents through adults in schools, hospitals, rehab facilities, and other settings. Handled a wide range of clients/patients from a variety of cultures and socioeconomic backgrounds, including those who were gifted, autistic, emotionally disturbed, and learning disabled.

MATCH YOUR ASSETS TO EMPLOYER REQUIREMENTS

List the position requirements in the left column. Next to each requirement, indicate how you can meet or exceed it.

Position Requirements	How Your Assets Meet or Exceed the Requirements
_____	_____
_____	_____
_____	_____
_____	_____
_____	_____
_____	_____
_____	_____
_____	_____
_____	_____
_____	_____
_____	_____
_____	_____
_____	_____
_____	_____
_____	_____
_____	_____
_____	_____

Step 2

Identify Matching Achievements That Prove Your Expertise

Make a list of all achievements that substantiate your expertise in your field. At this stage, jot down absolutely everything you can think of. (Later, you will select the ones that match your branding strategy.) Be sure to include achievements that demonstrate the requirements sought by prospective employers for the position(s) you seek. Of course, you can and should also include accomplishments that exceed what is required!

Note how each of the following examples matches an employer need or requirement with an achievement.

note This exercise is best accomplished by extracting and summarizing key accomplishments from your completed resume. You should not replicate the achievements in your resume word for word, but instead should include only their essence in order to whet the hiring manager's appetite for reading your resume. (Numerous achievement examples are included in the companion to this book, *Step-by-Step Resumes*.)

Job seeker: Pharmaceutical executive

Job requirement: Ability to increase sales through selective markets.

Achievement: Increased annual sales $3.5 million by implementing preferred provider agreements with managed care facilities.

Job seeker: Sales associate

Job requirement (for a management position): Provide leadership to a team of sales associates.

Achievement: Selected over 200 other sales associates for the firm's management training program.

Job seeker: Registered nurse

Job requirement: Able to cover several different units in a large hospital.

Achievement: Nine years of nursing experience in hospital and nursing home settings, including ICU, Telemetry, Open Heart Recovery, Emergency Room, and SICU.

note You will find numerous other achievement examples in the cover letter foundations, paragraphs, and samples throughout this book.

Job seeker: IT executive

Job requirement: Manage IT responsibilities for a large company.

Achievement: Spearheaded a total corporate connectivity initiative by directing the installation and configuration of multiple operating systems to run on the same server.

YOUR KEY ACCOMPLISHMENTS

Write your achievements in the space provided below or type them in a copy of this form (which is available on the CD).

1. _____

_____

2. _____

_____

3. _____

_____

4. _____

_____

5. _____

_____

6. _____

_____

7. _____

_____

8. _____

_____

9. _____

_____

10. _____

_____

After you identify your most important assets or features and related achievements, the next step in building your brand is to use these features to develop your benefits, and then your value proposition, and finally your return on investment to your prospective employers. Once you have all of that information, you will be able to create your brand message.

Step 2

DOCUMENT THE BENEFITS YOU OFFER TO EMPLOYERS

Just like any other marketing materials, your cover letter should identify the benefits of purchasing (or in this case, hiring) the product (in this case, you). For example, you wouldn't purchase a washing machine because it was "large." This particular feature might have you considering and worrying about other things, such as space constraints or the cost of doing your laundry. Effective advertising does not sell the features of a product; it sells the benefits of that product. In the case of the washing machine, the benefit is that it is "energy efficient," which means that it saves electricity, and therefore it costs less money to run (which is the value proposition offered to consumers).

The assets you defined in the previous sections are the features you have to offer your prospective employers. You make employers want these features when you explain how these features can help them. These are the *benefits* employers would derive from hiring you. These benefits are important to include in your cover letter because they make a compelling case to hire you. Identifying these benefits is a two-part process of first learning what the employers' needs are and then connecting your features with those needs. This process is similar to the process of matching your assets to employer requirements, but it takes a broader view.

Find Out Employers' Needs and Challenges

An employer *need* is a motivational/psychological feature that helps the employer meet a desired goal. As a job seeker, your aim is to proactively determine what some of these goals might be. In order to be able to meet employer needs, you have to offer employers ways in which you can solve their problems, resolve their challenges, or otherwise reach their goals.

To determine how you can best meet your prospective employers' needs, you need to have a good idea of what those needs are. Conducting some research to determine the types of challenges your prospective employers might face in the industry in which you are applying will help—especially if you are new to the field. You can go to their websites, request brochures, and ask others in the field. You can even request an information interview or call as a customer to see what they offer. If you have experience in the industry, jot down various types of challenges your previous employers faced and how you were able to help them overcome them.

They say that forewarned is forearmed. In seeking a position, this maxim holds true. If you know or can anticipate the type of challenges employers in your industry face, you can predetermine ways you can help them solve their challenges, which puts you a step ahead of other job candidates and helps you to become the type of candidate hiring managers seek. This information is also helpful when you are being interviewed.

In the following worksheet, state the various types of challenges your prospective employers might face and ways you might be able to help them meet and resolve those challenges. For example, a challenge for many employers is to increase market share and profits. Possible solutions for this challenge are to tap into untapped markets, use effective brand management, develop successful marketing campaigns, implement a sales support program, hire a public relations expert, implement better corporate communications, and the like.

EMPLOYER CHALLENGES AND POSSIBLE SOLUTIONS

Employer Challenges   **Possible Solutions**

1. _____   _____
                                          _____
                                          _____
2. _____   _____
                                          _____
                                          _____
3. _____   _____
                                          _____
                                          _____
4. _____   _____
                                          _____
                                          _____
5. _____   _____
                                          _____
                                          _____

Determine How Your Assets Help Employers

Select a dozen or more of your most important assets from the previous worksheets you filled in about your personal attributes, your transferable skills and areas of expertise, your education, your licenses and/or certifications, and other acquired knowledge. Choose the ones that play an important role in your being able to expertly fulfill your job responsibilities and achieve success for your employers.

Then use what you have learned about employer requirements to help you identify benefits that relate to the features you have selected. Use the following worksheet (which is also on the CD) to list your top features and their related benefits.

The more benefits you identify now, the more choices you have to include in your cover letter when you complete your draft. The following examples show how you can weave features and benefits into compelling cover letter statements. The bold text is the feature and the plain text is the benefit:

- ✔ Being a **good communicator and listener** helps me to learn about hurdles early on, resolve employee issues, and improve morale (thereby increasing productivity and decreasing employee turnover).

- ✔ Being an **out-of-the-box thinker** allows me to easily tackle problems and strategize new solutions (that elevate my employers' profitability).

- ✔ Being a **logical thinker** provides me with a practical, commonsense, decision-making process that takes the mystery out of problem solving (thereby increasing productivity and cutting costs).

- ✔ Being **security conscious** helps me to determine areas that require correction or more oversight (thereby eliminating accidents and potential lawsuits).

These examples provide more than just the benefit. The text in parentheses is the *value proposition* that these benefits provide. You will develop a value proposition later in this step.

WAYS YOUR FEATURES HELP EMPLOYERS

Write in your top features in the left column and then explain how each feature benefits employers in the right column.

Feature	Benefit
1.	
2.	
3.	
4.	
5.	
6.	
7.	
8.	
9.	
10.	
11.	
12.	

Step 2

You are now halfway through developing your own unique personal brand. If you are finding this step tedious, stop, get a cup of coffee, and refresh yourself. Just be sure to come back to this step with a fresh, open mind and complete it, because it is important to your career and your life.

DETERMINE YOUR COMPETITIVE EDGE

Compare yourself with other like-minded job candidates and individuals. Picture coworkers who possibly handled the same or a similar position or job function as you. Think about others whom you network or associate with. Then answer these questions:

✔ What do you have to offer versus your competition?

✔ Did you make or sell more (or better) products?

✔ Are you faster, more thorough, or more quality-oriented than others at your job?

✔ Have you won awards for your achievements? What were they for?

✔ Were you selected over others because of something you do well?

✔ Did you save or make money for your employers or otherwise increase their bottom line?

✔ Are you good at coming up with solutions to problems?

✔ Do you have additional knowledge, education, or other qualifications that exceed job requirements and help you perform your job better?

✔ Do you receive high performance evaluations? If so, what is noted that you do exceptionally well?

✔ Do you have a knack for getting along with people?

✔ Do people look up to you and respect your word?

✔ Do you outcompete others in any other way?

If you can answer yes to any of these questions or have other similar traits that make you stand out from others, then you already have a competitive edge. If you are having trouble coming up with your own competitive edge, think about what others may have said to you or about you about something you do well. Then also keep in mind what you know you do well on your job.

The following examples show the individual's competitive edge as well as the value proposition this edge provides to the prospective employer (in parentheses). I have provided a number of examples in this step, because it is difficult for most people to see how they might outcompete another candidate, even in a position they are thoroughly familiar with.

✔ **For a graphic designer or website developer:** The ability to write content as well as design pages is an uncommon feature (that allows the firm to save money on having to hire a copy writer). The knowledge of several web development or page layout programs as opposed to just one is another competitive edge (providing versatility to the firm and/or its clients). The ability to code sites or lay out pages quicker than most is another competitive edge (that increases productivity and helps cut costs).

✔ **For a sales manager:** Having knowledge or experience in various aspects of marketing and/or working directly with marketing specialists on marketing campaigns, for example, in addition to having sales experience will put you a cut above other competitors who only have sales experience. (Marketing experience allows you to perhaps make more seamless and comprehensive sales presentations, increase market share, and/or address prospective client questions more thoroughly and convincingly, thereby increasing sales for your employer.)

✔ **For a secretary or word processor:** A background in bookkeeping software might make you more attractive to an employer (because you can support both administrative and accounting functions, thereby saving the employer money on outsourcing), as would a thorough knowledge of MS Word where you have created tables, brochures, annual reports, or other specialized projects (providing employers with a more skilled candidate who is able to run with anything that comes his or her way).

✔ **For a resume writer or career coach:** The knowledge of various career development and career management areas, such as web portfolio development, personal branding, social networking profile development, interview skills training, job search coaching, and outplacement services, as opposed to just resume writing or career coaching alone, attracts more clients (because more and different services can be offered, thereby increasing income potential).

✔ **For a civil engineer:** Experience in designing commercial and residential structures or public and private buildings in addition to a civil engineering specialization such as highways, airports, bridges, power plants, pipelines, and/or transportation systems, for example, might help in solving structural problems on the job (thereby averting time delays and possible liability suits).

YOUR COMPETITIVE EDGE

In the space provided, make a list of everything you can think of that might make you stand out over your competition and give you the competitive edge.

1. _____
2. _____
3. _____
4. _____
5. _____
6. _____
7. _____
8. _____
9. _____
10. _____
11. _____
12. _____

DEVELOP YOUR VALUE PROPOSITION

Your *value proposition* is how your benefits and competitive edge create unique, added value to a hiring firm. It's how you can differentiate yourself from other candidates applying for the same position and showcase your value to a prospective employer. The value proposition answers the question, "How does this benefit help an employer?" Your benefits and value proposition, along with your return on investment (to be discussed in the next section), are what sell you to an employer.

Use the following worksheet to convert your benefits into the value propositions you have to offer your prospective employers. For examples of value propositions, refer to the bulleted lists in the "Determine How Your Assets Help Employers" and "Determine Your Competitive Edge" sections. The value propositions are in parentheses.

YOUR VALUE PROPOSITION

In the spaces provided, list each of your benefits from the previous "Ways Your Features Help Employers" worksheet and indicate how they can help your prospective employers, that is, the value proposition that you have to offer if they hire you instead of someone else.

Benefit	Value Proposition

You are now a good part of the way done with developing your personal brand. Need more coffee? A break? Or are you "good to go"?

UNCOVER YOUR RETURN ON INVESTMENT (ROI) TO PROSPECTIVE EMPLOYERS

With a shaky economy, job candidates generally think they have little opportunity to secure a position. That's because having the right qualifications for an available position is not enough. To get the position, you have to have good self-promotion, which includes an effective cover letter and resume. Determining your return on investment to prospective employers is a critical step in creating these documents because ROI shows employers why you are the best candidate for the position.

Your *return on investment* to a firm is a measurement that shows hiring managers the future value of hiring you. Your ROI is a statement of how you are able to fulfill your prospective employers' greatest need(s), that is, meet their challenges, solve their problems, and/or somehow enhance their bottom line. In essence, prospective employers will weigh the cost versus the ROI of hiring you.

Step 1 explained (in the section "Determine an Employer's Needs") how to find an employer's core need by asking yourself how fulfilling each lesser need helps the employer until you can no longer answer the question. The research you did about employer needs and requirements when identifying your assets and benefits earlier in this step is useful in determining your ROI.

YOUR ROI TO PROSPECTIVE EMPLOYERS

Use the space provided to explain how your assets, benefits, competitive edge, and value proposition will help you meet your prospective employer's greatest need.

_____

_____

_____

_____

_____

_____

_____

CREATE AND EDIT YOUR BRAND MESSAGE

Now that you have identified your assets/features, benefits, competitive edge, value proposition, and return on investment to employers, you have all of the essential ingredients to develop your brand message. Your brand message is a statement about who you are that encompasses everything that makes you unique and sets you apart in your own authentic professional niche. You will include this message (written in the first person) in your cover letter.

Step 1 included the following example of a brand message for a marketing specialist. You can use this example as a foundation for your own brand message, as shown in Personal Brand Message Foundation 1.

I develop strategic, innovative marketing campaigns (feature) that meet my employer's target audience's direct needs (benefit), thereby putting my employer ahead of its competition in the marketplace (competitive edge), increasing its market share, and helping it to sell more products and services (value proposition), which results in increased profits (return on investment).

PERSONAL BRAND MESSAGE FOUNDATION 1

I [develop/implement/manage/perform/conduct/other: _____] _____ [what?] that _____ [does what?], thereby _____ [accomplishing what?], which results in _____ [what benefits or ROI?] for your firm.

Personal Brand Message Foundation 2 and the examples that follow it show how this basic format can apply to many different careers.

PERSONAL BRAND MESSAGE FOUNDATION 2

As a(n) _____ [job title], I _____ [what you do, your features] for _____ [type of organizations you provide benefits to] so they can _____ _____ [what you help them achieve through your value proposition and ROI] through my _____, _____, and _____ [your competitive edge attributes].

Example: Marketing Specialist

As a marketing specialist, **I** develop and launch innovative new products and brands to new untapped target markets **for** forward-thinking companies **so they can** dramatically increase their revenues **through my** visionary creativity, innovative ideas, **and** knowledge of the consumer market.

Example: Customer Service Manager

As an experienced customer service manager, **I** direct and oversee sales, customer service, merchandising, front end, and warehouse areas **for** Fortune 500 grocery chains **so they can** improve staff performance, increase service levels, streamline supply flow, elevate customer loyalty, and increase sales **through my** consumer-needs awareness **and** value-added approach.

Example: Compliance Officer

As a proactive compliance officer, **I** am an objective reviewer and evaluator **for** various departments of large corporations **so they can** be sure that all business activities are in compliance with regulatory requirements and company policies and procedures **through my** ability to identify potential risk areas **and** immediately resolve compliance issues.

Example: Purchasing Agent

As a purchasing agent, **I** perform all facets of buying, merchandising, inventory control, and order processing **for** all departments of small to midsize businesses **so they can** successfully deliver products on time, increase purchasing service levels, and slash costs **through my** skillful contract negotiations **and** ability to control inventory to meet the firms' needs.

Example: Vice President of New Business Development

As a new business development executive, **I** develop visionary products, increase market share, drive sales and revenues, and elevate product profitability **for** forward-thinking technology firms **so they can** deliver profits to shareholders **through my** strategic planning leadership and direction, new program creation, **and** new business development initiatives.

If these foundations don't quite match with what you do or can fulfill for a prospective employer, there are numerous other brand messages contained within this book that you can use as a foundation.

REVISED DRAFT OF YOUR BRAND MESSAGE

Use the space provided to create a statement that includes all of your features, benefits, competitive edge, value proposition, and return on investment.

_____

_____

_____

_____

_____

_____

_____

Step 2

Determine the Best Strategy to Convey Your Brand

All branding—be it business branding or personal branding—requires a marketing strategy to work effectively. In this case, you need a marketing strategy for your personal brand in order to get a job. This strategy pulls together your features, benefits, value proposition, and return on investment in a cover letter statement that positions you as an excellent candidate who outcompetes your peers.

Here is an example:

> I will use my creativity and out-of-the-box thinking skills (features) to exhibit to a prospective employer how I can increase sales and profitability for their firm (return on investment) through the use of visionary and creative problem solving, innovative product launches, remerchandised brands, and effective advertising campaigns (benefits) that will increase market share and penetration (value proposition).

Now use the following worksheet to create your own brand strategy.

YOUR BRAND STRATEGY

Using the features, benefits, value proposition, and return on investment that you created in earlier sections of this step, write a brand strategy to use in your cover letter.

_____

_____

_____

_____

_____

_____

_____

Now that you know the branding strategy you plan to use, go back to the worksheet titled, "Your Key Accomplishments." Take a look at all the achievements you have already listed and identify the achievements that best support your brand message and strategy (the following worksheet provides space for you to list these). When you write the paragraphs in your cover letter, be sure that each of these achievements is listed or included in some fashion. The foundations throughout this book will show places you can insert these.

ACCOMPLISHMENTS THAT SUPPORT YOUR BRAND

Briefly list achievements that best support your personal brand and marketing strategy:

1. _____

_____

2. _____

_____

3. _____

_____

4. _____

_____

5. _____

_____

Develop Your Slogan/Tagline

A *slogan* or *tagline* is a memorable succinct phrase or motto that best sells you by summing up your brand in a nutshell. It reinforces your brand's position and promise and helps to set you apart from your competition. Developing a slogan isn't necessary to create your brand message, but if your slogan is poignant and memorable, it can be beneficial by way of its emotional impact, employer benefits, and image recall. Each time prospective employers see your brand—with your slogan as part of that brand—they will remember how you stood out from other job candidates (just another something that helps make employers want to seek you out).

When pondering a slogan for yourself, think in terms of what your greatest benefit would be to sell to prospective employers. What would get them excited? What benefits of your product—*you*—would you like them to know about and remember? Job search is all about persuasive selling, and your slogan is no exception. To get your creative juices flowing, here are some sample slogan ideas for various professions:

- ✔ **Construction superintendent:** "Bringing Projects in Within Budget and on Time, Every Time"
- ✔ **Sous chef:** "Serving Dining Patrons Since 2000" or "From Gourmet Appetizers to Fine Desserts"
- ✔ **Creative Director:** "Helping You to Brand Clients Better Than Their Competition"
- ✔ **Charter Pilot:** "Flying from the Caribbean to Mexico and Everywhere in Between"

Use the following worksheet to develop a tagline or slogan for your personal brand. When you have come up with one that captures your brand, be sure to place it on your final cover letter. You can put your slogan in quotation marks in the margin of your cover letter by using a larger, italic, or bold font; use it as a header at the top of your cover letter; or include it under your name. Step 9 provides more details and examples for how to incorporate a slogan into your cover letter.

CREATE A TAGLINE

Brainstorm and jot down all possible ideas and/or words that might work in a slogan or tagline that summarizes who you are as a brand and the benefits of hiring you.

_____

_____

_____

_____

Now write a punchy slogan (tagline) of one to nine words that states your value proposition. Develop and edit your tagline based on the ideas and critical words you listed above.

_____

_____

_____

This book gets easier from this point on. Throughout the remainder of this book, I have included fill-in-the-blank foundations that will help you with developing your cover letter and including your personal brand message.

Create Your Final Brand Message

Now that you have identified the features and benefits of hiring you, as well as your value proposition and return on investment to your prospective employers, it is time to develop your personal brand message. You can include your brand message right in your first cover letter paragraph and/or use it throughout the first three paragraphs. Additional information contained in your cover letter substantiates and backs up your value proposition claim (employer promise).

Compile what you have learned in the following worksheet. After you complete it, compare it with the one you prepared at the beginning of this step to be sure you didn't leave out anything important. Also take a look at how far you've come in developing and understanding your own unique personal brand!

YOUR REVISED PERSONAL BRANDING COMPONENTS

Use the space provided to document your features, benefits, competitive edge, value proposition, and return on investment to your prospective employers. Pick them up from the worksheets you completed throughout this step. Only list the ones you plan to include in your cover letter as part of your marketing strategy.

Assets/features:

_____

_____

Benefits:

_____

_____

Competitive edge:

_____

_____

Value proposition:

_____

_____

Return on investment (ROI):

_____

_____

Review each of the personal branding components in the preceding worksheet, and on a scrap piece of paper write them in various configurations and sentences to see what works best. Be sure to include as much content as you can in the least amount of words. Use the following worksheet to document your results. Check to be sure that all five critical personal branding components—features, benefits, competitive edge, value proposition, and return on investment—are included!

FINAL DRAFT OF YOUR BRAND MESSAGE

In the space provided, document and edit your final brand message—the one you will be including in your cover letter.

_____

_____

_____

_____

_____

_____

step 3

Write a Compelling First Paragraph

- Understand the Purpose of the First Paragraph
- Determine How to Use Your Personal Brand Message
- Draw the Reader In
- Include the Position Particulars
- Make the Reader Want to Read Further by Introducing Your Areas of Expertise
- Select a First Paragraph Foundation
- Write and Finalize Your First Paragraph

UNDERSTAND THE PURPOSE OF THE FIRST PARAGRAPH

Your first cover letter paragraph needn't and shouldn't be long. Two or three sentences work well. But you have a lot to accomplish in just a couple of sentences, so you need to write it strategically.

The first paragraph in your cover letter needs to accomplish four things:

1. Draw the reader in.

2. State the position you seek.

3. Identify where you heard about the position (if applicable).

4. Make the reader want to read further by introducing your areas of expertise.

This step explains various ways you can accomplish these things while also incorporating your personal brand.

DETERMINE HOW TO USE YOUR PERSONAL BRAND MESSAGE

tip

If your personal brand message is really strong and well stated, it could stand by itself as your entire cover letter. All you have to add is a line at the end in parentheses that states, "See resume for all of my qualifications and related achievements."

Now that you have developed your personal brand message and you know exactly what your personal brand is, you also know your features, benefits, competitive edge, value proposition, and return on investment to prospective employers—all critical components to include in your cover letter.

Keeping each of these components in mind as you develop your cover letter paragraphs, you have two options for how to include your unique branding information into your cover letter:

1. State your personal brand message exactly as you developed it in Step 2 and make that your very first cover letter paragraph, adding to it the particulars about the position you seek (these are specified in the section "Include the Position Particulars"). Because your brand statement includes your benefits and value proposition to entice your reader, it works exceptionally well as your first cover letter paragraph.

2. Create various personally branded statements that include your personal brand components separately or collectively throughout your cover letter. If you choose this method, you need to ensure that all five critical components are included within the cover letter.

note

These foundations are provided as an example and may or may not match what you have to offer; however, the remainder of the book provides tons of foundations from which you can select to find suitable paragraphs for your own cover letter.

To demonstrate how one brand plays out throughout a cover letter, I've provided five cover letter foundation paragraphs that you can fill in with information related to your brand. These foundation paragraphs are based on a cover letter I have created to highlight my own brand, which you can see broken up in the examples and in its entirety in Figure 3.1.

PERSONALLY BRANDED COVER LETTER PARAGRAPH 1 FOUNDATION

As a _____, _____, and _____ [your job title, certifi-
cations, degrees, or other assets], I bring to _____ [name of organization] _____ [number] years of
[global/national/industry-leading/other:_____] _____ [type of] expertise that can help your
[firm/clients/ other: _____] _____ [do what?]. As such, I am exploring
career opportunities as a _____ [job title] at _____ [name of organization] and am
attaching my resume for your review.

Sample personal brand message using the Paragraph 1 Foundation:

As a certified resume writer and career coach, personal branding strategist and marketer, creator of award-winning resume products, published author, **and** sought-after career speaker, **I bring to** Meadow University 20 **years of** industry-leading career management **expertise that can help your** students catapult their careers—right out of college! **As such, I am exploring career opportunities as a** career development director **at** Meadow University **and am attaching my resume for your review.**

PERSONALLY BRANDED COVER LETTER PARAGRAPH 2 FOUNDATION

Having _____ [action] of _____ [what or who?] during my career, I foster a _____ and _____ [personal characteristics] approach to meeting the
_____ [type of] needs of _____ [who or what?]. A [visionary thought leader/
other feature: _____], I am comfortable in an environment defined by _____,
_____ and _____ [employer- or industry-focused working conditions] and am
regarded as a [leading innovator/other feature: _____] at the forefront of _____
[what arena?].

Sample personal brand message using the Paragraph 2 Foundation:

Having championed the success **of** thousands of career-minded individuals **during my career, I foster a** comprehensive **and** innovative **approach to meeting the** career development **needs of** the twenty-first century job seeker. **A** visionary thought leader, **I am comfortable in an environment defined by** economic challenges, innovation, **and** technological advances **and am regarded as a** leading innovator **at the forefront of** strategic thinking, creativity, and change in the career management field.

PERSONALLY BRANDED COVER LETTER PARAGRAPH 3 FOUNDATION

I position _____ [whom or what?] in the top _____ [number] percent of
_____ [what?]. I accomplish this by strategically _____ [skills]
and developing _____ [what?]—critical in today's _____ [industry] world—by
_____ [skills].

Sample personal brand message using Paragraph 3 Foundation:

I position job seekers **in the top** 2 **percent of** candidates considered for jobs—even in a challenging environment. **I accomplish this by strategically** marketing and selling their benefits **and developing** their personal brand message **—critical in today's** work **world—by** defining their competitive edge, determining their value proposition, and capitalizing on their ROI to prospective employers**.**

PERSONALLY BRANDED COVER LETTER PARAGRAPH 4 FOUNDATION

My [industry-leading/other: _____] _____ [type of] expertise spans _____ , _____ , _____ , _____ , and _____ [areas of expertise]. To view information on any of these specializations, please [review my resume/go to my website/other: _____].

Sample personal brand message using Paragraph 4 Foundation:

My industry-leading career development **expertise spans** personal branding, resume and cover letter writing, career coaching, job searching, interview skills training, web resume development, positive online identity building, job board posting, social networking profile development, portfolio creation, **and more. To view information on any of these specializations, please** visit my Total Career Manager Center website at CareerImageBuilders.com. To view the groundbreaking resume and career products I have developed for and sell to career practitioners and job seekers worldwide, go to CareerCatapult.com**.**

PERSONALLY BRANDED COVER LETTER PARAGRAPH 5 FOUNDATION

If you would like your [firm/customers/patrons/other: _____] to _____ [employer goal], we should meet. I am confident that utilizing my [innovative techniques/trade secrets/other assets: _____] would help increase your [firm's/clients'/patrons'/other: _____] success rate in _____ [what area?] and, as such, contribute to _____ [name of organization's] growth and reputation. I will call you next week to see whether we can schedule a convenient time to discuss how my contributions can help _____ [name of organization] and its [clients/patrons/other: _____] and to learn more about your mission and goals. Thank you for your consideration!

Sample personal brand message using Paragraph 5 Foundation:

If you would like your students **to** outcompete others in their chosen profession after attending Meadow University, **we should meet. I am confident that utilizing my** innovative techniques and trade secrets **would help increase your** students' **success rate in** the business world **and, as such, contribute to** Meadow University's **growth and reputation. I will call you next week to see whether we can schedule a convenient time to discuss how my contributions can help** Meadow University **and its** students **and to learn more about your mission and goals. Thank you for your consideration!**

Figure 3.1 shows how these collective branding statements work together as one cover letter.

Evelyn U. Salvador, NCRW, JCTC

Phone: (555) 666-7777 • Fax: (555) 444-3333
Email: CareerCatapult@aol.com • Web Portfolio: EvelynSalvador.com

Mr. Alan Larkin
Human Resources Director
Meadow University
Smithville, IA 67891

Re: Career Development Director Position

Dear Mr. Larkin:

As a certified resume writer and career coach, personal branding strategist and marketer, creator of award-winning resume products, published author, and sought-after career speaker,[1] I bring to Meadow University 20 years of industry-leading career management expertise that can help your students catapult their careers—right out of college![2] I am exploring career opportunities as a career development director at Meadow University and am attaching my resume for your review.

Having championed the success of thousands of career-minded individuals during my career, I foster a comprehensive, innovative approach to meeting the career development needs of the twenty-first century job seeker. A visionary thought leader, I am comfortable in an environment defined by economic challenges, innovation, and technological advances and am regarded as a leading innovator at the forefront of strategic thinking, creativity, and change in the career management field.[3]

I position job seekers in the top 2 percent of candidates considered for jobs—even in a challenging environment. I accomplish this by strategically marketing and selling their benefits and developing their personal brand message—critical in today's world of work—by defining their competitive edge, determining their value proposition, and capitalizing on their ROI to prospective employers.[4]

My industry-leading career development expertise spans personal branding, resume and cover letter writing, career coaching, job searching, interview skills training, web resume and online career portfolio development, positive online identity building, job board posting, social networking profile development, portfolio creation, and more.[1] To view information on any of these specializations, please visit my Total Career Manager Center website at CareerImageBuilders.com. To view the groundbreaking resume and career products I have developed for and sell to career practitioners and job seekers worldwide, go to CareerCatapult.com. Links to other career development and business and personal branding websites are contained within these sites.

If you would like your students to outcompete others in their chosen profession after attending Meadow University,[3] we should meet. I am confident that utilizing my innovative techniques and trade secrets would help increase your students' success rate in the business world and, as such, contribute to Meadow University's growth and reputation.[5] I will call you next week to see whether we can schedule a convenient time to discuss how my contributions can help Meadow University and its students and to learn more about your mission and goals. Thank you for your consideration!

Sincerely,

Evelyn Salvador

Evelyn U. Salvador, NCRW, JCTC

Figure 3.1: Sample personally branded cover letter. Key: [1] assets, [2] value proposition, [3] competitive edge, [4] benefits, and [5] return on investment.

DRAW THE READER IN

Cover letters are like advertisements. If a headline in an ad doesn't catch your attention, do you continue reading about the product? Probably not. Likewise, many hiring managers skip reading applicant cover letters because the first sentence or two doesn't attract their attention. With so many applicants applying for positions, you need compelling cover letter statements that make hiring managers want to continue reading your cover letter, or they will pass it up entirely.

Instead of starting your first paragraph with a boring statement saying that you heard about a position and are enclosing your resume, think in terms of your prospective employer's needs. If you were the hiring manager filling the position you seek, exactly what would make you stand up and take notice? What "wow" factor might make you want to get to know this person?

As I mentioned in the preceding section, your personal brand message can be a great attention-getter. If you elect not to start your cover letter with your actual personal brand message, you will need to attract hiring managers in other ways. Following are some ideas:

✔ State your value proposition and/or return on investment right up top.

✔ State your passion, your track record, and/or your areas of expertise.

✔ Include your features and benefits to a prospective employer in your industry.

✔ Exhibit your competitive edge by stating what you have to offer.

In the following worksheet, jot down some ideas concerning what you have to offer that may catch the attention of your prospective employers and be sure to include them when you develop your cover letter draft.

IDEAS TO DRAW IN YOUR READER

Go back to the end of Step 2 where you developed each of the five components of your personal brand (in the worksheet titled "Your Revised Personal Branding Components"). Select components that would make a hiring manager stop and take notice, and list them below. Then expand those components into a paragraph with two or three sentences:

Idea 1: _____

_____

_____

Idea 2: _____

_____

_____

Idea 3: _____

_____

_____

Idea 4: _____

_____

_____

Idea 5: _____

_____

_____

INCLUDE THE POSITION PARTICULARS

Somewhere within your first cover letter paragraph you should address precisely what position you are seeking so the reader instantly knows what you are after without having to read through your entire cover letter to hunt for it, which they most probably will not do. In the examples at the beginning of this step, the position title appears at the very beginning of the paragraph.

Alternatively, you can state the job title right after the address section of your cover letter, as in the following example:

Re: Special Education Teacher position

Also include where you may have heard about the particular position, if applicable, such as on a particular job board, through a referral by a colleague, from a classified section of a newspaper, and so on.

In the following box, list the particulars you need to convey in your cover letter.

THE PARTICULARS YOU NEED TO CONVEY

Industry: _____

Position sought: _____

Where you heard of the position: _____

_____

Other: _____

MAKE THE READER WANT TO READ FURTHER BY INTRODUCING YOUR AREAS OF EXPERTISE

To make the reader of your cover letter want to read further, your first paragraph should also convey your primary area(s) of expertise (you listed these in Step 2 in the worksheet "Areas of Expertise"). List those in the following worksheet and be sure to include them in your first cover letter paragraph. Including your areas of expertise will also help when prospective employers search your cover letter and resume for applicable, matching keywords.

YOUR PRIMARY AREAS OF EXPERTISE

List your areas of expertise to be included in your first cover letter paragraph. Only include the areas that are directly related to the position you are applying for:

_____

_____

Write a sentence that includes your primary areas of expertise that are required for the position you seek. If you need help, refer to the following foundations.

_____

_____

_____

SELECT A FIRST PARAGRAPH FOUNDATION

The following 24 foundations are prewritten samples you can use by simply selecting applicable options and filling in the blanks with your own information. Or you can use them as a starting point to develop your own opening paragraph.

These foundations were created from actual cover letter paragraphs prepared by professional resume writers for their clients. The original submitted paragraphs are included as examples after each foundation. In the examples, the boldfaced words came from the foundation and the rest are applicable to the job seeker.

FIRST PARAGRAPH FOUNDATION 1

I believe my [broad experience/professional skill set/background/other: _____] in all [phases/aspects] of _____ [area or industry] coupled with my [master's/bachelor's/associate degree in _____ (major) or other feature: _____] uniquely qualifies me for a _____ [job title or type of] position in your [firm/company/organization]. I am enclosing my resume for your consideration.

EXAMPLE: CORPORATE TRAINER

I believe my broad experience **in all** phases **of** corporate training **coupled with my** master's degree in psychology **uniquely qualifies me for a** corporate trainer **position in your** firm. **I am enclosing my resume for your consideration.**

EXAMPLE: REGIONAL DIRECTOR OF SALES (CONTRIBUTED BY LAURIE BERENSON, CPRW)

I believe my professional skill set **in all** aspects **of** sales and sales management **coupled with my** strong knowledge of luxury goods **uniquely qualifies me for the** regional director of sales **position in your** company. **I am enclosing my resume for your consideration.**

EXAMPLE: SENIOR FINANCIAL SALES MANAGER (CONTRIBUTED BY LAURIE BERENSON, CPRW)

I believe my background **in all** phases **of** successfully building and managing client relationships **coupled with my** ability to provide ongoing, value-added client service **uniquely qualifies me for a** senior financial sales **position in your** investment firm. **I am enclosing my resume for your consideration.**

FIRST PARAGRAPH FOUNDATION 2

As a successful _____ [type of] [executive/manager/professional], I bring to your organization more than ____ [number] years of progressively responsible experience in _____, _____, and _____ [areas of expertise] for the _____ [type of] industry. My expertise lies in _____ and _____ [competitive edge knowledge]. My resume is enclosed for your consideration.

EXAMPLE: MANUFACTURING EXECUTIVE

As a successful manufacturing executive, **I bring to your organization more than** 13 **years of progressively responsible experience in** P&L direction, operations, finance management, marketing, labor relations, project management, **and** economic and business development **for the** paper manufacturing **industry. My expertise lies in** multimillion-dollar cost reductions **and** the development of proactive programs designed to drive and sustain revenues. **My resume is enclosed for your consideration.**

FIRST PARAGRAPH FOUNDATION 3

I am interested in exploring _____ [type of] opportunities within your firm and have enclosed my resume for your consideration. I believe my _____ and _____ [areas of expertise] experience together with my ability to _____ and _____ [skills] would assist your firm in meeting its _____ [type of] needs. My solid experience in _____ and _____ [areas of expertise] would serve your [firm/clients/patrons/other: _____] well.

EXAMPLE: GRAPHIC DESIGNER

I am interested in exploring graphic design **opportunities within your firm and have enclosed my resume for your consideration. I believe my** design **and** production **experience together with my ability to** manage special projects **and** create innovative and unique collateral pieces **would assist your firm in meeting its** graphic design **needs. My solid experience in** layout, design, four-color processing, prepress, **and** photo retouching **would serve your** clients **well.**

FIRST PARAGRAPH FOUNDATION 4

I believe my strong _____ and _____ [areas of expertise] experience coupled with my ability to _____ [skills] makes me an excellent candidate for a(n) _____ [job title] position within your organization. With broad experience in all phases of _____ [area of expertise], my forte is in _____ [what arena or niche?]. Based upon my _____ [type of] success, I am confident that I can be of considerable value to your organization. My resume is enclosed for your review.

EXAMPLE: ELECTRONIC ENGINEER

I believe my strong design **and** development **experience coupled with my ability to** integrate new software programs and cutting-edge technology with basic engineering and mechanical design principles **makes me an excellent candidate for an** electronic engineer **position within your organization. With broad experience in all phases of** running a tight business, **my forte is in** systems integration. **Based upon my** entrepreneurial **success, I am confident that I can be of considerable value to your organization. My resume is enclosed for your review.**

FIRST PARAGRAPH FOUNDATION 5

Developing the strategic roadmaps that help businesses define their _____ [what?], optimize _____ [what?], and maximize _____ [what?] is my expertise and my passion. My strengths in _____, _____, and _____ [areas of expertise] have been leveraged across multiple industries, including _____, _____, and _____ [which industries?], and have spanned _____ and _____ [type of firms].

EXAMPLE: MARKETING OR BRAND MANAGER (CONTRIBUTED BY BARBARA SAFANI, MA, CERW, MCRW, CPRW, CCM)

> **Developing the strategic roadmaps that help businesses define their** market differentiators, **optimize** brand reach, **and maximize** customer acquisition and retention **is my expertise and my passion. My strengths in** e-business transformation, brand unification, new market penetration, **and** product innovation **have been leveraged across multiple industries, including** consumer goods, technology, telecommunications, financial services, **and** advertising, **and have spanned** Fortune 50s, start-ups, **and** consulting practices.

FIRST PARAGRAPH FOUNDATION 6

Now that I have successfully revitalized _____ [name of company/division], overseeing a multimillion-dollar _____ [type of] project that _____ [benefits], I am seeking my next challenge. Proudly dedicating my career to _____ [doing what?], I am pleased to submit my resume for the _____ [job title] position advertised [on/in] _____ [where?]. I am confident that I will lead _____ [company name] in [developing/building/maintaining/other: _____] _____ _____ [what?].

EXAMPLE: GOLF COURSE SUPERINTENDENT (CONTRIBUTED BY AUGUST COHEN CARW, NCRW)

> **Now that I have successfully revitalized** ABC Country Club, **overseeing a multimillion-dollar** renovation **project that** returned the club to its premier status, **I am seeking my next challenge. Proudly dedicating my career to** executing significant restorations of classic golf courses and facilities, **I am pleased to submit my resume for the** golf course superintendent **position advertised** on Golf.net. **I am confident that I will lead** XYZ Country Club **in** maintaining its rich history and rewarding playing conditions.

FIRST PARAGRAPH FOUNDATION 7

Due to my _____ [industry] experience, I can provide your firm with _____ [competitive edge], particularly in regards to _____ [area of expertise]. As such, I am in a unique position to offer [insight/an enhanced ability] to _____ [do what?] in order to [strategize/develop/negotiate/achieve/other: _____] successful outcomes and _____ [value proposition] if given the opportunity to be a _____ [job title] with your firm. My resume is enclosed for your consideration.

EXAMPLE: GROUND OPERATIONS MANAGER (CONTRIBUTED BY BEVERLEY NEIL)

> **Due to my** airport **experience, I can provide your firm with** a first-hand understanding of airport culture and operations, **particularly in regards to** airport cost modeling to substantiate aeronautical and commercial lease pricing. **As such, I am in a unique position to offer** insight **to** communicate with the airports and government agencies **in order to** negotiate **successful outcomes and** form open, mutually beneficial relationships **if given the opportunity to be a** ground operations manager **with your firm. My resume is enclosed for your consideration.**

FIRST PARAGRAPH FOUNDATION 8

In today's tough economic climate where change is constant, it can be difficult to _____ [do what?]. With expertise in _____, _____, and _____ [areas of expertise], I can help _____ [company name] avoid many of the pitfalls associated with _____ [what?].

EXAMPLE: LAND ACQUISITION PROFESSIONAL (CONTRIBUTED BY ANGIE JONES, CPRW, CEIC)

In today's tough economic climate where change is constant, it can be difficult to identify a property's future potential**. With expertise in** market trends, pricing, growth, **and** supply, **I can help** Reed Enterprises **avoid many of the pitfalls associated with** the purchase of land or property**.**

FIRST PARAGRAPH FOUNDATION 9

Are you seeking a _____ [type of] _____ [job title] who believes in _____ [what?] and is a [change agent/other: _____] who earns respect by _____ [doing what?] and implementing key _____ [type of] initiatives on time and on budget while collaborating with _____ [who?]? If so, we should talk. My resume is enclosed for your review.

EXAMPLE: CHIEF INFORMATION OFFICER (CONTRIBUTED BY ANGIE JONES, CPRW, CEIC)

Are you seeking a hands-on chief information officer **who believes in** leading by example **and is a** change agent **who earns respect by** demonstrating a sound understanding of business goals and technology **and implementing key** technology **initiatives on time and on budget while collaborating with** a broad cross section of leaders**? If so, we should talk. My resume is enclosed for your review.**

FIRST PARAGRAPH FOUNDATION 10

The position of _____ [job title] for _____ [company name] matches my expertise, experience, and passion; therefore, it is with a high degree of [interest/confidence] that I seek this position and attach my resume for your review. I draw to your attention my _____ [competitive edge] and _____ [features], which combine to position me as a strong candidate for this role.

EXAMPLE: CHIEF EXECUTIVE OFFICER (CONTRIBUTED BY BEVERLEY NEIL)

The position of chief executive officer **for** CompTech **matches my expertise, experience, and passion; therefore it is with a high degree of** confidence **that I seek this position and attach my resume for your review. I draw to your attention my** years of leadership in the technology industry **and** fiscal responsibility, **which combine to position me as a strong candidate for this role.**

FIRST PARAGRAPH FOUNDATION 11

Working within the _____ [which?] industry to [sell/promote/provide/other: _____] beneficial [products/programs/projects/services/other: _____] is my passion. Throughout my career, building outstanding _____ [what?] and securing _____ [what?] have been major sources of challenge and [achievement/satisfaction/reward/other: _____] for me. My enclosed resume details my career thus far.

EXAMPLE: PERSONAL TRAINER (CONTRIBUTED BY BEVERLEY NEIL)

Working within the fitness **industry to** provide **beneficial** services **is my passion. Throughout my career, building outstanding** customer rapport **and securing** the sale **have been major sources of challenge and** achievement **for me. My enclosed resume details my career thus far.**

FIRST PARAGRAPH FOUNDATION 12

As soon as I saw your call for applications for a _____ [job title], I made putting this package together my first priority. That's because what drives me is _____ [what?], which is the underlying theme of my work as a _____ [what?]. In that role, I have delivered _____ [what results?] to _____ [whom?] that _____ [what benefits were a result?].

EXAMPLE: SPECIAL ASSISTANT (CONTRIBUTED BY DON ORLANDO MBA, CPRW, JCTC, CCM, CCMC)

As soon as I saw your call for applications for a special assistant**, I made putting this package together my first priority. That's because what drives me is** the lifelong conviction that strategic connections between cultures must bolster real world globalization, **which is the underlying theme of my work as a** Foundation Humanities Fellow. **In that role, I have delivered** effective classes in English and computer skills **to** learners in the developing world **that** enabled them to benefit from globalization faster than people without those skills.

FIRST PARAGRAPH FOUNDATION 13

The _____ [type of industry or market] needs of _____ [whom?] have changed dramatically over the past _____ [time period]. For _____ [number] years as a _____ [your job title] at _____ [current or previous employer], I have embraced change and introduced _____ [what?] that cater to the needs of _____ [whom?].

EXAMPLE: HIGHER EDUCATION SENIOR ADMINISTRATOR (CONTRIBUTED BY BARBARA SAFANI, MA, CERW, MCRW, CRPW, CCM)

The higher education **needs of** students, parents, and employers **have changed dramatically over the past** decade. **For** more than 10 **years as a** higher education senior administrator **at** ABC University and DEF College, **I have embraced change and introduced** creative and flexible curriculums **that cater to the needs of** the 21st-century student.

FIRST PARAGRAPH FOUNDATION 14

As an accomplished _____ [your job title], I excel at _____ and _____ [key skills]. I am proficient in _____, _____, _____, and _____ [transferable skills or areas of expertise] that you require and am _____ [competitive edge]. Throughout my attached resume, you will find links to some of my _____, _____, and _____ [type of website links].

Example: Application Developer (contributed by Reya Stevens, MA, MRW)

As an accomplished application developer, **I excel at** building rugged frameworks **and** writing clear, maintainable code. **I am proficient in** all of the languages, architecture, platforms, **and** tools **that you require and am** Adobe-certified in Flex. **Throughout my attached resume, you will find links to some of my** online code, articles, **and** demonstrations.

FIRST PARAGRAPH FOUNDATION 15

Creating something that people want, whether it's a(n) [product/program/entity/operation/technology/other: _____] or an idea, is what I do best. To succeed in today's [fiercely competitive business/other: _____] climate, you need vision, and that's what I have. I would like to put that vision and creativity to use in a position as a(n) _____ [job title] within your firm.

Example: New Business Development Director

Creating something that people want, whether it's a product **or an idea, is what I do best. To succeed in today's** fiercely competitive business **climate, you need vision, and that's what I have. I would like to put that vision and creativity to use in a position as a** new business development director **within your firm.**

FIRST PARAGRAPH FOUNDATION 16

_____, _____, and_____ [industry issues]—these are the critical issues facing _____ [type of] firms. With my expertise in _____, _____, _____, and _____ [areas of expertise], I can lead _____ [company name] in successfully confronting these tough issues. If I am given the opportunity to be your [job title], I will...

- _____ [do what?].
- _____ [do what?].
- _____ [do what?].

EXAMPLE: VICE PRESIDENT OF RESEARCH (CONTRIBUTED BY MARJORIE SUSSMAN, MRW, ACRW, CPRW)

Global competition, cost containment, **and** changing market conditions**—these are the critical issues facing** cutting-edge technology **firms. With my expertise in** nanotechnology, semiconductors, solar energy, **and** photonics**, I can lead** ABC Corporation **in successfully confronting these tough issues. If I am given the opportunity to be your** vice president of research**, I will...**

- Provide global perspective to identify opportunistic industry trends in the international business climate**.**
- Contain costs by continuously revisiting the value proposition of a business**.**
- Swiftly correct course to adapt to fluctuation in the business landscape, navigating change that determines the winner in today's business environment**.**

FIRST PARAGRAPH FOUNDATION 17

A true leader brings about positive change in alignment with strategic business objectives without organizational disruption. I am reputed for producing _____ [achievements] by _____ and _____ [doing what?]. This is the value and strength that I bring to the position of _____ [position title].

EXAMPLE: VICE PRESIDENT, LEARNING AND DEVELOPMENT (CONTRIBUTED BY KELLY WELCH, CPRW, MA, GPHR)

A true leader brings about positive change in alignment with strategic business objectives without organizational disruption. I am reputed for producing cost and operational efficiencies **by** building local and global relationships **and** devising win-win solutions**. This is the value and strength that I bring to the position of** VP, learning and development**.**

FIRST PARAGRAPH FOUNDATION 18

My resume reflects early and continued successes in _____ [area of expertise] and _____ [area of expertise]. I approach each project with a holistic understanding of business challenges, drawing upon a combination of winning experiences as _____ [job title] at _____ [current or most recent employer], as _____ [job title] at _____ [previous employer], and as _____ [position title] with _____ [past employer].

EXAMPLE: BUSINESS CONSULTANT (CONTRIBUTED BY KELLY WELCH, CPRW, MA, GPHR)

My resume reflects early and continued successes in entrepreneurship **and** full life cycle consulting**. I approach each project with a holistic understanding of business challenges, drawing upon a combination of winning experiences as** senior human capital consultant **at** ABC Corporation**, as** human capital planning consultant **at** XYZ Business Consulting**, and as** HR strategist and entrepreneur **with** technology startup LMN.com**.**

FIRST PARAGRAPH FOUNDATION 19

Your advertisement for a _____ [job title] was forwarded to me by my colleague _____ [referral name], who recognized that my blend of experience in _____, _____, and _____ [areas of expertise] would be an ideal fit. Please consider me as an applicant for this role. My qualifications include practical use of _____ [what?] along with the ability to _____ [do what?]. This background is enhanced by a [master's/ bachelor's/associate] degree in _____ [major].

EXAMPLE: SCHOOL PROGRAM DIRECTOR (CONTRIBUTED BY CHARLOTTE WEEKS, CCMC, CPRW)

Your advertisement for a school program director **was forwarded to me by my colleague** Michael Thomas**, who recognized that my blend of experience in** adult education, high school instruction, **and** corporate training **would be an ideal fit. Please consider me as an applicant for this role. My qualifications include practical use of** educational best practices **along with the ability to** train teachers**. This background is enhanced by a** master's **degree in** English**.**

FIRST PARAGRAPH FOUNDATION 20

After successfully directing and operating the _____ [type of] department of a(n) $_____ [amount] corporation, I am seeking new challenges with a cutting-edge organization such as _____ [prospective employer]. My ____[number]-year _____ [type of] career encompasses multiple promotions in which I used my _____, _____, and _____ [which?] skills to [drive/ elevate/increase] [business development/sales/revenues/profits/other: _____].

EXAMPLE: INFORMATION SYSTEMS DIRECTOR (CONTRIBUTED BY CHARLOTTE WEEKS, CCMC, CPRW)

After successfully directing and operating the information systems **department of an** $800 million **corporation, I am seeking new challenges with a cutting-edge organization such as** ABC Corporation**. My** 15**-year** leadership **career encompasses multiple promotions in which I used my** strategic planning, organizational leadership, **and** change management **skills to** drive business development and sales**.**

FIRST PARAGRAPH FOUNDATION 21

With more than _____ [number] years of _____ [type of] experience and a consistent track record of [increasing profitability/improving service/decreasing costs/other:_____], I am confident that I can do the same for _____ [whom or what?] at _____ [prospective employer]. A _____ [asset], I have _____ [accomplishment]. As such, I am enclosing my resume for your review.

EXAMPLE: TEACHER (CONTRIBUTED BY CHARLOTTE WEEKS, CCMC, CPRW)

With more than 15 **years of** teaching **experience and a consistent track record of** increasing student test scores in math, reading, and writing**, I am confident that I can do the same for** the children **at** ABC Academy**. A** winner of multiple teaching awards**, I have** led students to improve their behavior through strong classroom management**. As such, I am enclosing my resume for your review.**

EXAMPLE: HEALTH CARE OPERATIONS EXECUTIVE

With more than 9 **years of** health care **experience and a consistent track record of** increasing profitability and improving service**, I am confident that I can do the same for** the medical facilities **at** GreenHealth. **A** successful change leader**, I have** dramatically improved faltering programs in a relatively short amount of time. **As such, I am enclosing my resume for your review.**

FIRST PARAGRAPH FOUNDATION 22

Improving the cost effectiveness of _____ [area of expertise] is critical in today's business environment. My _____ [job area] experience using _____ and _____ [core competencies] would add measurable value to your _____ [which?] function(s). I am enclosing my resume for your consideration.

EXAMPLE: RETAIL MANAGER (CONTRIBUTED BY LAURIE BERENSON, CPRW)

Improving the cost effectiveness of store operations **is critical in today's business environment. My** department management **experience using** disciplined analysis **and** cross-functional coordination **would add measurable value to your** store development **function. I am enclosing my resume for your consideration.**

FIRST PARAGRAPH FOUNDATION 23

With progressive responsibility in _____, _____, and _____ [areas of expertise] in the _____ [which?] industry, my background and hands-on knowledge make me a [strong match/ excellent candidate] for a _____ [type of] position within your [firm/organization].

EXAMPLE: SALES AND MARKETING MANAGER (CONTRIBUTED BY LAURIE BERENSON, CPRW)

With progressive responsibility in management, marketing, **and** sales **in the** tourism **industry, my background and hands-on knowledge make me a** strong match **for a** management **position within your** organization**.**

FIRST PARAGRAPH FOUNDATION 24

Understanding the _____ [type of] industry as intimately as I do, I appreciate the [seasonal changes/ economic fluctuations] that toss a company between "a few jobs on" to "absolutely insanely busy." During these times of maximum capacity, I offer you my expert _____ [type of] services, confident in my ability to always hit the ground running to achieve outstanding results.

EXAMPLE: FREELANCE EVENT MANAGER (CONTRIBUTED BY BEVERLEY NEIL)

Understanding the event management **industry as intimately as I do, I appreciate the** seasonal changes **that toss a company between "a few jobs on" to "absolutely insanely busy." During these times of maximum capacity, I offer you my expert** contractual **services, confident in my ability to always hit the ground running to achieve outstanding results.**

WRITE AND FINALIZE YOUR FIRST PARAGRAPH

In the following worksheet, write your first cover letter paragraph. Be sure you include the four important elements your first paragraph should contain (that is, draw your reader in, state the position you seek, identify where you heard about the position, and make the reader want to read further) as well as your five critical personal branding components (that is, your features, benefits, competitive edge, value proposition, and return on investment to your prospective employer).

YOUR FIRST PARAGRAPH

Using the foundations and ideas presented in this step and your own thoughts, write the first paragraph of your cover letter.

_____

_____

_____

_____

_____

_____

Step 3

step 4

State Your Qualifications and Benefits

- A Winning Cover Letter Formula
- Develop Your Second Paragraph
  - List the Job Requirements and Your Matching Qualifications
  - State the Benefits of Your Qualifications
  - Identify and Include the Value Proposition of Your Benefits
  - State Your Return on Investment (ROI)
  - Include Your Competitive Edge
- Review Second Paragraph Foundations and Examples
- Finalize Your Second Cover Letter Paragraph

A WINNING COVER LETTER FORMULA

Now that you have developed your first cover letter paragraph to attract and spark the interest of your prospective employers, think in terms of this sequence for the remainder of your cover letter:

- ✔ The first paragraph attracts your audience via your personal brand message or other "wow" factor.
- ✔ The second paragraph explains what you have to offer through your matching qualifications and value proposition.
- ✔ The third paragraph validates your value proposition describing your related achievements.
- ✔ The fourth (optional) paragraph sparks additional interest via a related story or eye-opening comment.
- ✔ The fifth paragraph summarizes the letter and closes with a statement of interest and a call to action.

This formula is not the be-all, end-all method of building a cover letter. It is, however, one that works exceptionally well and makes sense. And when the sentences are constructed well, the result is a compelling, marketing-savvy, solid cover letter that stands out from the competition. If, however, you find another, equally good formula to include all five of the critical components of your personal brand, that will work as well.

Using the method in this book, your second paragraph should explain your qualifications as they relate to the position you seek and the value of what your qualifications have to offer prospective employers if they were to hire you. (It should also include your return on investment if you have not already stated it in your first paragraph.) Exhibiting your competitive edge over other candidates is also important.

The way to accomplish all of this is to first select and match your qualifications directly with the prospective employer's stated requirements, similar to what you did in Step 2. Doing so shows you are a perfect match for the position, which makes you a very viable applicant.

DEVELOP YOUR SECOND PARAGRAPH

The process of developing the second paragraph of your cover letter is similar to the one you went through when developing your personal brand in Step 2. However, in this step, you will be selecting only the most relevant and important points for inclusion.

Your second paragraph should primarily include your features and benefits as they relate to and match the job requirements of the position you seek. If your first paragraph fully includes or explains your value proposition and return on investment, you should not repeat the same information. If, however, while going through the worksheet process in this step, you uncover new or additional valuable information, you can either add it here or go back and refine it in your first paragraph.

The following example shows the type of information you will be compiling and developing for your second cover letter paragraph within the various sections of this step. This example provides an overall picture of how to match position requirements with features and then use that information to develop a second cover letter paragraph. This process involves asking yourself a series of questions.

Suppose you are a sales manager who has to address the following job requirement:

Develop and execute new business development initiatives.

What features or assets do you have that meet this requirement?

> Seven years of experience spearheading new business development initiatives, programs, and campaigns, such as point-of-sale materials, community outreach programs, new brand launches, remerchandised products, add-on sales promotions, and sales lead qualifications.

What are the benefits of these features and assets? Or (using the Marketing 101 method) how does that help?

> My new business development initiatives promote a consumer-sensitive approach, sell trust, educate consumers, elevate consumer awareness, and create consumer need and desire.

What value do your benefits offer the prospective employer? (Or how does that help?)

> Improves product visibility, turns singular sales into multiple sales, increases average dollar transactions and sales tickets, raises levels of saleable merchandise, and grows untapped markets.

What return on investment does your value proposition have to prospective employers? (Or how does that help?)

> Elevates sales and profitability so they surpass projections and goals, increases the account base, and establishes the firm's presence in the marketplace.

What is your competitive edge? What do you do that excels over others?

> My consumer market knowledge and experience enable me to devise any number of effective sales and marketing initiatives through visionary strategizing, conceptualizing, planning, development, and execution that directly target consumer needs.

Here is the final cover letter paragraph for this example:

> I have seven years of experience spearheading new business development initiatives, programs, and campaigns that promote a consumer-sensitive approach, sell trust, educate consumers, elevate consumer awareness, and create consumer need and desire. The programs I develop and execute improve product visibility, turn singular sales into multiple sales, increase average dollar transactions, raise levels of saleable merchandise, and grow untapped markets, resulting in elevated sales and profitability that surpass projections, increase the account base, and establish my employer's presence in the marketplace. My consumer market knowledge and experience enable me to devise any number of effective sales and marketing initiatives through visionary strategizing, conceptualizing, planning, development, and execution that directly target and match consumer needs.

The following sections take you through this process one part at a time and help you develop each part of the second paragraph individually for all of your main job requirements. Each section of this step is set up with separate worksheets to record your work. Alternatively, you can use the larger, all-encompassing worksheet at the end of this chapter to compile all of your information, whichever is easier for you.

To save time, you can also type your information into the files contained on the accompanying CD. Simply pop in the CD, open the Worksheets folder, and then click on the Second Paragraph folder to access the worksheets for this step.

List the Job Requirements and Your Matching Qualifications

tip One way to write your second paragraph is to simply make a bulleted list or table of both the job requirements and your matching qualifications. Another way is to use the second paragraph foundations near the end of this step to input your relevant qualifications as indicated.

Go back to Step 2 and review the various job requirements you listed as important for your job position in the "Prospective Employer's Requirements" worksheet. For each job requirement, ask yourself: "What assets/features do I have that meet this requirement?" These specific features are your *qualifications.* Select the important requirements for the position you seek where you can show you have matching (or very similar) qualifications.

Here are two sample job requirements and qualifications for a sales manager:

✔ **Job requirement:** Five years of experience in sales management

Matching qualification: Seven years of experience in sales management and marketing

✔ **Job requirement:** Monitor sales and operational expenses of new product rollouts

Matching qualification: Experience reviewing and evaluating sales and operational reports to monitor sales and expenses associated with product planning, training, and rollout

JOB REQUIREMENTS AND QUALIFICATIONS

In the space provided, make a brief list of the job requirements for the position you want and indicate your matching qualifications. Be sure to include each of these in your second cover letter paragraph.

1. Job requirement: _____

   How met: _____

2. Job requirement: _____

   How met: _____

3. Job requirement: _____

   How met: _____

4. Job requirement: _____

   How met: _____

5. Job requirement: _____

   How met: _____

6. Job requirement: _____

   How met: _____

7. Job requirement: _____

   How met: _____

8. Job requirement: _____

   How met: _____

9. Job requirement: _____

   How met: _____

10. Job requirement: _____

    How met: _____

Step 4

State the Benefits of Your Qualifications

Each of your qualifications is beneficial to your prospective employers in some way. When you review each of your qualifications, ask yourself the question, "What does this do for the firm or its clients?" or "What benefit can a firm derive from my qualifications?" The answers become your benefits.

In the sales manager example, the manager's seven years of experience was one of his qualifications:

✔ **Qualification:** Seven years of experience spearheading new business development initiatives, programs, and campaigns, such as point-of-sale materials, community outreach programs, new brand launches, remerchandised products, add-on sales promotions, and sales leads qualifications.

✔ **Benefit of this qualification:** My new business development initiatives promote a consumer-sensitive approach, sell trust, educate consumers, elevate consumer awareness, and create consumer need and desire.

Step 4

BENEFITS OF YOUR QUALIFICATIONS

List your qualifications from the "Job Requirements and Qualifications" worksheet in the following Qualification column. Next to each of your qualifications write the benefit that that particular qualification has to an employer. You can select your top benefits from the "Ways Your Features Help Employers" worksheet you completed in Step 2.

Qualification	Benefit
1.	1.
2.	2.
3.	3.
4.	4.
5.	5.
6.	6.
7.	7.
8.	8.
9.	9.
10.	10.

Identify and Include the Value Proposition of Your Benefits

Now that you know the benefits of each of your qualifications, ask yourself the question: "How do these benefits create value for my prospective employer?"

Take a look at how the sales manager answered this question:

✔ **Benefit:** My new business development initiatives promote a consumer-sensitive approach, sell trust, educate consumers, elevate consumer awareness, and create consumer need and desire.

✔ **Value proposition:** Improves product visibility, turns singular sales into multiple sales, increases average dollar transactions and sales tickets, raises levels of saleable merchandise, and grows untapped markets.

The following worksheet provides a place for you to detail your value proposition.

VALUE PROPOSITION OF YOUR BENEFITS

In the following Benefit column, copy the benefits from your "Benefits of Your Qualifications" worksheet. Next to each of your benefits, state the value proposition that benefit has to your prospective employer. You can select these from the worksheet in Step 2 titled "Your Value Proposition."

Benefit	Value Proposition
1.	1.
2.	2.
3.	3.
4.	4.
5.	5.
6.	6.
7.	7.
8.	8.
9.	9.
10.	10.

Step 4

State Your Return on Investment (ROI)

If you have already included your ROI in your first cover letter paragraph, it is not necessary to do so again, and you can skip to the next section—unless of course you can think of additional returns on investment to your prospective employers.

If you haven't yet mentioned your ROI in your cover letter, you need to work it into the second paragraph. Start by examining the value proposition you listed for each of your benefits. For each value proposition, ask yourself, "What return on investment does this value have for my prospective employer?" Or ask, "What results do my achievements offer an employer?"

Here is how these ideas connect in the sales manager example:

✔ **Value proposition:** Improves product visibility, turns singular sales into multiple sales, increases average dollar transactions and sales tickets, raises levels of saleable merchandise, and grows untapped markets.

✔ **Return on investment:** Elevates sales and profitability that surpasses projections and goals, increases account base, and establishes the firm's national presence in the marketplace.

ROI ON YOUR VALUE PROPOSITION

Copy the value propositions you came up with in the preceding worksheet into the following Value Proposition column. Next to each of your value propositions, write the return on investment it offers your prospective employer. Look at the "Your ROI to Prospective Employers" worksheet in Step 2 for inspiration.

Value Proposition	ROI Based on Value Proposition
1. _____	1. _____
2. _____	2. _____
3. _____	3. _____
4. _____	4. _____
5. _____	5. _____
6. _____	6. _____
7. _____	7. _____
8. _____	8. _____
9. _____	9. _____
10. _____	10. _____

Include Your Competitive Edge

When you compared yourself with other like-minded job candidates and individuals in Step 2, what did you come up with as your competitive edge? To find your competitive edge, ask yourself, "What do I have to offer that my competition may not?" Or ask, "In what areas do I excel over others?"

The following is the sales manager's competitive edge:

> My consumer market knowledge enables me to devise any number of effective sales and marketing initiatives through visionary strategizing, conceptualizing, planning, development, and execution that directly target consumer needs.

Take everything that makes you stand out from the competition and narrow it down to the most important points (the following worksheet provides space to do this). These are what you need to include in your second paragraph.

YOUR KEY COMPETITIVE EDGE COMPONENTS

Copy the top 6 or so of the 12 items you listed in the "Your Competitive Edge" worksheet in Step 2 into the space provided. You will want to be sure to include each of those items when you write your second cover letter paragraph.

1. _____

   _____

2. _____

   _____

3. _____

   _____

4. _____

   _____

5. _____

   _____

6. _____

   _____

REVIEW SECOND PARAGRAPH FOUNDATIONS AND EXAMPLES

By now you should have a clear understanding of what your features (qualifications), benefits, value proposition, return on investment, and competitive edge are. Plug the items you have identified in the worksheets throughout this step into the second paragraph foundations provided in this section. Try this with a variety of foundations that seem to work well for your situation. After you have reviewed the foundations you completed, select the very best one for your second cover letter paragraph—or write one of your own that includes your qualifications and value proposition.

 **note** The 19 cover letter foundations that follow are also available on the CD in the back of this book to make them even easier to use. All you have to do is type in the missing words.

SECOND PARAGRAPH FOUNDATION 1

During my _____ [number] years of _____ [type of] experience, I have been involved in [all facets/just about every facet] of _____ [primary responsibility]—from _____ and _____ [what functions?] to _____ and _____ [primary functions]. I have utilized my _____, _____, and _____ [type of] skills to [successfully/effectively] _____ [do what?].

EXAMPLE: CORPORATE TRAINER

During my 9 **years of** corporate training **experience, I have been involved in** just about every facet **of** training **—from** program design **and** instruction **to** monitoring **and** follow up in the real world. **I have utilized my** communication **and** listening **skills to** effectively train people at all employee and management levels.

SECOND PARAGRAPH FOUNDATION 2

I am experienced in _____, _____, and _____ [doing what?] for my employers. I believe my _____ [type of] expertise, _____ [skill or attribute] abilities, and _____ [type of] skills are a perfect combination for a(n) _____ [type of] professional. I am confident that the enthusiasm and experience I can bring to your organization will prove to be assets in achieving your firm's goals as they have been for others.

EXAMPLE: GRAPHIC DESIGNER

I am experienced in assessing client needs, tackling difficult challenges, meeting tight deadlines, ensuring quality control, **and** utilizing creative Photoshop filters to design and produce high-end visual communications **for my employers. I believe my** graphic design **expertise,** artistic **abilities, and** computer **skills are a perfect combination for a** design **professional. I am confident that the enthusiasm and experience I can bring to your organization will prove to be assets in achieving your firm's goals as they have been for others.**

SECOND PARAGRAPH FOUNDATION 3

In addition to my expertise in _____, _____, and _____ [areas of expertise], I am actively involved in _____ [what area?] as well as _____ [what area?]. I am committed to [embracing modern technological improvements for _____ (area)/other: _____] while _____ [doing what?].

EXAMPLE: GOLF COURSE SUPERINTENDENT (CONTRIBUTED BY AUGUST COHEN)

In addition to my expertise in turf management, long-range planning, **and** fiscal oversight, **I am actively involved in** several local golfing organizations **as well as** the Golf Course Superintendents Association of America. **I am committed to** embracing modern technological improvements for course management **while** preserving the character, tradition, and aesthetic of old courses with respect for their natural environment.

SECOND PARAGRAPH FOUNDATION 4

Complementing my ability to _____ [do what?] and effectively _____ [do what?] are equally strong qualifications in _____, _____, _____, and _____ [areas of expertise]. I am able to provide strategic direction with appropriate tactical action plans to meet those needs while responding to the constantly changing demands of the _____ [type of] industry. I lead by example and provide strong [decision making/problem solving/staff development/other: _____] skills.

EXAMPLE: MANUFACTURING EXECUTIVE

Complementing my ability to implement six-digit cost-reduction programs, spearhead the development of systemized tracking programs, **and effectively** introduce new CNC equipment **are equally strong qualifications in** product development, program strategy, direction setting, product positioning, **and** data tracking. **I am able to provide strategic direction with appropriate tactical action plans to meet those needs while responding to the constantly changing demands of the** manufacturing **industry. I lead by example and provide strong** decision-making and problem-solving **skills.**

SECOND PARAGRAPH FOUNDATION 5

My solid experience in _____ [qualifications] would serve your firm well in the areas of _____, _____, and _____ [benefits]. I have a proven track record for _____ and _____ [value proposition] for my employers.

EXAMPLE: ELECTRONIC ENGINEER

My solid experience in digital design, embedded systems, microprocessors/microcontrollers, mechanical design, and electronic/mechanical integration **would serve your firm well in the areas of** costing, new product development, increased productivity, quality control, **and** increased profits. **I have a proven track record for** decreasing company costs, streamlining operations, increasing production and manufacturing efficiency, **and** procuring profitable contracts **for my employers.**

SECOND PARAGRAPH FOUNDATION 6

For the past _____ [number] years, I have served as a _____ [position title] for _____ [organization name]. My expertise lies in _____ [what field?], including _____, _____, _____, and _____ [areas of expertise]. I offer extensive experience in _____ and _____ [qualifications] and have established a reputation as a leader in _____ [competitive edge], which _____ [value proposition].

EXAMPLE: IT SECURITY SOLUTIONS ARCHITECT (CONTRIBUTED BY ANGIE JONES, CPRW, CEIC)

For the past eight **years, I have served as a** security solutions architect **for** ABC Corporation. **My expertise lies in** Data Loss Prevention (DLP)**, including** solutions to protect data at rest, in motion, and in use. **I offer extensive experience in** network security monitoring **and** the development of Network Intrusion Prevention solutions **and have established a reputation as a leader in** rapid prototyping**, which** allows for near immediate solutions to resolve business-critical situations.

SECOND PARAGRAPH FOUNDATION 7

I have served as a(n) _____ [title] for _____ [current employer] for the past _____ [number] years and as a _____ [title] for _____ [past employer] prior to that. My roles included _____, _____, and _____ [functions] and involved clearly communicating [goals/decisions/recommendations/procedures/other: _____] to [other departments/clients/coworkers/other:_____]. I am able to work with _____ and _____ [who?] to understand [requirements/strategy/operations/other: _____] related to _____ [what?] in order to _____ [benefit or value proposition].

EXAMPLE: COMPUTER PROGRAMMER (CONTRIBUTED BY ANGIE JONES, CPRW, CEIC)

I have served as a project leader **for** ABC Company **for the past** seven **years and as a** senior programmer **for** XYZ Company **prior to that. My roles included** both pre-sales support **and** customer delivery **and involved clearly communicating** recommendations **to** the appropriate parties. **I am able to work with** IT **and** business owners **to understand** requirements and strategy **related to** the assigned product line **in order to** design business solutions.

SECOND PARAGRAPH FOUNDATION 8

Throughout the past _____ [number] years, I have been [actively/heavily] involved in the [strategic/tactical/other: _____] planning required to align _____ [type of] initiatives with budget dollars in the support of [business/mission-critical/other: _____] needs for _____ [whom or what?]. I have established a reputation built on _____ [type of] excellence through the delivery of [innovative/practical/cost-effective/other: _____] solutions that [increase efficiency/boost performance/elevate revenues/other: _____]. Prior to this, I spent [a number of/_____ (number)] years working as a(n) _____ [job title].

EXAMPLE: CHIEF INFORMATION OFFICER (CONTRIBUTED BY ANGIE JONES, CPRW, CEIC)

Throughout the past 12 **years, I have been** heavily **involved in the** tactical **planning required to align** technology **initiatives with budget dollars in the support of** mission-critical **needs for** the State of Nebraska. **I have established a reputation built on** operational **excellence through the delivery of** practical, cost-effective **solutions that** increase efficiency and boost performance. **Prior to this, I spent** a number of **years working as a(n)** application analyst.

SECOND PARAGRAPH FOUNDATION 9

With more than _____ [number] years of _____ [type of] experience, I know how to drive the _____ [area of expertise] **process to** [maturity/completion/other: _____] and clearly communicate [goals/decisions/recommendations/other: _____] to the appropriate parties. My expertise lies in _____, _____, and _____ [areas]. I am recognized for my innate ability to [coach/motivate/inspire/train/develop/other: _____] staff members to reach their full potential.

EXAMPLE: CHIEF INFORMATION OFFICER (CONTRIBUTED BY ANGIE JONES, CPRW, CEIC)

With more than 17 **years of** IT **experience, I know how to drive the** solution development **process to** maturity **and clearly communicate** goals **to the appropriate parties. My expertise lies in** network design, administration, security, application development, **and** integration. **I am recognized for my innate ability to** motivate **staff members to reach their full potential.**

SECOND PARAGRAPH FOUNDATION 10

A true leader _____ [value proposition]. I am reputed for _____ [benefit] and _____ [benefit] through _____ [competitive edge]. This is the value and strength that I can bring to the position of _____ [job title] at _____ [name of prospective employer]. Throughout my career, I have provided _____ [what?], created _____ [what?], and _____ [did what?], thereby [winning/providing/resulting in/other: _____] _____ [what benefits and ROI?].

EXAMPLE: VICE PRESIDENT (CONTRIBUTED BY KELLY WELCH, CPRW, MA, GPHR)

A true leader brings about positive change in alignment with strategic business objectives without organizational disruption. **I am reputed for** producing cost **and** operational efficiencies **through** building local and global relationships and devising win-win solutions. **This is the value and strength that I bring to the position** of vice president **at** ABC Company. **Throughout my career, I have provided** turnaround leadership, **created** alliances and partnerships, **and** reengineered organizations, **thereby** winning greater profitability, providing best in class learning strategies and curricula, and motivating teams to perform their best.

SECOND PARAGRAPH FOUNDATION 11

With my expertise in _____ and _____ [areas of expertise], I am able to _____ [do what?] and _____ [do what?]. I approach each [challenge/situation/problem/project/accountability/other: _____] with a holistic understanding of business challenges, drawing upon a combination of winning experiences as _____ [job title] at _____ [employer], as _____ [job title] at _____ [employer], and as _____ [job title] at _____ [employer].

EXAMPLE: MANAGEMENT CONSULTANT (CONTRIBUTED BY KELLY WELCH, CPRW, MA, GPHR)

With my expertise in organization **and** talent performance, **I am able to** conceptualize change strategies and modeling to accompany existing service offerings and/or serve as a differentiator for conventional service lines or projects. **I approach each** engagement **with a holistic understanding of business challenges, drawing upon a combination of winning experiences as** senior human capital consultant **at** ABC Corporation, **as** human capital planning consultant **at** XYZ Corporation, **and as** HR strategist and entrepreneur **at** DEFCompany.com.

SECOND PARAGRAPH FOUNDATION 12

Currently, I serve as _____ [job title] of the _____ [which?] department at _____ [firm name]. I was brought in to turn around an underperforming department and went well beyond expectations by spearheading the creation of _____ [what?], improving _____ [what area?] through _____ [type of] initiatives, and _____ [achieving what?].

EXAMPLE: DEPARTMENT ADMINISTRATOR (CHARLOTTE WEEKS, CCMC, CPRW)

Currently, I serve as department administrator **of the** emergency **department at** ABC Foundation and University. **I was brought in to turn around an underperforming department and went well beyond expectations by spearheading the creation of** a standardized revenue cycle, **improving** staff morale **through** team-building **initiatives, and** leading this former division to acquire departmental status.

SECOND PARAGRAPH FOUNDATION 13

My number one criteria is _____ [your mission or goal in work]. I achieve that by _____ [skills or competitive edge]. I always make it a practice to get to know _____ [who?] so that _____ [benefit]. I also believe _____ [another work goal], so _____ [skill] is essential. My _____ [type of] expertise and ability to _____ [primary skill] are a perfect combination for the _____ [industry] field. For these reasons and more, I feel confident that I can apply my skills to work well within your firm.

EXAMPLE: CORPORATE TRAINER

My number one criteria is to ensure that my training results in the highest retention levels possible with the ability to put into practice what is learned in class. **I achieve that by** making the classes enjoyable, adding humor, and relating lessons to real business situations. **I always make it a practice to get to know** my trainees **so that** I can take them from where they are comfortable and bring them forward—whatever the subject matter. **I also believe** that what is taught in class needs to be carried through in business practice, **so** evaluating and monitoring results and making modifications, as necessary, **are essential. My** public speaking **expertise and ability to** be an effective team player and team builder **are a perfect combination for the** training **field. For these reasons and more, I feel confident that I can apply my skills to work well within your firm.**

SECOND PARAGRAPH FOUNDATION 14

Improving the _____ [what function(s)?] of _____ [what area?] is critical in today's business environment. My _____ [type of] experience utilizing _____ and _____ [features or methods] would add measurable value to your _____ [type of] function.

EXAMPLE: STORE MANAGER (CONTRIBUTED BY LAURIE BERENSON, CPRW)

Improving the cost effectiveness **of** store operations **is critical in today's business environment. My** departmental management **experience utilizing** disciplined analysis **and** cross-functional coordination **would add measurable value to your** store development **function.**

SECOND PARAGRAPH FOUNDATION 15

With more than _____ [number] years of _____ [type of] experience and a stunning track record of __ _____ [doing what?], I am confident that I can do the same for [clients/customers/ patrons/other: _____] at _____ [prospective employer]. A winner of multiple awards, I have been recognized by _____ [whom?] for my dedication to _____ [field]. In addition to _____ [doing what?], I have _____ [done what?].

EXAMPLE: TEACHER (CONTRIBUTED BY CHARLOTTE WEEKS, CCMC, CPRW)

With more than 15 **years of** teaching **experience and a stunning track record of** increasing student test scores in math, reading, and writing, **I am confident that I can do the same for** the children **at** ABC Academy. **A winner of multiple awards, I have been recognized by** students and their parents **for my dedication to** teaching. **In addition to** instructing students in their daily subjects, **I have** led them to improve their behavior through strong classroom management.

SECOND PARAGRAPH FOUNDATION 16

My most recent position was at _____ [organization name], a _____ [type of organization]. While there, I repeatedly _____ [did what?] and _____ [did what?]. Along with _____ [abilities], I have proven that I can _____ [do what?].

EXAMPLE: TEACHER (CONTRIBUTED BY CHARLOTTE WEEKS, CCMC, CPRW)

My most recent position was at ABC Elementary, **a** Chicago public school. **While there, I repeatedly** raised student test scores **and** mentored teachers to do the same with their classes. **Along with** interacting well with coworkers, **I have proven that I can** lead by overseeing teachers involved in an after-school program that was designed to provide student enrichment and individual instruction in math.

SECOND PARAGRAPH FOUNDATION 17

After successfully _____ [doing what?], I am seeking new challenges with a _____ [type of] organization such as _____ [prospective employer]. My _____ [number]-year _____ [type of] career encompasses multiple promotions in which I used my _____, _____, _____ and _____ [type of] skills to _____ [do what?]. While _____ [position title] and _____ [position title] at _____ [previous employer], I utilized my _____ and _____ [which?] abilities to _____ [do what?].

EXAMPLE: INFORMATION TECHNOLOGY DIRECTOR (CONTRIBUTED BY CHARLOTTE WEEKS, CCMC, CPRW)

After successfully directing and operating the information systems department of an $800 million corporation, **I am seeking new challenges with a** cutting-edge **organization such as** The ABC Company. **My 15-year** leadership **career encompasses multiple promotions in which I used my** strategic planning, organizational leadership, **and** change management **skills to** drive business development. **While** vice president of information technology **and** vice president of interactive services **at** XYZ Restaurants, **I utilized my** leadership **and** financial **abilities to** initiate and develop cost-savings activities.

SECOND PARAGRAPH FOUNDATION 18

More than _____ [number] years in top-tier roles of multimillion-dollar [firms/organizations/other: _____] as well as _____ [what area(s)?] has afforded me the opportunity to continuously sharpen my talent for [driving revenue/catalyzing aggressive growth/other: _____]. I can...

- _____ [benefit]–_____ _____[achievement or feature].

- _____ [benefit]–_____ _____[achievement or feature].

- _____ [benefit]–_____ _____[achievement or feature].

EXAMPLE: VICE PRESIDENT (CONTRIBUTED BY MARJORIE SUSSMAN, MRW, ACRW, CPRW)

More than 20 **years in top-tier roles of multimillion-dollar** organizations **as well as** emerging start-ups **has afforded me the opportunity to continuously sharpen my talent for** driving revenue and catalyzing aggressive growth. **I can...**

- Build business opportunities—I led negotiations that made ABC Corporation the preferred supplier of EUV scanners for the #1 provider of lithography systems in the semiconductor industry.

- Breathe life into new organizations—I built and propelled a sales organization to strategic partnerships and profitable growth throughout countries in Europe, the Middle East, and Asia.

- Communicate across cultural boundaries—I held leadership roles in operations, sales, and product development for major firms in Europe as well as the United States. I am fluent in German and Dutch.

SECOND PARAGRAPH FOUNDATION 19

I have an innate ability to _____ [do what?] in order to [create/achieve/obtain/
other: _____] _____ [what benefit(s)?] as evidenced in my roles as
_____ and _____ [job title(s)].

EXAMPLE: CHILDREN'S TELEVISION SHOW HOST (CONTRIBUTED BY BEVERLEY NEIL, CRW, CERW)

I have an innate ability to speak in a way that captures children's attention **in order to** create a sense of relationship through the screen, across the stage, or in the classroom **as evidenced in my roles as** both a primary **and** a secondary school teacher.

FINALIZE YOUR SECOND COVER LETTER PARAGRAPH

Now that you have analyzed your prospective employers' requirements and identified your qualifications and benefits that correspond to those requirements, it's time to shape that information into a stellar second paragraph. The previous examples showed many ways you can do this. You may find it helpful to start by gathering the information you created in this step in the following worksheet. Or you can go right to drafting your second paragraph.

SECOND PARAGRAPH DEVELOPMENT

Use the space provided to compile the information you have identified in this chapter.

Job requirement: _____

Qualifications that meet requirement: _____
_____

Benefits of your qualifications: _____
_____

Value proposition of benefit: _____
_____

ROI of value proposition: _____
_____

Your competitive edge: _____
_____

Job requirement: _____

Qualifications that meet requirement: _____
_____

Benefits of your qualifications: _____
_____

Value proposition of benefit: _____
_____

ROI of value proposition: _____
_____

Your competitive edge: _____
_____

Job requirement: _____

Qualifications that meet requirement: _____

_____

Benefits of your qualifications: _____

_____

Value proposition of benefit: _____

_____

ROI of value proposition: _____

_____

Your competitive edge: _____

_____

Job requirement: _____

Qualifications that meet requirement: _____

_____

Benefits of your qualifications: _____

_____

Value proposition of benefit: _____

_____

ROI of value proposition: _____

_____

Your competitive edge: _____

_____

Job requirement: _____

Qualifications that meet requirement: _____

_____

Benefits of your qualifications: _____

_____

Value proposition of benefit: _____

_____

ROI of value proposition: _____

_____

Your competitive edge: _____

_____

Step 4

YOUR SECOND PARAGRAPH

On the following lines, write your second cover letter paragraph. You can use a foundation or sentences from the examples given in this step or write one of your own.

_____

_____

_____

_____

_____

_____

_____

_____

_____

_____

Step 5

Summarize Your Key Accomplishments

- Select Achievements to Validate Your Skill Statements
- Summarize Your Achievements in Concise Statements
- Review Examples and Select a Third Paragraph Foundation
- Write Your Third Paragraph

SELECT ACHIEVEMENTS TO VALIDATE YOUR SKILL STATEMENTS

As discussed in Steps 1 and 2, your personal brand states what you have to offer. In the first and second paragraphs of your cover letter, you have established your personal brand by highlighting your assets and introducing the value and benefits you offer. In your third cover letter paragraph, you need to substantiate and validate your statements by exhibiting achievements you have accomplished for your current or previous employers as proof that you can handle the things you say you can. In this way, the third paragraph of the cover letter shows prospective employers what their return on investment would be if they were to hire you.

To do this, you first need to select accomplishments that come closest to matching and validating the qualifications, benefits, and value proposition you have made to your prospective employer in previous cover letter paragraphs. Refer to the "Your Key Accomplishments" worksheet that you completed in Step 2 for a list of accomplishments you can choose from. You also can select achievements from your resume.

YOUR MATCHING ACCOMPLISHMENTS

In the space below, summarize the achievements that substantiate and validate the qualifications, benefits, and value proposition you offered the prospective employer in the first two paragraphs of your cover letter:

1. _____

   _____

2. _____

   _____

3. _____

   _____

4. _____

   _____

5. _____

   _____

SUMMARIZE YOUR ACHIEVEMENTS IN CONCISE STATEMENTS

Your cover letter should showcase your past achievements and connect them to your prospective employers' needs in a way that whets their appetite to read your resume to learn more about how you may have,

for example, increased sales, elevated profitability, cut costs, streamlined operations, increased productivity, or raised customer service levels. Therefore, your achievement statements should be brief and written in a different fashion than your resume.

In addition, you should use numbers in your achievement statements whenever possible. If you have not already done so in your resume, be sure to quantify all of your achievements to the best of your ability in terms of dollar amounts,

 tip If you do not readily have these numbers available to you, now is a good time to go find them. You can review previous performance evaluations, business or sales reports, or speak directly to your supervisor about getting these numbers.

percentages, or other important numbers that relate to your field. When it comes to your resume and cover letter, numbers speak louder than words to a hiring manager. Stating that you increased sales, productivity, or customer service levels, for example, is not as powerful as saying you elevated annual sales by $350,000, increased productivity by 35 percent, or that you brought customer service levels up to 98 percent.

My preferred method when summarizing a client's achievements is to write a very short paragraph that highlights how he or she contributed to the bottom line of an employer, as shown in Foundations 1, 2, 3, 4, 13, and 14.

Other professional resume writers describe client achievements in somewhat more detail. The remaining foundations exemplify this method. Either way works, but remember to be concise and not replicate the contents of your resume.

Step 5

REVIEW EXAMPLES AND SELECT A THIRD PARAGRAPH FOUNDATION

Review the following foundations and samples to get an idea of how you might state your achievements.

THIRD PARAGRAPH FOUNDATION 1

I have a proven track record of [increasing sales and profits/elevating profits/decreasing costs/streamlining operations/increasing productivity/other: _____]. Notable achievements include _____, _____, _____, and _____ [your most significant accomplishments]. Please see the attached resume for details.

EXAMPLE: MANUFACTURING EXECUTIVE

I have a proven track record of decreasing costs, streamlining operations, and increasing productivity. **Notable achievements include** reducing overtime costs by 17 percent, decreasing annual production costs in excess of $675,000, streamlining in-house operations, decreasing job turnaround times, **and** increasing production accuracy and safety performance levels. **Please see the attached resume for details.**

THIRD PARAGRAPH FOUNDATION 2

Throughout my career, I have consistently demonstrated my ability to _____ [benefit or value provided] by _____ [skills] to ensure attainment of goals. I have gained a solid reputation for _____ and _____ [personal attributes or areas of expertise] resulting in _____ _____ [what ROI?] for my employers.

EXAMPLE: ELECTRONIC ENGINEER

Throughout my career, I have consistently demonstrated my ability to revitalize the production strength of an organization **by** identifying problem areas, devising and implementing effective manufacturing controls, and supervising all daily activities **to ensure attainment of goals. I have gained a solid reputation for** integrity, reliability, **and** skill in coordinating all integral functions **resulting in** strong profits and expanded product lines **for my employers.**

THIRD PARAGRAPH FOUNDATION 3

As _____ [job title] for _____ [most recent employer] for the past _____ [number] years, I have _____ [state your accomplishments]. Additionally, I have _____ _____ [additional accomplishment]. Other areas of expertise include _____, _____, _____, and _____ [areas of expertise].

EXAMPLE: GRAPHIC DESIGNER

As graphic designer **for** Draper Advertising **for the past** two **years, I have** designed and produced brochures, four-color ads, newsletters, and logos and have overseen all prepress processes for print production. **Additionally, I have** assisted in website design and development. **Other areas of expertise include** creating magazine layouts, developing effective advertising campaigns, **and** creating direct mail pieces using Mac OS and various software programs, including Adobe InDesign, Photoshop, Illustrator, and Dreamweaver.

THIRD PARAGRAPH FOUNDATION 4

Currently as _____ [job title] of _____ [employer name], I have taken [the company/my department/other: _____] from _____ [dollar amount, percentage, or other measurement] to _____ [dollar amount, percentage, or other measurement] in [annual sales/market share/other:_____]. I also have received [awards/promotions/commendations/other: _____] for _____ _____ [primary achievements].

EXAMPLE: ELECTRONIC ENGINEER

Currently as president and founder **of** XYZ Corporation, **I have taken the** company **from** start-up **to** $4.5 million **in** annual sales. **I also have received** various awards **for** being one of the fastest-growing systems integrators in the country.

THIRD PARAGRAPH FOUNDATION 5

A sample of my achievements in _____ [areas of expertise] include

- Earning _____ [what?] from _____ [whom?], honoring my _____ [achievement honored].

- Overseeing _____ [whom or what?], resulting in _____ [benefits].

- Developing _____ [what?] that identified and resolved _____ [employer/industry issues].

- Managing_____ [what?], _____ [benefit to past employer].

- Initiating_____ [what?] to _____ [benefit].

EXAMPLE: A GOLF COURSE SUPERINTENDENT (AUGUST COHEN, CARW, NCRW, CPRW)

A sample of my achievements in developing and maintaining Eastbrook Country Club **include**

- **Earning** the "Top 50 Classic Courses" award **from** *Golf World* magazine, **honoring my** improvements.

- **Overseeing** engineers, landscape designers, utility staff, and a $5 million budget, **resulting in** a successful renovation to the pool area and clubhouse.

- **Developing** a long-range golf course improvement plan **that identified and resolved** all issues regarding bunkers, tees, drainage, cart paths, and tree care.

- **Managing** the successful refurbishment of 95 bunker complexes, delivering project 30% under budget at $900,000.

- **Initiating** programs **to** restore lost features of the course.

THIRD PARAGRAPH FOUNDATION 6

In reviewing my resume, you will find that I have more than _____ [number] years of experience _____, _____, _____, and _____ [doing what?] for _____ [whom or what?].

My expertise includes

- Planning, developing, and supervising _____ [what?].

- Prospecting for _____ [what?].

- Preparing _____ [what?]

- Acquiring _____ [what?].

- Managing _____ [what?].

- Reviewing _____ [what?].

EXAMPLE: REAL ESTATE PROFESSIONAL (CONTINUED BY ANGIE JONES, CPRW, CEIC)

In reviewing my resume, you will find that I have more than 15 **years of experience** identifying, sourcing**, and** acquiring land and residential, commercial, and hospitality properties **for** investors**.**

My expertise includes

- **Planning, developing, and supervising** the acquisition or divestiture of property and land rights**.**
- **Prospecting for** potential land/property acquisition opportunities**.**
- **Preparing** preliminary pro forma financial analysis for land and/or property opportunities**.**
- **Acquiring** property or land and entitling the land necessary to meet organizational goals and projections**.**
- **Managing** the preparation and approval of all entitlement documents required for new land purchases**.**
- **Reviewing** title reports and coordinating title objection letters to sellers**.**

THIRD PARAGRAPH FOUNDATION 7

I look forward to making an immediate contribution to the needs of _____ [prospective employer] **by offering**

- _____ [feature/asset] —_____ [related achievement].
- _____ [feature/asset] —_____ [related achievement].
- _____ [feature/asset] —_____ [related achievement].

EXAMPLE: HUMAN RESOURCES PROFESSIONAL (CONTRIBUTED BY KELLY WELCH, CPRW, MA, AND GPHR)

I look forward to making an immediate contribution to the needs of XYZ Industries **by offering**

- Unparalleled collaboration—I secured NOP Company's executive management commitment and then integrated a 200-person multidisciplinary project team to launch a change management program for a $50 million worldwide ERP/SAP implementation**.**
- Creative problem solving—At DEFCompany.com, I led the conception and launch of client-validated technology with a business model that transformed online recruitment models and reduced time-to-hire by 75%**.**
- Proven change leadership—At QRS Incorporated, I was the youngest professional in my division (HR) and was selected to join the leadership team of the most important project for the organization. I led the transformation of cross-company HR processes from a noncollaborative culture to successful implementation, raising client satisfaction from 30% to 100% and gaining recognition as key collaboration expert**.**

THIRD PARAGRAPH FOUNDATION 8

Highlights of my qualifications include

- _____ [core competency]: _____ [related achievement].
- _____ [core competency]: _____ [related achievement].
- _____ [core competency]: _____ [related achievement].

Step 5

EXAMPLE: RETAIL MANAGER (CONTRIBUTED BY LAURIE BERENSON, CPRW)

Highlights of my qualifications include

- Handling global, large-scale, complex situations: Supported 15 presidents, 25+ brands, and 75 business units worldwide relative to corporate store design, architecture, and construction and retail, wholesale, and franchisee growth.
- Implementing new ideas and processes with an eye towards operating results: Reduced operating costs for 600+ stores with new web-based store facilities systems and significantly improved forecasting accuracy by establishing comprehensive budgeting systems.
- Supervising large groups and budgets to achieve company objectives: Successfully managed more than 50 employees, 250 projects annually, and a $200 million budget while improving organizational efficiency and monitoring key metrics.

THIRD PARAGRAPH FOUNDATION 9

I offer a brief overview of my expertise and invite you to peruse my resume, which provides more in-depth information:

- History of undertaking challenging _____ [type of] assignments, including _____, _____, and _____ [what?]. I have repeatedly been sought out to undertake these and other [projects/events/other: _____] due to my _____ [features], which _____ [benefit], and my ability to _____ [value proposition].
- Instinctive knowledge and ability to _____ [skills] and to implement _____ [what?].
- Vital ability to _____ [area of expertise] and to_____ [area of expertise].
- Excellent _____ [type of] qualifications include _____ and _____ [what degrees, certifications, software, or special knowledge?], which I have found invaluable when combined with my _____ and _____ [features].

EXAMPLE: EVENT PLANNER (CONTRIBUTED BY BEVERLEY NEIL)

I offer a brief overview of my expertise and invite you to peruse my resume, which provides more in-depth information:

- **History of undertaking challenging** stage and event management **assignments, including** 7-day international family conferences consisting of 600 adults and 650 children, an outdoor rock concert with 6 bands in a remote mining town, **and** a number of progressive dinners and unique venue special events. **I have repeatedly been sought out to undertake these and other** events **due to my** methods of operation, **which** remove all stress from the client, **and my ability to** make my employer look good.
- **Instinctive knowledge and ability to** read the room **and to implement** rapid changes when required.
- **Vital ability to** communicate instructions clearly and confidently to all event participants **and to** motivate and inspire large groups.
- **Excellent** academic **qualifications include** a Bachelor of Arts with a major in drama and design from the Albert University of Technology **and** a Certificate in Priority Management, **which I have found invaluable when combined with my** natural organizational expertise **and** career experience.

THIRD PARAGRAPH FOUNDATION 10

Please consider these relevant points detailed further in my attached resume:

- [Designed/Developed/Implemented/Managed/Other: _____] _____ [what?] used to produce _____ [what?] in support of _____ [what endeavor?]. As a result, _____ [benefits].

- Undertook _____ [what?] for _____ [whom?]. Negotiated _____ [type of] agreements for _____ [what?] and _____ [did what?].

- Reviewed _____ [what?] to ensure _____ [what?].

- Qualifications include _____, _____, and _____ [other features].

EXAMPLE: OPERATIONS MANAGER (CONTRIBUTED BY BEVERLEY NEIL)

Please consider these relevant points detailed further in my attached resume:

- Designed, implemented, and managed performance platform **used to produce** critical corporate costing data **in support of** government applications at both primary and secondary airports throughout Australia. **As a result,** the applications realized additional revenues, projected to be $37 million (+13.8%) in 2010 and $110 million (+86%) in 2011.

- **Undertook** an extensive review of supplier contracts **for** a multibillion-dollar global corporation. **Negotiated** nationwide **agreements for** multiple services across a network of 1500 retail outlets **and** recommended preferred suppliers for endorsement at board level.

- **Reviewed** domestic terminal infrastructure agreements **to ensure** maximum recovery of outgoings, return on infrastructure investment, and appropriate management of planned projects.

- **Qualifications include** a master's of commerce in accounting, economics, and law **and** a bachelor's of commerce in business finance and strategic business leadership.

THIRD PARAGRAPH FOUNDATION 11

Although my resume reflects my notable accomplishments, it does not reflect my passion for _____ and _____ [doing what?], which are what I do best. I have consistently succeeded by

- Pioneering _____ [related achievement].

- Redesigning and executing _____ [related achievement].

- Managing _____ [related achievement].

- Developing effective _____ [related achievement].

EXAMPLE: SALES MANAGER (CONTRIBUTED BY MARJORIE SUSSMAN, MRW, ACRW, CPRW)

Although my resume reflects my notable accomplishments, it does not reflect my passion for bringing out the best in others **and** causing transformation in business strategy, staff performance, and financial results, **which are what I do best. I have consistently succeeded by**

- **Pioneering** big ideas and inspiring teams to go above and beyond preconceived limits for the greater good.
- **Redesigning and executing** organizational initiatives to improve performance and increase productivity.
- **Managing** meaningful relationships with internal and external clients.
- **Developing effective** products and programs that attract new business.

THIRD PARAGRAPH FOUNDATION 12

I draw to your attention my [past history/current involvement/experience] and [strengths/transferable skills/expertise/knowledge/other: _____], which combine to position me as a strong candidate for this role:

- The challenges of [spearheading/championing/analyzing/formulating/executing/other: _____] _____ [what?], [growing/enhancing/elevating/other: _____] _____ [what?], and [turning around/renewing/improving/helping/other: _____] struggling [departments/territories/stores/clients/other: _____] have been my life. Inherent in all these challenges are the skills and experience required to _____ and to _____ [benefits] while improving _____ [benefit].
- I am experienced in _____ [primary skill or achievement], _____ [related skills].
- I am well known for my exceptional _____ and _____ [competitive edge] skills, both with _____ [related skill] and _____ [related skill]—_____ [benefit], which invariably achieves outstanding results.

Step 5

EXAMPLE: CHIEF EXECUTIVE OFFICER (CONTRIBUTED BY BEVERLEY NEIL)

I draw to your attention my experience and skills, **which combine to position me as a strong candidate for this role:**

- **The challenges of** analyzing, formulating, and executing strong operational strategies and sales and marketing initiatives; growing new enterprises; **and** turning around **struggling** companies and territories **have been my life. Inherent in all of these challenges are the skills and experience required to** increase profitability **and to** identify and secure outside sources of income **while improving** operations from within.
- **I am experienced in** organizing social and corporate box events on major race days for up to 40 guests, negotiating and overseeing all aspects, including food and beverage service and staff communication.
- **I am well known for my exceptional** communication **and** people **skills, both with** bringing out the best in my staff **and** in building exceptional rapport with peers, suppliers, clients and others—taking relationships to a respectful, personal level, **which invariably achieves outstanding results.**

THIRD PARAGRAPH FOUNDATION 13

With a stunning track record of increasing [profitability/sales/income/revenues/other: _____] and improving [service/efficiency/other: _____], I am confident that I can do the same for your [firm/clients/other: _____] seeking a _____ [job title]. A successful change leader, I have dramatically improved _____ [what?] in a relatively short amount of time.

EXAMPLE: HEALTH CARE EXECUTIVE (CONTRIBUTED BY CHARLOTTE WEEKS, CCMC, CPRW)

With a stunning track record of increasing profitability **and improving** service for medical facilities, **I am confident that I can do the same for your** clients **seeking a** health care operations executive. **A successful change leader, I have dramatically improved** faltering programs **in a relatively short amount of time.**

THIRD PARAGRAPH FOUNDATION 14

The ability to _____ [do what?] is one of my strongest skills. In the attached resume, you will see details of my multiple successes at _____ [former employer]. In addition, I have greatly improved _____ [what?]. By _____ [doing what?], I have also reduced expenditures without compromising [quality/service/productivity/other: _____].

EXAMPLE: HEALTH CARE MANAGER (CONTRIBUTED BY CHARLOTTE WEEKS, CCMC, CPRW)

The ability to develop a comprehensive strategy from an understanding of the big picture **is one of my strongest skills. In the attached resume, you will see details of the multiple successes at** ABC Hospital. **In addition, I have greatly improved** the financial situation of an area not typically profitable for hospitals. **By** tightly managing finances, **I have also reduced expenditures without compromising** quality.

THIRD PARAGRAPH FOUNDATION 15

_____ [primary skill] is what I do best. I would like to _____ [benefit] now for _____ [prospective employer] as its next _____ [position title]. Please consider the following examples of my past achievements as harbingers of what I could do for _____ [prospective employer]:

- _____ [achievement]. How? By _____ [skills used in achievement].

- _____ [general achievement] by _____ [skills] and _____ [related numbers].

- _____ [general achievement] by _____ [skills] and _____ [related numbers].

You will find more details of these and other accomplishments on my enclosed resume.

EXAMPLE: VICE PRESIDENT OF OPERATIONS (CONTRIBUTED BY REYA STEVENS, MA, MRW)

Building sustainable growth and profitability **is what I do best. I would like to** build value **now for** American Conglomerate **as its next** vice president of operations. **Please consider the following examples of my past achievements as harbingers of what I could do for** American Conglomerate**:**

- I converted a start-up R&D organization bearing a 65% sales loss into a profitable and growing manufacturing and marketing company, with gross margins at 50+%. **How? By** expanding sales to existing customers; creating new, high-margin products for other markets; zealously seeking out inefficiencies; and streamlining operations.

- I grew a division of a midsized company **by** cultivating strategic relationships with large customers and suppliers, negotiating long-term agreements, developing innovative solutions to reduce costs for all involved, **and** increasing sales by nearly 500%.

- I turned around a failing business unit of a Fortune 500 company **by** modernizing operations, expanding product offerings, revamping supplier networks, **and** growing sales by an average of 23% annually.

You will find more details of these and other accomplishments on my enclosed resume.

THIRD PARAGRAPH FOUNDATION 16

My well-rounded [resume/portfolio/curriculum vitae] includes the following:

[CAREER AREA] CREDENTIALS

- A _____ [degree level] degree in _____ [subject]

- _____ [number] years of _____ [career area] experience _____ [specific example]

- [Certifications/Credentials/Awards] including _____ [what?]

[CAREER AREA] SUCCESSES

- _____ [did what?] to _____ [benefit].

- _____ [did what?] for _____ [who?].

- Early _____ [career area] positions in _____ [previous employer or field] allowed me to _____ [desirable skill or experience]. I rose to the challenge of _____ [achievement].

EXAMPLE: TEACHER/SCHOOL PSYCHOLOGIST (CONTRIBUTED BY ROLETA FOWLER VASQUEZ, CPRW, CEIP)

My **well-rounded** teaching portfolio **includes the following:**

Current and Socially Relevant Teaching **Credentials**

- **A** recently completed MS **degree in** school psychology, preceded by a BA in liberal studies
- 10 **years of** teaching **experience** at K–12, adult, and special needs levels with an additional 5 semesters as a school psychologist/intern
- Certifications **including** school psychology and multiple subject teaching credential with emphasis on cross-cultural language and development (CLAD), highly qualified teacher, Reading First, and Math Matters

Teaching **Successes**

- Developed and implemented curriculum **to** raise student learning and performance benchmarks 92–100 percent.
- Spearheaded a student study team **for** students with behavioral and academic problems.
- **Early** teaching **positions in** the XYZ School System **allowed me to** work with students and parents from multicultural backgrounds. **I rose to the challenge of** developing and teaching courses that blend literacy, problem solving, and social skills.

THIRD PARAGRAPH FOUNDATION 17

In the attached resume, you will find multiple ways I can add value, including

- _____ [area of expertise]: _____ [achievement].
- _____ [area of expertise]: _____ [achievement].
- _____ [area of expertise]: _____ [achievement].

EXAMPLE: SCHOOL PROGRAM DIRECTOR (CONTRIBUTED BY CHARLOTTE WEEKS, CCMC, CPRW)

In the attached resume, you will find multiple ways I can add value, including

- Training teachers and staff**:** I have facilitated multiple training sessions for educators in public and private schools, as well as professionals in business environments.
- Developing and implementing successful programs**:** I have created customized programs for both teachers and students, after assessing the unique needs of the audience.
- Presenting to school leaders**:** I have successfully persuaded administrators and department leaders to purchase educational materials.

THIRD PARAGRAPH FOUNDATION 18

Highlights of my [strengths/qualifications] include

- _____ [feature or area of expertise]. _____ [achievement or benefit].
- _____ [feature or area of expertise]. _____ [achievement or benefit].
- _____ [feature or area of expertise]. _____ [achievement or benefit].

EXAMPLE: CORPORATE TRAINER (CONTRIBUTED BY LAURIE BERENSON, CPRW)

Highlights of my strengths **include**

- Program development. I design and deliver training materials for technical and business skill development, including a creative—and successful—plan to increase training opportunities for customer service representatives in a call center environment without taking away from their phone time.
- Skills assessment. I analyze and interpret quality monitoring data to best enhance workplace productivity, office functionality, and employee peak performance. I proposed and facilitated new peer feedback sessions (where) participants benefited by learning from each other.
- Coaching techniques. I develop and utilize effective one-on-one coaching methods. I co-created a thriving in-house model for coaching customer service representatives on results of their monitoring. I created a related training module and employed technique in actual coaching sessions.

EXAMPLE: FINANCIAL SALES MANAGER (CONTRIBUTED BY LAURIE BERENSON, CPRW)

Highlights of my qualifications **include**

- Top-notch client service. I successfully built a strong client base and retained client relationships over time by providing accurate service and attention to detail at every point.
- Calm under pressure. As a Fed Funds trader, I remained level-headed and effectively multitasked in extremely tense situations. I react quickly to new information to add value for clients.
- Valued team player. I am respected by colleagues for long-standing commitment to improve the team's performance—whether training new hires, mentoring a junior associate, or taking on additional projects outside the scope of my responsibilities—in addition to meeting and exceeding individual sales goals.

Step 5

THIRD PARAGRAPH FOUNDATION 19

For now, I want to concentrate on what years of experience have equipped me to offer [you/your team/your customers/other: _____]. What I do isn't magic; this professional code guides me:

- Being _____ [attribute] isn't good enough. I must _____ [skill] in order to _____ [benefit].
- Being _____ [attribute] isn't good enough. I must _____ [benefit].
- Being _____ [attribute] isn't good enough. I want _____ [benefit].

Proof of that kind of performance is too important to be diluted by the usual resume format. So I've included a leadership addendum on the next page. I chose these examples of my passion in action because I am confident they are transferable to your industry.

EXAMPLE: CHIEF EXECUTIVE OFFICER (CONTRIBUTED BY DON ORLANDO, MBA, CPRW, JCTC, CCM, CCMC)

For now, I want to concentrate on what years of experience have equipped me to offer you, your team, and your customers. **What I do isn't magic; this professional code guides me:**

- **Being** passionate about my business **isn't good enough. I must** instill systemic passion, helping every team member trace his or her daily efforts to our profitability, **in order to** align every team member's personal goals with our corporate aims.

- **Being** productive **isn't good enough. I must** have every employee, every vendor, every customer see his or her personal growth tied to ABC Company's corporate growth.

- **Being** sales driven **isn't good enough. I want** our customers to see us as their success partner, believing that using ABC Company's per-seat, on-demand services is their own good idea.

Proof of that kind of performance is too important to be diluted by the usual resume format. So I've included a leadership addendum on the next page. I chose these examples of my passion in action because I am confident they are transferable to your industry.

WRITE YOUR THIRD PARAGRAPH

Fill in the blanks of one of the foundations provided in the preceding section or write your own achievement statements to complete the third paragraph of your cover letter.

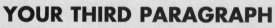

YOUR THIRD PARAGRAPH

In space provided, document your third cover letter paragraph.

_____

_____

_____

_____

_____

_____

_____

Step 5

Step 6

Personalize Your Message

- Determine Whether to Include a Fourth Paragraph
- State Why You Want This Job
- Address Industry or Company Issues or Needs
- Tell a Compelling Story
- Review Fourth Paragraph Foundations
- Write Your Fourth Paragraph

DETERMINE WHETHER TO INCLUDE A FOURTH PARAGRAPH

Each paragraph of your cover letter should convey something of significance to a prospective employer. The fourth paragraph, though optional, is no exception. In the first three paragraphs, you have caught and held your hiring manager's attention through your personal brand, your qualifications, and your matching achievements. Use the optional fourth paragraph to write something outlandish or eye opening to maintain a hiring manager's interest enough to want to read your resume and hire you.

This optional paragraph may be beneficial to include in your cover letter if you have something else compelling to share with a hiring manager. To determine whether you do, ask yourself these questions:

✔ Do I have a passion for my field of work or study?

✔ Do I really enjoy doing what I do?

✔ Is there a reason why I most want to work for a particular company?

✔ Have I helped any employers or their clients in an outstanding manner with terrific results?

✔ Can I meet my prospective employers' needs so well that I have something else to offer that I have not already addressed?

> **note** If you have an interesting story or something compelling to share that would interest a hiring manager, it belongs in your cover letter! Making your cover letter interesting is how you entice the reader to continue reading in order to learn more about you.

✔ Is there a compelling reason to hire me over anyone else in my field?

✔ Can I explain why I am changing fields or careers or have employment gaps (or any other "red flags") by converting this issue into an asset or a positive message?

✔ Do my prospective employers have difficult challenges that I know I can face head on?

✔ Can I meet any other job requirements that I have not already mentioned?

If you answered yes to any of these questions, you should include a fourth paragraph in your cover letter.

STATE WHY YOU WANT THIS JOB

It may seem obvious, because you are sending your resume and cover letter to a company, that you are seeking a certain position. However, stating *why* you are interested in working for a particular company or in a particular industry, field, or position exhibits that you are particularly interested in the company or position as opposed to just broadcasting your resume to every company.

A particular field or type of work might interest you for any number of reasons:

✔ You might have longed to work in a particular industry all your life.

✔ An early experience might have struck your interest and compelled you to make this work your life's passion.

✔ You might have touched on a particular type of work in another profession and decided you want to do that work full-time.

✔ You might enjoy working with a particular set of circumstances or type of people or certain issues, such as students, seniors, animals, or the environment.

✔ You might enjoy working in a field where helping others thrive or do well really fulfills you.

✔ You might have a talent that can be applied only in a particular field of work.

✔ You might have worked in another profession for a number of years only to find that you had another calling.

Letting hiring managers know you have a real passion or talent for doing the type of work you do and/or are applying for shows them you are not just any candidate trying to get any job. It also shows that you are more apt to stay in a position for a length of time and do well for your employer because passionate people generally excel at what they do.

Following are examples of how you can develop a cover letter paragraph around your passion for a particular kind of work.

EXAMPLE: INFORMATION TECHNOLOGY DIRECTOR (CONTRIBUTED BY CHARLOTTE WEEKS, CCMC, CPRW)

My passion for bringing technology leadership to business situations is what drives me to create innovative solutions. For example, when promoted to director of IT at ABC Company, I took on an underperforming department. To turn around its negative image, I set about analyzing the staff and level of customer service and quickly brought about changes. In a short time, the IT department was recognized and respected by the executive committee.

EXAMPLE: TELEVISION HOST/REPORTER (CONTRIBUTED BY BEVERLEY NEIL)

Presenting to any age group on any topic is to me an exhilarating experience. However, my particular passion is in presenting to children and in bringing information and segments to life. I have an innate ability to speak at the best level to capture children's attention–not "down to," but "with" in order to create a sense of relationship through the screen, across the stage, or in the classroom as I did in my roles as both a primary and secondary school teacher.

EXAMPLE: SENIOR COLLEGE ADMINISTRATOR (CONTRIBUTED BY BARBARA SAFANI, MA, CERW, NCRW, CPRW, CCM)

My passion for education and my expertise in analyzing processes and people have contributed to my successes in program development; curriculum redesign; blended, virtual, and experiential learning; and administrative process reengineering.

Step 6

STATE YOUR PASSION

In the space provided, explain your passion for your field and state why you want the job for which you are applying:

_____

_____

_____

_____

_____

_____

_____

ADDRESS INDUSTRY OR COMPANY ISSUES OR NEEDS

All professions have different sets of needs, challenges, goals, and/or missions. You may know and understand some of these better than other job candidates—or even a prospective employer's current employees. You may have a unique set of attributes, qualifications, talents, or ideas (your competitive edge) that enables you to help a prospective employer meet its needs better than other people can. Or you may have some interesting thoughts concerning that profession or how a business can grow through your unique talents or expertise. Following are examples of how you can develop a cover letter paragraph around these and other such circumstances.

EXAMPLE: MARKETING SPECIALIST (CONTRIBUTED BY BARBARA SAFANI, MA, CERW, NCRW, CPRW, CCM)

Developing the strategic roadmaps that help businesses define their market differentiators, optimize brand reach, and maximize customer acquisition and retention is my expertise and my passion. My strengths in e-business transformation, brand unification, new market penetration, and product innovation have been leveraged across multiple industries including consumer goods, technology, telecommunications, financial services, and advertising and span Fortune 50s, start-ups, and consulting practices.

EXAMPLE: SENIOR COLLEGE ADMINISTRATOR (CONTRIBUTED BY BARBARA SAFANI, MA, CERW, NCRW, CPRW, CCM)

The higher education needs of students, parents, and employers have changed dramatically over the past decade. For more than 10 years, as a higher education senior administrator at ABC University and XYZ College, I have embraced change and introduced creative and more flexible curriculums that cater to the needs of the 21st-century student.

EXAMPLE: TEACHER/SCHOOL PSYCHOLOGIST (CONTRIBUTED BY ROLETA FOWLER VASQUEZ, CPRW, CEIP)

As our state cuts more budgets, one thing I know is that educational quality must prevail. Where education fails, a community fails. Dual qualifications as a teacher and school psychologist allow me to deliver excellent educational and socio-psychological services, even in times of dwindling budgets. As a school psychology major, I have special interest and success in reprogramming and mainstreaming difficult students. Along this theme, I welcome any school counselor or teacher opportunities that will allow me to protect and serve the students, the community, and your educational institution.

EXAMPLE: SPECIAL ASSISTANT (CONTRIBUTED BY DON ORLANDO, MBA, CPRW, JCTC, CCM, CCMC)

Like you, many application packages I've reviewed didn't give me clear and compelling confidence that the authors understood the problems I would ask them to solve. In addition, I rarely saw transferable examples of the ability to think critically, remove obstacles effectively, and do both in a "real world" tempo. I have tried to avoid those distractions in the documents you are about to read. That's why my resume may not look like others you have seen.

Right at the top is my pledge of value to you and the foundation. I've included a leadership addendum, which is four extended examples to illustrate not just how I can perform, but the critical thinking and communication skills that define value. As you read, I hope a central thought stands out clearly: I am very comfortable connecting social institutions with private entities to produce synergies that overcome formidable obstacles.

Step 6

EXAMPLE: MANAGEMENT CONSULTANT (CONTRIBUTED BY KELLY WELCH, CPRW, MA, GPHR)

I have a passion for opening new business avenues using strategic collaboration. I analyze client challenges, identify issues, and partner to offer solutions that complement and expand existing offerings. This model delivers high performance and lasting results within client service lines.

With my expertise in organization and talent performance, I am able to conceptualize change strategies and modeling to accompany existing service offerings and/or to serve as a differentiator for conventional service lines or projects. I approach each engagement with a holistic understanding of business challenges, drawing upon a combination of winning experiences as senior human capital consultant at ABC Corporation, human capital planning consultant at DEF, Inc., and as HR strategist and entrepreneur with GHI Company.

EXAMPLE: SALES PROFESSIONAL (CONTRIBUTED BY DON ORLANDO, MBA, CPRW, JCTC, CCM, CCMC)

I come with a track record of making my customers look so good that they choose me, personally, to become their preferred supplier. You'll find seven proofs of my contributions on the next pages, the kinds of contributions I'd like to offer ABC Company. I've chosen each example in my resume to reflect the following personal, professional code that guides all I do:

- Making the sales numbers is good; building the relationships that keep those numbers growing is better.
- Meeting the customers' stated needs is good; learning their business well enough to anticipate their next need is better.
- Knowing who the competitors are is good; knowing how to act faster than they can is better.

My employer likes what I do for it, and, more important, my customers like what I do for them. But my industry is a stable one that lacks big challenges. Hence I am "testing the waters" with this confidential application.

YOUR APPROACH TO MEETING AN ORGANIZATION'S NEEDS

In the space provided, address how you can meet your prospective employers' business needs and/or challenges with your unique skills and experience:

_____

_____

_____

_____

_____

_____

_____

_____

Step 6

TELL A COMPELLING STORY

A relevant story always sparks interest. Telling such a story in your cover letter lets the hiring manager see the person behind the piece of paper. A story reveals qualities that hiring managers may not otherwise have discovered in the rest of your cover letter.

When writing your own compelling story, think in terms of what you might share with a hiring manager during an interview as an event or project that brought you to your profession or reflects your beliefs about the field. Any story that is suitable for an interview can be included in your cover letter.

EXAMPLE: MINISTER (ROLETA FOWLER VASQUEZ, CPRW, CEIP)

As a minister with 20-plus years at the pulpit, I fully understand broadcast media's power to reach the world with the Gospel and compassionate life solutions. I have fielded just about every question imaginable, responding authoritatively, gracefully, and humorously regarding religion and its role in modern life, morality, sexuality, politics, business, education, and law. My views draw upon considerable biblical training (a doctorate in theology/divinity), current theological thinking, live feedback from my audiences, and, of course, my own experiences as a husband, father, and human being.

I honed my gift in live broadcasting while serving as a guest theologian, expert, and panelist on several well-known radio and television syndicated broadcasts, including those hosted by Daniel Pastor (Hartford Communications), James Stuart, and the Church Television Network (CTN). In fact, I have appeared on several airings of CTN's *Spread the Word*.

YOUR INTERESTING STORY

If you have an interesting story to tell, write it here:

_____

_____

_____

_____

_____

REVIEW FOURTH PARAGRAPH FOUNDATIONS

If you have not already created a fourth paragraph from the examples provided in this step, take a look at the following foundations to see if any of them fit your set of circumstances. These foundations were derived from paragraphs submitted by professional resume writers for their clients. You can use these samples by filling in the blanks with your own information and/or as a starting point to develop your own paragraph.

Again, this fourth paragraph is optional. Only use this cover letter space if you have something else compelling to offer. Otherwise, leave it out.

FOURTH PARAGRAPH FOUNDATION 1

Consistently Achieve _____ [what?]

There can be only one reason for these results: a consuming passion for _____ [your field]! Working within the _____ [which?] industry and with individuals to [sell/promote/educate/other: _____] on a beneficial [mission/product/program/project/goal/other:_____]—this has been my [lifeblood/passion/interest/other: _____].

EXAMPLE: PERSONAL TRAINER (CONTRIBUTED BY BEVERLEY NEIL)

Consistently Achieve Top 10 Out of 350 Nationwide

There can be only one reason for these results: a consuming passion for personal training**! Working within the** health **industry and with individuals to** sell, promote, and educate **on a beneficial** product or program**—this has been my** lifeblood**.**

FOURTH PARAGRAPH FOUNDATION 2

My love of _____ [job-related area] is long-standing. As a member of _____ [professional or skill-related group], I have undertaken _____ [achievement] and have a real joy in participating in _____ [what?]. I am excited by the possibility of contributing to _____ [prospective employer] and truly believe that my _____ [feature] will _____ [benefit] and I will _____ [value proposition] as a _____ [job title].

EXAMPLE: TELEVISION HOST/REPORTER (CONTRIBUTED BY BEVERLEY NEIL)

My love of the environment and our wildlife **is long-standing. As a member of** two different styles of bushwalking clubs**, I have undertaken** walks of up to five days **and have a real joy in participating in** and observing the natural environment and our unique wildlife. **I am excited by the possibility of contributing to** the *Wildlife for Kids* television show **and truly believe that my** presentation style **will** enthrall, involve, and motivate children **and I will** deliver audience-grabbing performances **as a** television host/reporter**.**

Step 6

FOURTH PARAGRAPH FOUNDATION 3

I believe in really _____ [doing what?], finding that this always brings its own rewards in _____ [what areas?]. I have also always believed in _____ [other beliefs] and consistently working to the highest standard of professionalism. I am confident that these innate belief systems, in conjunction with my ability to _____ [do what?] position me as an ideal candidate for this role.

EXAMPLE: PERSONAL TRAINER (CONTRIBUTED BY BEVERLEY NEIL)

I believe in really listening and showing the customer respect, **finding that this always brings its own rewards in** trust, open communication, and increased sales. **I have also always believed in** hard work, loyalty, **and consistently working to the highest standard of professionalism. I am confident that these innate belief systems, in conjunction with my ability to** rapidly assimilate new information and techniques, **position me as an ideal candidate for this role.**

FOURTH PARAGRAPH FOUNDATION 4

My search for companies who share my passion for success put _____ [prospective employer] at the top of my list. Here's why: As the _____ [job title] of a successful company, I took it as job number one to_____ [do what?]. And because nobody told me it couldn't be done, I made it happen. Now that _____ [separation circumstances], I want that dream to come true again, this time in a partnership with _____ [prospective empployer]. I would never make such a bold suggestion if I couldn't offer a strong return on investment for both of us.

EXAMPLE: CHIEF EXECUTIVE OFFICER (CONTRIBUTED BY DON ORLANDO, MBA, CPRW, JCTC, CCM, CCMC)

My search for companies who share my passion for success put ABC Company **at the top of my list. Here's why: As the** CEO **of a successful company, I took it as job number one to** replicate my passion in every member of my team. **And because nobody told me it couldn't be done, I made it happen. Now that** my company has been sold to a public entity, **I want that dream to come true again, this time in a partnership with** ABC Company. **I would never make such a bold suggestion if I couldn't offer a strong return on investment for both of us.**

FOURTH PARAGRAPH FOUNDATION 5

All _____ [type of] companies want _____s [job title] who not only exhibit _____ [type of] expertise, but who also _____ [do what?]. Few _____s [job title] can deliver all of these results. I can, and I would like to deliver them for _____ [prospective employer] as your new _____ [job title]. I am passionate about _____ [doing what?]. I achieve this by _____ [doing what?]. In this way, I _____ [benefit].

EXAMPLE: APPLICATION DEVELOPER (CONTRIBUTED BY REYA STEVENS, MA, MRW)

All technology **companies want** software developers **who not only exhibit** technical **expertise, but who also** save time and money while increasing client satisfaction. **Few** developers **can deliver all of these results. I can, and I would like to deliver them for** Excellent Software **as your new** Flex developer. **I am passionate about** ensuring that my applications meet my clients' needs. **I achieve this by** asking key questions and using an "active listening" process at the outset of a project. **In this way, I** avoid the costly mid- or end-project disruptions that result from unclear initial communications.

WRITE YOUR FOURTH PARAGRAPH

The fourth paragraph is a place to add that something extra that gives the hiring manager some insight about you as a person. There are three different methods you can use to do this:

✔ State your passion by explaining why you want this particular job.

✔ Demonstrate your knowledge of industry issues and address the particular needs of the prospective employer through your competitive edge or ROI.

✔ Tell a memorable story that shows your strengths as an employee.

Review the examples and worksheets in this step to help you choose the method that provides the most impact in your situation and write the paragraph in the following worksheet.

YOUR FOURTH PARAGRAPH

From the paragraphs you developed in this step or adapted from the foundations, write and finalize your fourth cover letter paragraph in the space provided.

_____
_____
_____
_____
_____
_____
_____

step 7

Close with a Statement of Interest and a Call to Action

- State Your Interest
- Include Your Call to Action
- Review and Choose a Closing Paragraph Foundation
- Write Your Last Cover Letter Paragraph
- Close Your Cover Letter
  - Your Complimentary Close
  - Your Signature
    - Signature Analysis and the Hiring Process
    - Signature Size
  - Your Typed Name

STATE YOUR INTEREST

Cumulatively, your cover letter paragraphs should entice your reader to want to get to know you better through reading your resume and calling you in for an interview. Specifically, your last paragraph should include one or all of the following things:

✔ A strong statement of your interest in working in your particular field and/or for the prospective employer (if you didn't include this information in the optional fourth paragraph)

✔ A brief reminder of your benefits

✔ A description of your ability to contribute to your prospective employer's mission or bottom line

Though it might seem obvious to a job candidate, stating your interest in working in your specific field or niche and/or for that prospective employer in particular provides an additional reason for the hiring manager to consider you. Use the following worksheet to create a rough draft of a sentence or two that explains why you want this particular job at this particular company. This statement should be altered to fit each prospective employer.

YOUR STATEMENT OF INTEREST

In the space provided, summarize what you have to offer and why you want the job. Include your return on investment if you have not already stated it in preceding paragraphs.

_____

_____

_____

_____

_____

_____

_____

INCLUDE YOUR CALL TO ACTION

Your closing paragraph should also include your call to action. A *call to action* is a short statement in a promotional message that urges the reader to do something to act upon the offer being made. It provides the next step, such as "Call now" or "Click here." No promotional message is complete without a call to action—your cover letter is no exception. In a cover letter, your call to action is typically a statement of what you plan to do next, such as "I will call you to follow up." It could also be a suggestion of what you would like the prospective employer to do with the promotional information you presented in your cover letter and attached resume.

 note How much information you have available to you about the open position (among other factors) will determine what your call to action will be. As a job candidate, you should inform the prospective employer what you plan to do, such as call or send an email message, as opposed to requesting that the company contact you. However, you may not know the hiring manager's direct phone number or email address if you are responding to a blind job posting that does not list specific employer contact information. In this case, you can encourage the employer to contact you. The foundations later in this step show examples of various ways you can do this.

Many job seekers are reluctant to follow up with employers because they do not want to seem pushy. Yet following up after sending out a cover letter and resume is actually proper career etiquette and in a job seeker's best interest. I suggest following up in approximately five business days after mailing or emailing your cover letter and resume.

tip Double-check that you have included a phone number and/or email address on your cover letter and all pages of your resume. If the pages are separated, you want to make it easy for the employer to contact you.

By following up with a phone call or email message, you demonstrate your continued interest in the position and your desire to work for the prospective employer. Sometimes, that action alone sparks an employer's interest. Following up also gives you an opportunity to ask about the status of a position, that is, if it has been filled, if it is still under consideration, or if something has temporarily or permanently interrupted the hiring process. Knowing the status of a position can either shed worries and provide hope or help you determine whether you should move on to seek a different opportunity.

REVIEW AND CHOOSE A CLOSING PARAGRAPH FOUNDATION

You can write your own closing paragraph or select one from the following foundations. You should personalize the last paragraph with your prospective employer's name, the position title sought, and/or the brief version of your resume contributions. Then close with what you plan to do or request that the employer do to respond.

CLOSING PARAGRAPH FOUNDATION 1

I believe _____ [prospective employer] will benefit from my _____ [type of] approach to [operational excellence/enhancing the bottom line/improving productivity/other: _____]. I look forward to speaking with you soon to discuss how my expertise can bring immediate and lasting results to your company. I will contact you soon to set up an interview, or you may contact me at _____ [phone number].

CLOSING PARAGRAPH FOUNDATION 2

Thank you for your time and consideration, [Mr./Ms.] _____ [hiring manager's last name]. I look forward to the possibility of discussing the opportunity of contributing my _____ [benefits] to your highly [innovative/motivated/productive/other: _____] team. May I hear from you soon?

CLOSING PARAGRAPH FOUNDATION 3

I am excited by the possibility of contributing to _____'s [prospective employer] mission to _____ [do what?] and truly believe my _____ [assets] will _____ [do what?] and deliver _____ [what benefits/ROI?]. I would like to hear more about your firm's [mission/unique needs/challenges/other: _____]. I will call you in a few days to arrange a time to do that.

CLOSING PARAGRAPH FOUNDATION 4

Because your organization has the kind of culture in which I thrive, I would like to explore how I might serve the _____ [prospective employer] team by _____ [doing what?]. I will call you next week to see if you can put me on your calendar for that purpose.

CLOSING PARAGRAPH FOUNDATION 5

I am excited by the prospect of an opportunity to work with _____ [prospective employer]. I would like to meet with you to discuss my _____ [type of] qualifications in more detail and would appreciate a personal interview. I will [call/email] you next week to follow up.

CLOSING PARAGRAPH FOUNDATION 6

Excited by the prospect of an opportunity with your company and [impressed by the strength of your brand/other quality you admire: _____], I would be delighted to learn more about the opportunities and challenges your firm faces and to explore how I could best help _____ [prospective employer] define, meet, and exceed its goals. I will call in a week to arrange an interview.

CLOSING PARAGRAPH FOUNDATION 7

I would welcome the chance to meet with you to discuss _____'s [prospective employer] business needs and my qualifications in more detail. I am confident that I can deliver results similar to those described above for your firm and look forward to a personal interview. Please call me at _____ [phone number] or email me at _____ [email address] at your earliest convenience for a mutual return on investment.

CLOSING PARAGRAPH FOUNDATION 8

I would like to discuss our mutual interests and explore some ideas I have for _____'s [prospective employer] expanding presence in the marketplace. With my qualifications and track record of success, I would be a valuable contributor to your _____ [which?] efforts. I will contact you next week to arrange a meeting.

CLOSING PARAGRAPH FOUNDATION 9

I would love the opportunity to find out how I could help _____ [prospective employer] meet its challenges and satisfy its needs. I will call you in a week to see whether we can arrange an interview.

Step 7

CLOSING PARAGRAPH FOUNDATION 10

I look forward to the opportunity to discuss with you how my diverse [background/experience/qualifications/other: _____] in _____ [what arena?] would be an asset to _____ [prospective employer] in the areas of _____, _____, and _____ [areas of expertise]. I will call you next week to see if you have time to schedule an interview.

CLOSING PARAGRAPH FOUNDATION 11

Please permit me to present some ideas I have formulated for _____ [prospective employer] at your earliest convenience by calling me at _____ [phone number].

CLOSING PARAGRAPH FOUNDATION 12

I look forward to meeting with you to discuss how I can _____ [do what?] while helping _____ [prospective employer] meet the challenges of _____ [what?] to achieve its current and future goals. Please contact me at _____ [phone number] or _____ [email address].

CLOSING PARAGRAPH FOUNDATION 13

I am certain that my [experience/competencies/other: _____] would be immediately transferable toward the _____ [position sought] role and to the continued success of _____ [prospective employer] and its [clients/customers/patrons/other: _____]. I look forward to the opportunity to speak with you soon to discuss my qualifications and the organization's objectives in further detail.

CLOSING PARAGRAPH FOUNDATION 14

The enclosed resume sheds more light on my abilities to [penetrate new markets/develop new business opportunities/ other: _____]. I look forward to discussing some ideas I have on _____ [relevant industry topics] and will contact you early next week with the hope of scheduling an introductory meeting.

Step 7

CLOSING PARAGRAPH FOUNDATION 15

By providing an opportunity for me to describe my [contribution/participation/commitment/other: _____] within the _____ [which?] industry, a personal conversation and interview would reveal my suitability and passion for this role. I hope we may speak soon. Thank you for your time and consideration.

CLOSING PARAGRAPH FOUNDATION 16

I am confident in my ability to make an immediate and lasting contribution to your organization and would welcome an interview at your earliest convenience. I look forward to speaking with you soon.

CLOSING PARAGRAPH FOUNDATION 17

These proven abilities can contribute to _____'s [prospective employer] continued growth. I look forward to speaking with you further and will call next week to arrange a mutually convenient time. Should you wish to contact me, my telephone number and e-mail address are provided above. Thank you for your consideration.

CLOSING PARAGRAPH FOUNDATION 18

My distinctive blend of [practical knowledge/formal education/enthusiasm/other: _____] and _____ _____ [what skills or features?] would be an ideal match for a _____ [type of] company. I would welcome the opportunity to speak with you and will call to follow up. Thank you for your time and consideration.

CLOSING PARAGRAPH FOUNDATION 19

If _____ [prospective employer] could benefit from a visionary [executive/professional], I would welcome the opportunity to speak with you in more detail. I will call next week to schedule a meeting. Or I can be reached at the telephone number and email address listed above.

CLOSING PARAGRAPH FOUNDATION 20

If you feel that your company would benefit from having someone with my [qualifications/background/expertise/education/skills/other: _____], I would appreciate hearing from you. Please call me at _____ [phone number] so that we can meet. Thank you for your time and consideration.

CLOSING PARAGRAPH FOUNDATION 21

I am confident in my ability to make an immediate and lasting contribution to your organization and would welcome an interview at your earliest convenience. Please contact me to discuss a mutual return on investment. I look forward to speaking with you soon.

CLOSING PARAGRAPH FOUNDATION 22

In the _____ [which?] field I have found my niche, and I excel in this arena. If you are looking for a(n) [strategic/innovative/flexible/diverse/other: _____] professional able to infuse creative ideas into cohesive strategies within time-critical goals and rigid budgets, I would like to explore this opportunity with you. Please call me at your earliest convenience.

CLOSING PARAGRAPH FOUNDATION 23

Though secure in my current position, I am seeking a new challenge in _____ [type of] operations. I am open to relocation and am particularly interested in opportunities _____ [where?]. I can be reached at the telephone number and email address listed above. Thank you for your time and consideration.

CLOSING PARAGRAPH FOUNDATION 24

I am confident my experience [developing/executing/implementing/managing/overseeing/preparing/conducting/performing/other: _____] _____ [what?] would be valuable to your company's _____ [what challenge or goal?]. I look forward to hearing from you for a personal interview at your earliest convenience.

CLOSING PARAGRAPH FOUNDATION 25

I am confident that the [dedication/experience/enthusiasm/other: _____] I can bring to your [firm/organization/company] will prove to be an asset in [achieving your firm's goals/meeting your firm's challenges/other: _____]. I would welcome the opportunity to meet with you and look forward to hearing from you for a personal interview at your earliest convenience. Please call me at _____ [phone number]. Thank you for your consideration!

CLOSING PARAGRAPH FOUNDATION 26

Please call me at your earliest convenience for the opportunity to discuss in person how my diverse experience will be an asset for _____'s [prospective employer] _____ [type of] [challenge/mission/objective]. I look forward to meeting with you.

CLOSING PARAGRAPH FOUNDATION 27

I would very much like to discuss a _____ [job title or type of] position within your company and would appreciate hearing from you regarding any existing or future openings you might have. Thank you for your time and consideration.

Step 7

CLOSING PARAGRAPH FOUNDATION 28

Thank you in advance for your time and consideration. I look forward to hearing from you for a personal interview at your earliest convenience and would welcome the opportunity to meet with you. I will follow up next week to see whether we can set up a time to meet.

CLOSING PARAGRAPH FOUNDATION 29

I am confident my experience _____ [doing what?] would be valuable to your firm's _____, _____, and _____ [functions/mission/objectives/goals]. Thank you in advance for your time and consideration. I look forward to hearing from you for a personal interview at your earliest convenience.

CLOSING PARAGRAPH FOUNDATION 30

Currently exploring new opportunities, I am confident in my ability to make an immediate and lasting contribution to your organization and would welcome an interview at your earliest convenience.

CLOSING PARAGRAPH FOUNDATION 31

For all of these reasons, I feel I would be an asset to your firm. I would welcome the opportunity to discuss my background and accomplishments with you in greater detail and to learn more about your company and its goals. I will contact you next week to answer any questions you may have.

WRITE YOUR LAST COVER LETTER PARAGRAPH

In the unlikely event you have not chosen one of the preceding foundations to complete your cover letter, write your last paragraph in the following box. Be sure your closing paragraph includes your call to action, whether you are planning to follow up with the firm or trying to encourage the prospective employer to call you.

YOUR CLOSING PARAGRAPH

Write your closing paragraph in the space provided. You can use some of the foundations and/or mix and match sentences or partial sentences to create your own final statement.

_____

_____

_____

_____

_____

Step 7

CLOSE YOUR COVER LETTER

Like any other business letter, your cover letter should end with the following:

✔ A complimentary close

✔ Your signature

✔ Your typed name

This may seem straightforward, but as with everything else on the cover letter, the details are important. They can be the difference between being interviewed and being ignored.

Your Complimentary Close

You can choose to be business formal and end your cover letter with "Sincerely," "Very truly yours," or "Cordially," but it is recommended that you select a more up-to-date, contemporary close that is more personal, such as "Regards," "Warm regards," or "Best regards." Do, however, keep your close professional and not too casual. The close is always followed by a comma, with the first word in uppercase and any additional words in lowercase.

Your Signature

Your signature should be one of the following:

✔ Your full signature with your legal/given name

✔ The actual signature you always use

✔ Your signature with the preferred name you are known by

For example, you may choose to sign "Larry Jones" instead of "Lawrence Jones" In order to give the prospective employer a heads-up as to what to call you. If you have a difficult first name to pronounce and go by a more common name, you may elect to sign your cover letter using your common or preferred name.

Once you have decided what to sign as your name, put some thought into how to sign your name as well. Make sure the size and style of your signature reflect the personal traits you want to emphasize. The following sections explore this idea in more detail.

SIGNATURE ANALYSIS AND THE HIRING PROCESS

Graphology—or handwriting analysis—is the study of handwriting as an indicator of the writer's character, disposition, or psychological makeup. Significance is placed on the size of the handwriting, handwriting slope, and formation of letters, amongst other writing features.

Have you heard the expression "You are what you eat"? Well, in the handwriting analysis arena, the expression is, "You are what you write." With this idea in mind, some larger firms have job candidates' signatures analyzed before making job offers. This practice is especially prevalent in Europe.

According to Elaine Quigley, a leading expert graphologist and former chair of the British Institute of Graphologists, handwriting analysis is now an accepted method of assessing people in organizations, such as for interviewing, recruitment, team-building, counseling, and career planning. Ms. Quigley describes graphology as "brain writing" and states that there are at least 300 different handwriting features that are analyzed and interpreted to understand people through their handwriting.

I don't want to dwell on this topic, but I do want you to be informed so that you can play it safe when you sign your name. Fiona MacKay Young, a certified career development practitioner, certified handwriting analyst, and personality assessment specialist, highlights how handwriting can reflect the "soft skills" employers are looking for (her website is www.potentiality.biz):

- ✔ **Slant of writing:** A slight slant to the right indicates that you are emotionally responsive. A slight upward slant shows optimism. These qualities are important in communication and interpersonal skills.
- ✔ **T-bars:** Long t-bars indicate enthusiasm. Heavy t-bars show self-motivation, and high t-bars show ambition. All of these characteristics demonstrate leadership potential and a commitment to the job.
- ✔ **Loops:** Upper loops indicate imagination, and long and wide lower loops demonstrate flexibility. Both of these traits are desirable in a workplace that's constantly changing.

Review your assets and benefits from Step 2, and then determine whether you are sending the right message through your signature. You may need to make some small modifications to your standard signature—at least the one you include in your cover letter or job application. Or maybe how you already write sends the message you want to convey regarding your personal brand as it pertains to the position you seek and no changes are needed.

Signature Size

The size of your signature matters, too. Keep your signature neat, not too large, and not too small, unless you are fully aware of how the size of your handwriting is interpreted and can use it to your advantage in your particular field or for a certain position.

The size of your handwriting, specifically your signature, denotes your need to be noticed (large writing) or unnoticed (small writing) and your ability to take notice to what is going on around you. It depicts whether you focus on the big/global picture or the small/local one. Both perspectives have their pros and cons, depending on the job involved.

- ✔ **Large and bold signatures:** These can be construed as signed by a person who is assertive, an extrovert, someone who is aware of the outside world, comfortable with him or herself, and can take on leadership roles. It says, "Notice me!" Though it generally denotes that the person is good at multitasking, the drawback is it also depicts an inability to concentrate and oversee details.
- ✔ **Small signatures:** These might be construed as being written by someone who prefers to be unnoticed, an introspective person who can concentrate and focus well and who is good with details and organization. However, the smaller the writing, the lesser one's ability is to see what is going on around them as they are more in tune to their own inner world, making them good at working independently in detail-oriented positions.
- ✔ **Average-sized signature:** This signature size depicts the ability to be realistic, logical, and practical. A person with this signature is thought to be grounded and able to handle life's everyday challenges.

Your Typed Name

Your typewritten name should be your full name, followed by any earned certifications. Including your middle initial, if you have one, is optional. Use the same name that you have included in your masthead on your cover letter and resume.

If your name, for example, is Lawrence, but you prefer to be called "Larry," you can elect to include the name everyone knows you by as well, such as "Lawrence (Larry) Jones."

With some names today, it is difficult to ascertain whether you are male or female. If you worry this may cause a problem in any way or want to be sure prospective employers know whether they are calling a male or a female, you can elect to include your middle name instead of just an initial. For example, if your name is Terry M. Smith, you can use "Terry Maria Smith" or "T. Maria Smith."

step 8

Complete Your Cover Letter Draft

- Pull Your Cover Letter Together
- Ensure Your Cover Letter Contains the Five Critical Components of Your Personal Brand
- Sprinkle Your Cover Letter with Industry-Specific Keywords
  - Industry-Specific Keywords by Profession
  - Keyword-Rich Paragraph Examples
- Make Your Cover Letter the Best It Can Be

PULL YOUR COVER LETTER TOGETHER

Copy the final paragraphs you created in Steps 3 through 7 in the following worksheet.

COMPLETE COVER LETTER DRAFT

Dear _____ [name]:

First paragraph from Step 3:

_____

_____

_____

_____

Second paragraph from Step 4:

_____

_____

_____

_____

Third paragraph from Step 5:

_____

_____

_____

_____

Fourth paragraph (optional) from Step 6:

_____

_____

_____

_____

Fifth (closing) paragraph from Step 7:

_____

_____

_____

Warm regards,

[Your Signature]
[Your Name]

Enclosure: Resume

Now that your cover letter draft is complete, make sure you perfect the details before sending it out. Like your resume, your cover letter should be sprinkled with industry-specific keywords and should be written in marketing-savvy language, that is, in compelling statements that include your personal brand. When your cover letter is written well, your target audience—your prospective employers—should say, "I want to contact this person!"

ENSURE YOUR COVER LETTER CONTAINS THE FIVE CRITICAL COMPONENTS OF YOUR PERSONAL BRAND

The importance of conveying your personal brand cannot be overstated. If your brand message contains the "wow" factor, it should leave hiring managers with the feeling that if they don't call you quickly enough, they might lose you to another firm—no matter how difficult the economic climate might be.

As you remember from Steps 1 and 2, your brand message should include the following:

- ✔ **Your features:** What you have to offer
- ✔ **Your benefits:** How your features help an employer
- ✔ **Your competitive edge:** What you do better than others
- ✔ **Your value proposition:** What value your benefits have to prospective employers
- ✔ **The prospective employer's return on investment:** How prospective employers will benefit from hiring you

If any of these components are missing in your final cover letter draft, go back to Step 2 to work on them. Remember, your personal brand message is what will put you in the top 2 percent of candidates because your value proposition and return on investment to prospective employers are what compel them to call. So be sure you've included all the personal brand components in your cover letter!

Review, edit, and tweak your personal brand message to be sure it is convincing, compelling, and persuasive. When you read it, you should think, "I would hire me!"

SPRINKLE YOUR COVER LETTER WITH INDUSTRY-SPECIFIC KEYWORDS

Many employers today electronically scan the resumes they receive directly into databases. Human resources professionals then search these databases for suitable candidates to fill open positions by entering keywords that match the job requirements. Cover letters and resumes must contain these keywords in order to be retrieved and seen. If your cover letter and resume do not contain these important keywords or keyword phrases, they may never be read.

Keywords are an important component of both your resume and cover letter. They signify your areas of expertise or qualifications and showcase your experience and knowledge. The best way to ensure you have included all related keywords an employer may search for is to review job postings or descriptions thoroughly and include any such words where you have matching expertise in the area in your cover letter as well as your resume. Check your cover letter draft against the "Areas of Expertise" worksheet in Step 2 to see whether you included all important keywords and terms.

Industry-Specific Keywords by Profession

In the next few pages, you will find numerous industry-specific keywords for various business professions. Check the boxes next to the keywords for the areas in which you are knowledgeable. Circle all areas in which you are highly proficient and that directly relate to your profession.

If you have enough circled items, you can skip including the items that are only checked in your cover letter, unless the job description requires that particular area of expertise. Look over your cover letter draft and insert any important keywords that you may have left out.

If you do not find keywords that relate to your profession or areas of expertise in the examples given, the last box provides space for you to insert keywords for your specific profession. (If you are in need of keywords for a profession other than those that follow, you can send an email message to me at CareerCatapult@aol. com to request them.)

ADMINISTRATIVE AND GENERAL BUSINESS KEYWORDS

- Account servicing
- Administration
- Administration management
- Administrative processes
- Administrative support
- Back-office operations
- Billing and invoicing
- Bookkeeping
- Budget administration
- Budget development
- Building contracts
- Business analysis
- Business plans
- Business start-up
- Client correspondence
- Client relations
- Communications
- Compliance
- Computer troubleshooting
- Contract development
- Contract negotiations
- Copying
- Correspondence
- Customer service
- Data entry
- Data processing
- Deliveries

- Document preparation
- Document processing
- Executive assistance
- Faxing
- Fulfillment
- General office administration
- Goods transfers
- Interdisciplinary team meetings
- Inventory control
- Labor relations
- Logistics management
- Mail opening and sorting
- Management support
- Manufacturing
- Materials distribution
- Materials scheduling
- Merchandising
- Negotiations
- Networking
- Office management
- Office services
- Operations management
- Order processing
- Payroll issues
- Policy and procedure development
- Printing

- Procurement
- Product and service delivery
- Production
- Productivity improvement
- Progress update reports
- Project development
- Project life cycle
- Project management
- Project prioritizing
- Project scheduling/timelines
- Purchasing
- Quality assurance
- Quality control
- Recordkeeping
- Records management
- Research and analysis
- Security
- Shipping and receiving
- Stock distribution
- Strategizing client needs
- Switchboard operations
- Transportation
- Travel arrangements
- Vendor relations
- Word processing
- Workflow management

COMPLIANCE KEYWORDS

- Audit plan development
- Audit reports
- Automated controls
- Automated procedures
- Compliance
- Controls

- Control programs
- Corporate operations
- Data integrity
- Decision-making assistance
- Documentation review
- Efficiency evaluations

- Financial systems
- Government regulations
- In-process testing
- Information systems
- Inspections
- Internal and external reviews

Step 8

- ❏ Inventory audits
- ❏ Management procedures
- ❏ Management protocols
- ❏ Manual procedures
- ❏ Methods development
- ❏ Operations audits
- ❏ Policy effectiveness
- ❏ Record accuracy verification

- ❏ Quality assurance (QA)
- ❏ Quality assurance audits
- ❏ QA performance reports
- ❏ QA/QC conceptualization
- ❏ QA/QC documentation
- ❏ QA/QC implementation
- ❏ QA/QC programs and systems

- ❏ Quality control (QC)
- ❏ Quality control process development
- ❏ Records examinations
- ❏ Regulatory compliance
- ❏ Service levels
- ❏ Stability studies
- ❏ Testing systems

FINANCE KEYWORDS

- ❏ Budgeting
- ❏ Budgeting analysis
- ❏ Business administration
- ❏ Business analysis
- ❏ Business case development
- ❏ Business development
- ❏ Business functions and processes
- ❏ Business models preparation
- ❏ Business opportunity development
- ❏ Business partners and vendors
- ❏ Business practices application
- ❏ Business problem solving
- ❏ Business process improvement identification
- ❏ Business process management
- ❏ Business requirements

- ❏ Business requirements writing
- ❏ Business transformation
- ❏ Business-to-business e-commerce
- ❏ Capital budgeting
- ❏ Compensation
- ❏ Contract administration
- ❏ Contract administrative support
- ❏ Cost/benefit analysis
- ❏ Cost/integrated scheduling
- ❏ Cost control practices
- ❏ Cost management
- ❏ Cost performance indexing
- ❏ Earned value analysis
- ❏ Enterprise budgeting
- ❏ Enterprise project management system

- ❏ Enterprise resource planning
- ❏ Enterprise-level scheduling development
- ❏ Estimating
- ❏ Finances and costs management
- ❏ Financial and management reporting
- ❏ General administration
- ❏ Inventory management
- ❏ Personnel management
- ❏ Purchasing
- ❏ Standard business processes
- ❏ Strategic business plan execution
- ❏ Strategic business plan development

INVENTORY CONTROL KEYWORDS

- ❏ Access control installation
- ❏ Access control inventory
- ❏ Access control maintenance
- ❏ Access control support
- ❏ Asset protection
- ❏ Bill paying
- ❏ Bookkeeping assistance

- ❏ Business letter writing
- ❏ Card control inventory
- ❏ Collaborative vendor forecasting
- ❏ Computer networking
- ❏ Control form inventory
- ❏ Control inventory management

- ❏ Control inventory module software
- ❏ Correct English usage
- ❏ Customer access control
- ❏ Customer service
- ❏ Detailed clerical work
- ❏ Direct importing

Step 8

(continued)

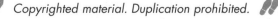

INVENTORY CONTROL KEYWORDS (CONTINUED)

- ❏ Distribution process
- ❏ Electronic security systems
- ❏ Employee safety
- ❏ Facilities
- ❏ File organizing and maintenance
- ❏ Grammar and punctuation
- ❏ Human resources
- ❏ Integrated systems
- ❏ Inventory access control
- ❏ Inventory accounting
- ❏ Inventory accounting tools software
- ❏ Inventory accuracy software
- ❏ Inventory control management
- ❏ Inventory control point
- ❏ Inventory control processing
- ❏ Inventory control software
- ❏ Inventory control spreadsheet

- ❏ Inventory control system
- ❏ Inventory management software
- ❏ Inventory shrinkage
- ❏ Inventory shrinkage reduction
- ❏ Inventory tracking software
- ❏ Invoice process
- ❏ Loss prevention
- ❏ Loss reduction
- ❏ Naval inventory control
- ❏ Office practices and procedures
- ❏ Online stock control
- ❏ Operating equipment
- ❏ Order entry
- ❏ Order process
- ❏ Personnel accountability
- ❏ Policies, procedures, and processes

- ❏ Production inventory control
- ❏ Purchasing
- ❏ Quality control
- ❏ Quality control access inventory
- ❏ Reception
- ❏ Recordkeeping
- ❏ Retailing
- ❏ Secure asset storage
- ❏ Security and asset protection
- ❏ Software license transactions
- ❏ Spare parts inventory control
- ❏ Spreadsheet and database tools
- ❏ Statistical process control
- ❏ Stock control
- ❏ Store operations
- ❏ Tool control and inventory

INFORMATION TECHNOLOGY KEYWORDS

- ❏ Analysis and design
- ❏ Application and data architecture coordination
- ❏ Applications development methodologies
- ❏ Architecture landscapes development
- ❏ Capacity planning
- ❏ Client/server development methods
- ❏ Coding practices
- ❏ Configuration and release management
- ❏ Contemporary testing methodologies
- ❏ Contract IT staffing

- ❏ Database design concepts
- ❏ Data mining
- ❏ Data modeling
- ❏ Data requirements
- ❏ Data warehousing
- ❏ Defect management leadership
- ❏ Deployment management
- ❏ Development tools and technologies
- ❏ Development and testing
- ❏ Hardware/software changes
- ❏ High-volume solution development
- ❏ Industry portfolio management tools

- ❏ Industry technology trends and offerings
- ❏ Information technology development processes
- ❏ Information technology governance
- ❏ Information technology organization management
- ❏ Information technology processes
- ❏ Information technology program management
- ❏ Integration planning
- ❏ Intranet systems development methods
- ❏ Large organization navigation

- ❏ Leading-edge technology project development
- ❏ Major third-party IT services provider
- ❏ Multitier architecture
- ❏ Multitier development environments
- ❏ New technologies and practices
- ❏ New technology development
- ❏ Project management tools and techniques

- ❏ Quality methods
- ❏ Release and version control
- ❏ Requirements gathering
- ❏ Resource breakdown structure
- ❏ Service level management
- ❏ Service level measurement
- ❏ Software design review
- ❏ Software development life cycle
- ❏ Software development methodologies

- ❏ Software development project management
- ❏ Software measurement
- ❏ Software package evaluation and implementation
- ❏ Software processes
- ❏ Software quality management
- ❏ Solutions design and development
- ❏ Standard software modeling practices

PURCHASING KEYWORDS

- ❏ Adjustments
- ❏ Acquisition management
- ❏ Barter arrangements
- ❏ Bidding
- ❏ Blanket orders
- ❏ Capital equipment acquisition
- ❏ Client and vendor records
- ❏ Client interface
- ❏ Comparative cost analyses
- ❏ Competitive bidding
- ❏ Computer equipment
- ❏ Contract change orders
- ❏ Contract terms and negotiations
- ❏ Delivery scheduling
- ❏ Distribution management
- ❏ Expediting
- ❏ High-volume processing

- ❏ International trade
- ❏ Inventory control/management
- ❏ Leasing
- ❏ Logistics management
- ❏ Materials management
- ❏ Materials replenishment ordering
- ❏ Merchandise pricing
- ❏ Merchandise sales projections
- ❏ Merchandising
- ❏ Negotiations
- ❏ Office machinery
- ❏ Office supplies
- ❏ Order processing
- ❏ Overseas importing
- ❏ Phone systems
- ❏ Pricing negotiations
- ❏ Procurement

- ❏ Production materials
- ❏ Production schedule monitoring
- ❏ Production scheduling
- ❏ Promotional items
- ❏ Purchase orders
- ❏ Purchasing
- ❏ Request for proposal (RFP)
- ❏ Request for quotation (RFQ)
- ❏ Strong follow-up
- ❏ Supplier management
- ❏ Trade shows
- ❏ Vendor bids
- ❏ Vendor relations
- ❏ Vendor partnerships
- ❏ Warehousing
- ❏ Warehouse management

RESEARCH KEYWORDS

- ❏ Activity coordination, product level
- ❏ Activity coordination, project level
- ❏ Activity coordination, task level

- ❏ Activity management
- ❏ Analytical methods
- ❏ Biomedical research proposals
- ❏ Business opportunities identification

- ❏ Competitive studies
- ❏ Complex data interpretation
- ❏ Computer management
- ❏ Conflict management

Step 8

(continued)

RESEARCH KEYWORDS (CONTINUED)

- Contractual data interpretation
- Cross-organizational activity
- Customer needs identification
- Data analysis
- Data compilation
- Data gathering
- Data verification
- Demographic research
- Details clarification
- Fact verification
- Hardware installation
- Independent research
- Information augmentation
- Information gathering and analysis
- Legal research
- Market analysis and definition
- Market research
- Market results comparison
- Marketplace dynamics
- Materials gathering
- Materials sourcing
- Mathematical principles
- Meeting deadlines
- Multilevel task balancing
- Multivariate analysis

- Performance audits
- Policy analysis
- Policy improvement
- Practical data evaluation
- Presentation development
- Product results comparison
- Profitability studies
- Project coordination
- Project monitoring
- Project planning
- Proposal writing
- Qualitative marketing techniques
- Qualitative research methods
- Quantitative marketing techniques
- Quantitative research
- Quantitative research methods
- Records maintenance
- Research analysis
- Research compilation
- Research coordination
- Research development
- Research evaluation
- Research interpretation
- Research methods
- Research oversight

- Research planning
- Research principles and practices
- Research program development
- Research program implementation
- Research skills
- Research studies
- Research verification
- Sales projections
- Segmentation
- Social science analysis techniques
- Solutions identification
- Solutions recommendation
- Source materials
- Standardizing market research
- Statistical analysis
- Statistical information analysis
- Statistical techniques
- Target audience identification
- Technical quantitative skills
- Technical writing
- Time results comparison
- Trends identification
- Work prioritization

TRAINING AND DEVELOPMENT KEYWORDS

- ❑ Adjunct training materials
- ❑ Budget development and management
- ❑ Career development activities
- ❑ Compliance
- ❑ Computer-assisted training courses
- ❑ Consultation
- ❑ Course materials
- ❑ Coursework development
- ❑ Employee assistance
- ❑ Employee counseling
- ❑ Implementation
- ❑ Instructor training seminars
- ❑ Long-range strategizing

- ❑ Management consultation
- ❑ Management practices
- ❑ Management trainee programs
- ❑ Management training and development
- ❑ Maximizing employee potential
- ❑ Monitoring training
- ❑ New hire training centers
- ❑ On-the-job training programs
- ❑ Organizational development
- ❑ Orientation sessions
- ❑ Planning
- ❑ Program compliance
- ❑ Program development

- ❑ Program scheduling
- ❑ Specialized training courses
- ❑ Staff training and development
- ❑ Strategic planning
- ❑ Training classes
- ❑ Training concepts and practices
- ❑ Training coordination
- ❑ Training programs
- ❑ Training direction
- ❑ Training needs assessments
- ❑ Train-the-trainer programs
- ❑ Video instructional courses
- ❑ Workshops

KEYWORDS FOR YOUR SPECIFIC PROFESSION

In the lines below, make a list of keywords you have found in job descriptions or postings for people in your profession:

_____

_____

_____

_____

_____

_____

_____

Circle the words that appear most frequently in the jobs you are most interested in and are strong areas of expertise for you. Make sure these words are part of your cover letter (and resume).

Step 8

Keyword-Rich Paragraph Examples

The following keyword-rich cover letter paragraphs include industry-specific keywords that exhibit a job candidate's qualifications and areas of expertise in his or her profession:

I facilitate management oversight of the firm's advertising projects, including project scope, planning, scheduling, budgeting, creative team selection, and quality and cost control—keeping in line with all business objectives. I also provide leadership and direction in the production of client ad campaigns, packaging, direct mail, annual reports, corporate identity, and website projects.

Directing the engineering division and activities for petroleum production plant engineers, I oversee specifications, plans, designs, and cost estimates and lead engineering research and analysis, including planning, evaluation and assessment, concept and design, coordination, simulation, testing, construction, and quality control.

I lead, coordinate, and manage multiple technology areas, including voice and data communication, administrative computer systems, analog and digital technology, website presence, multimedia development, and land-based and wireless networks.

I manage the functional areas of procurement and asset utilization, property purchases and sales, distribution support and safety, corporate affairs, property management, materials and supplies purchasing, contract establishment, and corporate governance systems.

Step 8

MAKE YOUR COVER LETTER THE BEST IT CAN BE

Use these tips to polish the text of your cover letter:

- ✔ **Convey a positive, professional, and personal tone.** Ensuring you have included the five critical components of personal branding will make your cover letter powerful, compelling, and marketing savvy. Conveying a positive and personal tone is equally important to show who you are as the person behind the piece of paper. Make all sentences positive and professional, and wherever you can infuse a personal tone, do so. Use words and phrases such as, "My passion for this position stems from…" or "The experience I gained from (a particular) position helped to position me for…" or "Working for your firm would truly be enjoyable to me because…."

- ✔ **Delete any irrelevant, redundant, or misdirected information.** Check for and omit any irrelevant, redundant, misdirected, or negative points. If you perform some functions in your current job or performed them in past jobs that do not support your job search objective or are not included in the job description of the position you are seeking, do not include them. Focus on making all of your cover letter statements relevant to the position you seek.

  Also, don't bore your reader by repeating information in your resume or stating the same information twice in your cover letter. Instead, touch on the many facets of who you are and what you have to offer insofar as your qualifications, knowledge, expertise, education, and/or personal attributes (your features).

- ✔ **Condense, condense, condense!** Your cover letter should be no longer than one page. Review each sentence in your cover letter to see whether there is a way to make it more concise and poignant without losing content. Omit any unnecessary words. Make every word count! Focus on what you have to convey without saying more than is necessary to convince the prospective employer that you are a viable candidate for the position. If you still have cumbersome sentences or paragraphs in your cover letter, review the numerous foundations in this book for ideas on how to replace what isn't working.

- ✔ **Make sure your cover letter is error-free: check grammar, spelling, and vocabulary usage.** The biggest pet peeve of hiring managers is when they read a cover letter or resume that contains spelling and other errors. Most will not even consider a job candidate if they find errors. For example, while conducting some research for this book, I ran across a website where the very first sentence started with "People doesn't…" With the exception of scrolling down to see what fool wrote it, I immediately stopped reading and dismissed the entire site as not having anything of value to offer me or my readers.

  You've worked through all the steps to develop your personal brand and create your compelling cover letter, so be sure you don't have it tossed out due to errors. Use MS Word's spell-check and grammar-check to ensure you correct any errors. Also check your punctuation and word capitalization, as well as any other errors, and be sure to correct them! Then proofread the entire cover letter, not once or twice, but three times to make sure your letter contains *no errors*.

- ✔ **Sleep on it. Review it again. Pass it around for comment.** Getting an outside, objective opinion on your cover letter before sending it out is always a good idea. Try to find someone in your profession or in human resources who can provide an objective, professional opinion about your cover letter.

In the next step, you will be formatting your cover letter and including personal branding elements that visually set your cover letter apart from others so that it is read.

step 9

Format and Design Your Cover Letter

- Follow the Cover Letter Formatting Guidelines
- Select a Professional Letterhead Design or Create One of Your Own
- Add Brand Identification Elements
  - Add a Slogan or Tagline
  - Add Testimonials
  - Add a Mission Statement
- Create an Email Version of Your Cover Letter
- Send It Out!

FOLLOW THE COVER LETTER FORMATTING GUIDELINES

Now that you are done writing your cover letter, you can move on to formatting and designing it into a professional presentation. Just as the content of your cover letter is important to get your foot in the door, the design and look of your cover letter are important to ensuring that it is noticed and read.

Use the following instructions when you are formatting and designing your cover letter, whether you are using a design template from the CD or creating one of your own. Keeping it organized, crisp, and clean looking is key.

1. **Make your contact information (your masthead) clear and readable.** Be sure your contact information is clear and large enough to stand out from the rest of your cover letter. Setting the font size for your name at 14 to 16 points works well, and a 12 point setting works well for your address, phone number, email address, and/or web portfolio URL. Adding a rule that extends from your left margin to your right margin gives it a clean, clear look.

2. **Use white space effectively.** You do not have to fill your page with text. In fact, your cover letter and resume should contain plenty of white (blank or unused) space. White space makes your letter more inviting to read. Adjust the font size and spacing between lines and paragraphs to make it attractive and fit the space well. A one-inch margin (or slightly less) works well for the top and bottom of the page and both sides. You can adjust these margins according to how long your cover letter is, but don't try to cram a lot of text on the page.

note Font size is relative to the font you choose. So if you change the font you are using, you will probably have to adjust the font size as well. For example, Verdana 9 point is about the same size as Times New Roman 11 point.

3. **Choose an appropriate font and font size.** Generally speaking, your cover letter should be easy to read and should be one point size larger than your resume. The cover letter and resume should also use the same font. To ensure that your cover letter and resume look the same when they are sent via email and opened on a hiring manager's computer as they did when you created them, you should use a font that is installed on all computers, such as Times New Roman, Arial, or Verdana.

4. **Decide on a one- or two-column format.** You can elect to set up a margin in the left-hand side of your cover letter to include bulleted areas of expertise, testimonials, your slogan, or a mission statement, as discussed in this step. (This type of margin is often called a *scholar's margin.*) This step and the accompanying CD show both formats.

5. **Use italics to set information apart.** Use italics to separate subordinate information, such as achievements in a bulleted list. Italicizing information in your scholar's margin separates it and makes it stand out from the rest of your cover letter.

SELECT A PROFESSIONAL LETTERHEAD DESIGN OR CREATE ONE OF YOUR OWN

A job seeker can gain significantly higher interview odds when his or her cover letter and resume are visually appealing and stand out from the crowd in a professional way.

The following images show nine letterhead designs that you can use as is from the accompanying CD or alter to create one for yourself. Either way, they are examples of suitable professional designs for your cover letter letterhead. If you decide to use a design on the CD, you can paste the information you compiled right into the MS Word document file. You can also review the many cover letter samples contained in Step 10 to help you create a suitable cover letter design for yourself.

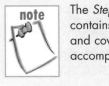

note The *Step-by-Step Resumes* book contains coordinating resume and cover letter designs on its accompanying CD.

Figure 9.1: Letterhead Design 1.

Figure 9.2: Letterhead Design 2.

Step 9

YOUR NAME   **PROFESSIONAL TITLE**
Street Address, Town, ST 00000 • Phone: (000) 000-0000 • Email: xxxxxxxxx@xxxxx.xxx

Dear Human Resources Professional:

Xxxxxxxxxxxxxxxxxxxxxxxxxxxxxxxxxxxxxxxxxxxxxxxxxxxxxxxxxxxxxxxxxxxx
x xxxxxxxxxxxxxxxxxxxxxxxxxxxxxxx. Xxxxxxxxxxxxxxxxxxxxxxxxxxxxxxxxx
xxxxxxxxxx. Xxxxxxxxxxxxxxxxxxxxxxxxxxxxxxxxxxxxxx.

Xxxxxxxxxxxxxxxxxxxxxxxxxxxxxxxxxxxxxxxxxxxxxxxxxxxxxxxxxxxxxxxxxxxx
xxxxxxxxxxxxxxxxxxxxxxxxxxxxxxxxxxxxx. Xxxxxxxxxxxxxxxxxxxxxxxxxxxx
xxxxxxxxxx. Xxxxxxxxxxxxxxxxxxxxxxxxxxxxxxxxxxxxxxxxxxxxxxxxxxxxxx
xxxxxxxxxxxxxxxxxxxxxxxxxxxxxxxxxxxxxxxxxxxxxxxxxxxxxx.

Xxxxxxxxxxxxxxxxxxxxxxxxxxxxxxxxxxxxxxxxxxxxxxxxxxxxxxxxxxxxxxxxxxxx
xxxxxxxxxxxxxxxxxxxxxxxxxxxxxxxxxxxxx. Xxxxxxxxxxxxxxxxxxxxxxxxxxxx
xxxxxxxxxx. Xxxxxxxxxxxxxxxxxxxxxxxxxxxxxxxxxxxxxxxxxxxxxxxxxxxxxx
xxxxxxxxxxxxxxxxxxxxxxxxxxxxxxxxxxxxxxxxxxxxxxxxxxxxxx.

Xxxxxxxxxxxxxxxxxxxxxxxxxxxxxxxxxxxxxxxxxxxxxxxxxxxxxxxxxxxxxxxxxxxx
xxxxxxxxxxxxxxxxxxxxxxxxxxxxxxxxxxxxx. Xxxxxxxxxxxxxxxxxxxxxxxxxxxx
xxxxxxxxxx. Xxxxxxxxxxxxxxxxxxxxxxxxxxxxxxxxxxxxxxxxxxxxxxxxxxxxxx
xxxxxxxxxxxxxxxxxxxxxxxxxxxxxxxxxxxxxxxxxxxxxxxxxxxxxx.

Xxxxxxxxxxxxxxxxxxxxxxxxxxxxxxxxxxxxxxxxxxxxxxxxxxxxxxxxxxxxxxxxxxxx
xxxxxxxxxxxxxxxxxxxxxxxxxxxxxxxxxxxxx. Xxxxxxxxxxxxxxxxxxxxxxxxxxxx
xxxxxxxxxx. Xxxxxxxxxxxxxxxxxxxxxxxxxxxxxxxxxxxxxx.

Best regards,

Your Name

cc: Resume

YOUR SLOGAN/TAGLINE HERE

Figure 9.3: Letterhead Design 3.

YOUR NAME
Your Professional Title
Street Address, Town, ST 00000 • Phone: 000-000-0000
Email: xxxxxx@xxxxx.xxx • Web Portfolio: YourName.com

Dear Hiring Manager:

Xxxxxxxxxxxxxxxxxxxxxxxxxxxxxxxxxxxxxxxxxxxxxxxxxxxxxxxxxxxxxxxxxxxx
xxxx xxxxxxxxxxxxxxxxxxxxxxxxxxxxxxx. Xxxxxxxxxxxxxxxxxxxxxxxxxxxxxxx.
Xxxxxxxxxxxxxxxxxxxxxxxxxxxxxxxxxxxxxxxx.

Xxxxxxxxxxxxxxxxxxxxxxxxxxxxxxxxxxxxxxxxxxxxxxxxxxxxxxxxxxxxxxxxxxxx
xxxxxxx xxxxxxxxxxxxxxxxxxxxxxxxxxxxxx. Xxxxxxxxxxxxxxxxxxxxxxxxxxxx
xxxxxxxxxx. Xxxxxxxxxxxxxxxxxxxxxxxxxxxxxxxxxxxxxxxxxxxxxxxxxxxxxx.
Xxxxxxxxxxxxxxxxxxxxxxxxxxxxxxxxxxxxxxxxxxxxxxxxxxx.

Xxxxxxxxxxxxxxxxxxxxxxxxxxxxxxxxxxxxxxxxxxxxxxxxxxxxxxxxxxxxxxxxxxxx
xxxxx xxxxxxxxxxxxxxxxxxxxxxxxxxxxx. Xxxxxxxxxxxxxxxxxxxxxxxxxxxxxx
xxxxxxxxxx. Xxxxxxxxxxxxxxxxxxxxxxxxxxxxxxxxxxxxxxxxxxxxxxxxxxxxxx.
Xxxxxxxxxxxxxxxxxxxxxxxxxxxxxxxxxxxxxxxxx
xxxxxxxxxxxxxxxxxxxxxxxxxxxxxxxxxxxxxxxxxxxxxx.

Xxxxxxxxxxxxxxxxxxxxxxxxxxxxxxxxxxxxxxxxxxxxxxxxxxxxxxxxxxxxxxxxxxxx
xxxxxxx xxxxxxxxxxxxxxxxxxxxxxxxxxxx. Xxxxxxxxxxxxxxxxxxxxxxxxxxxxxx.
Xxxxxxxxxxxxxxxxxxxxxxxxxxxxxxxxxxxxxxxxxxxxxxxxxxx
xxxxxxxxxxxxxxxxxxxxxxxxxx. Xxxxxxxxxxxxxxxxxxxxxxxxxxxxxxxxxxxxxx
xxxxxxxxxxxxxxxxxxxxxxxxxxxxxxxxxxxxxxxxx.

Xxxxxxxxxxxxxxxxxxxxxxxxxxxxxxxxxxxxxxxxxxxxxxxxxxxxxxxxxxxxxxxxxxxx
xxxxxxxxxxxxxxxxxxxxxxxxxxxxxxxxxxxxx. Xxxxxxxxxxxxxxxxxxxxxxxxxxxx.
Xxxxxxxxxxxxxxxxxxxxxxxxxxxxxxxxxxxxxxxxxx.

Sincerely,

Your Name

cc: Resume

YOUR SLOGAN/TAGLINE HERE

Figure 9.4: Letterhead Design 4.

Your Name   Street Address, Town, ST 00000
Phone: (000) 000-0000
Email: xxxxxxxx@xxxxxxxx.xxx
Web Portfolio: YourName.com

Dear Hiring Manager:

Xxxxxxxxxxxxxxxxxxxxxxxxxxxxxxxxxxxxxxxxxxxxxxxxxxxxxxxxxxxxxxxxxxxx
xx xxxxxxxxxxxxxxxxxxxxxxxxxxxxxxxxxxxxxxxxxxxxxxxxxxxxxxxxxxxxxxxxx
xxxxxxxxxxxxxxxxxxxxxxxxxxxxxxxxxxxxxxxxxx.

Xxxxxxxxxxxxxxxxxxxxxxxxxxxxxxxxxxxxxxxxxxxxxxxxxxxxxxxxxxxxxxxxxxxx
xxxxxxxxxxxxxxxxxxxxxxxxxxxxxxxxxxxxxxxxxxxxxxxxxxxxxxxxxxxxxxxxxxxx
xxxxxxxxxxxxxxxxxxxxxxxxxxxxxxxxxxxxxxxxxxxxxxxxxxxxxxxxxxxxxxxxxxxx
xx xxxxxxxxxxxxxxxxxxxxxxxxxxxxxxxxxxxxxxxxxxxxxxxxxxxxxxxxxxxxx.

Xxxxxxxxxxxxxxxxxxxxxxxxxxxxxxxxxxxxxxxxxxxxxxxxxxxxxxxxxxxxxxxxxxxx
xxxxxxxxxxxxxxxxxxxxxxxxxxxxxxxxxxxxxxxxxxxxxxxxxxxxxxxxxxxxxxxxxxxx
xxxxxxxxxxxxxxxxxxxxxxxxxxxxxxxxxxxxxxxxxxxxxxxxxxxxxxxxxxxxxxxxxxxx
xx xxxxxxxxxxxxxxxxxxxxxxxxxxxxxxxxxxxxxxxxxxxxxxxxxxxxxxxxxxxxx.

Xxxxxxxxxxxxxxxxxxxxxxxxxxxxxxxxxxxxxxxxxxxxxxxxxxxxxxxxxxxxxxxxxxxx
xxxxxxxxxxxxxxxxxxxxxxxxxxxxxxxxxxxxxxxxxxxxxxxxxxxxxxxxxxxxxxxxxxxx
xxxxxxxxxxxxxxxxxxxxxxxxxxxxxxxxxxxxxxxxxx.

Sincerely,

Your Name

cc: Resume

Your Slogan Here

Figure 9.5: Letterhead Design 5.

YOUR NAME
Street Address, Town, ST 00000   Phone: (000) 000-0000
Web Portfolio: YourName.com   Email: xxxxxxx@xxxxxxxx.xxxxx

Dear Human Resources Professional:

Xxxxxxxxxxxxxxxxxxxxxxxxxxxxxxxxxxxxxxxxxxxxxxxxxxxxxxxxxxxxxxxxxxxx
xxxxxxxxxxxxxxxxxxxxxxxxxxxxxxxxxxxxxxxxxxxxxxxxxxxxxxxxxxxxxxxxxxxx
Xxxxxxxxxxxxxxxxxxxxxxxxxxxxxxxxxxxxxxxxxxxxxx.

Xxxxxxxxxxxxxxxxxxxxxxxxxxxxxxxxxxxxxxxxxxxxxxxxxxxxxxxxxxxxxxxxxxxx
xxxxxxxxxxxxxxxxxxxxxxxxxxxxxxxxxxxxxxxxxxxxxxxxxxxxxxxxxxxxxxxxxxxx
Xxxxxxxxxxxxxxxxxxxxxxxxxxxxxxxxxxxxxxxxxxxxxxxxxxxxxxxxxxxxxxxxxxxx
xxxxxxxxxxxxxxxxxxxxxxxxxxxxxxxxxxxxxxxxxxxxxxx.

Xxxxxxxxxxxxxxxxxxxxxxxxxxxxxxxxxxxxxxxxxxxxxxxxxxxxxxxxxxxxxxxxxxxx
xxxxxxxxxxxxxxxxxxxxxxxxxxxxxxxxxxxxxxxxxxxxxxxxxxxxxxxxxxxxxxxxxxxx
Xxxxxxxxxxxxxxxxxxxxxxxxxxxxxxxxxxxxxxxxxxxxxxxxxxxxxxxxxxxxxxxxxxxx
xxxxxxxxxxxxxxxxxxxxxxxxxxxxxxxxxxxxxxxxxxxxxxx.

Xxxxxxxxxxxxxxxxxxxxxxxxxxxxxxxxxxxxxxxxxxxxxxxxxxxxxxxxxxxxxxxxxxxx
xxxxxxxxxxxxxxxxxxxxxxxxxxxxxxxxxxxxxxxxxxxxxxxxxxxxxxxxxxxxxxxxxxxx
Xxxxxxxxxxxxxxxxxxxxxxxxxxxxxxxxxxxxxxxxxxxxxxxxxxxxxxxxxxxxxxxxxxxx
xxxxxxxxxxxxxxxxxxxxxxxxxxxxxxxxxxxxxxxxxxxxxxx.

Xxxxxxxxxxxxxxxxxxxxxxxxxxxxxxxxxxxxxxxxxxxxxxxxxxxxxxxxxxxxxxxxxxxx
xxxxxxxxxxxxxxxxxxxxxxxxxxxxxxxxxxxxxxxxxxxxxxxxxxxxxxxxxxxxxxxxxxxx
Xxxxxxxxxxxxxxxxxxxxxxxxxxxxxxxxxxxxxxxxxxxxx.

Best regards,

Your Name

cc: Resume

INSERT YOUR SLOGAN HERE

Figure 9.6: Letterhead Design 6.

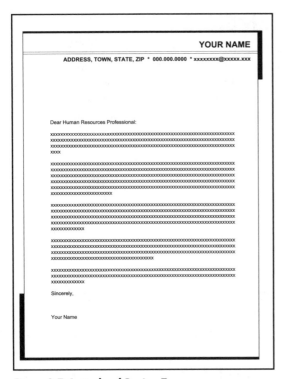

Figure 9.7: Letterhead Design 7.

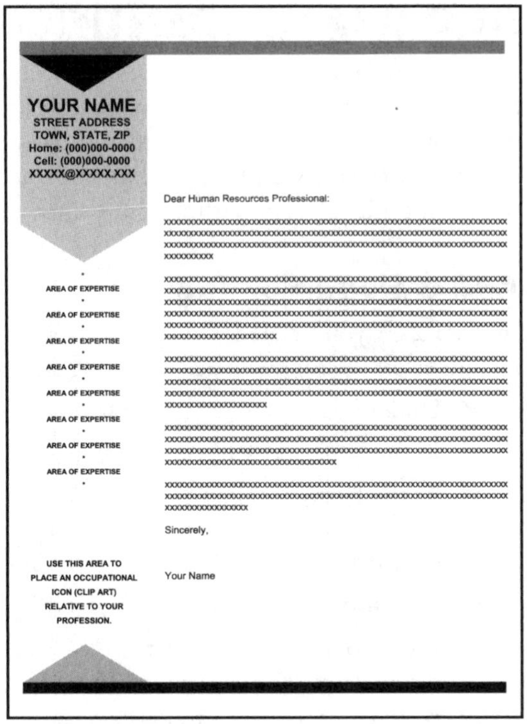

Figure 9.8: Letterhead Design 8.

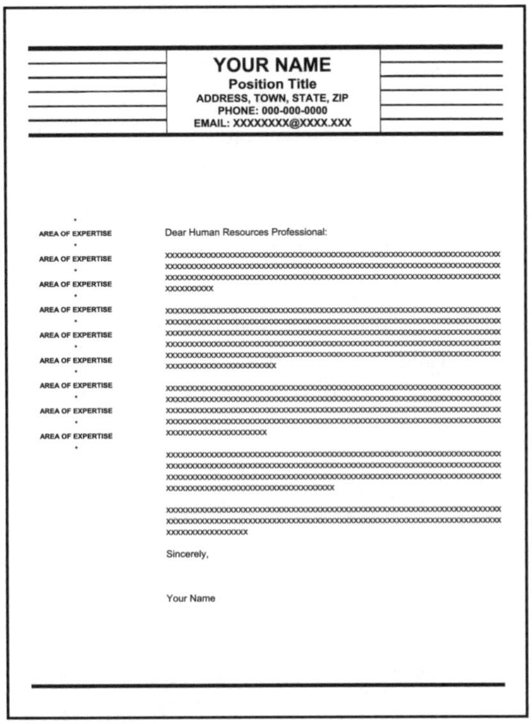

Figure 9.9: Letterhead Design 9.

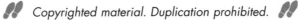

ADD BRAND IDENTIFICATION ELEMENTS

In a pile of bland cover letters, the ones that hiring managers notice first are the ones they read first. And if after attracting their attention, your cover letter presents content that compels them to call you, you have met your goal of getting noticed in order to get your foot in the door. One way to get your cover letter noticed is to infuse it with brand identification elements. The following sections show you how. Keep in mind that this is an optional step, but it might be just the thing that makes your cover letter really stand out.

Add a Slogan or Tagline

In Step 2, if you created a slogan or tagline that exemplifies your personal brand message, you can now include it on your cover letter in one of these three places:

- ✔ Under your name in your masthead
- ✔ In the left-hand scholar's margin
- ✔ At the bottom of your letter in larger italics

Step 2 provided some examples of slogans and taglines. Here are a few more to spur your imagination:

- ✔ **Aviation Mechanic:** "There Isn't a Plane I Can't Repair"
- ✔ **Elementary Teacher:** "Helping Students Take Positive Steps Toward their Future" or "Gaining Enthusiasm, Participation, and Lesson Retention"
- ✔ **Registered Nurse:** "Providing Caring, Professional Medical Care from Infants to Geriatrics"
- ✔ **Sales Manager:** "Meeting Challenges, Overcoming Obstacles, and Closing Sales" or "Successfully Uncovering and Fulfilling Customer Needs"

Add Testimonials

Including testimonials or endorsements on your cover letter is another way to grab the attention of your prospective employer and add interest to your presentation. Stating what others have said about your performance also adds credence to the information you convey in your cover letter.

Testimonials can include excerpts from letters of recommendation, reference letters, customer thank you letters, vendor satisfaction letters, performance evaluation comments, internship summaries, staff memos, customer surveys, and other commendations.

Adding one to three testimonials in the scholar's margin of your cover letter will make your presentation stand out. Try to select comments from a variety of sources in your field, such as superiors, professors, customers or clients, vendors, peers and subordinates, and others who speak to your various abilities. Following are examples:

"Sandy is a strong leader. She bases decisions on what is best for the guests and creates a positive environment for employees."

—James Turner, Regional Director, Stamford Brew House

"Janet is a an excellent trainer and team worker. She shows dedication and commitment in all she does."

—John Jones, Area Director, Pasta Grill Restaurant

Step 9

Add a Mission Statement

Including a *mission statement* in your cover letter is another way to verbally brand yourself. A mission statement shows you are serious about your profession. Generally a mission statement used in your cover letter is a promise of the value you offer or a strong belief concerning your profession.

A mission statement should be short and to the point and can be written for any position. It basically states what your mission is specific to your targeted career goal—what you plan to do or have done, what you believe in (be sure it is something the prospective employer believes in, too!), why your profession is important to you, or another promise or value-added statement of some sort that will pique the recruiter's attention and show your enthusiasm, contribution, and/or vested interest in your career.

Here are some sample mission statements:

"Each step a child takes in his life has an effect on his future. I would like to help students take positive steps by creating an educational experience conducive to learning."

"If the customer is happy and you are making a sale, it's a win/win. I believe in making customers happy."

"An effective case manager takes time to listen, treats others the way she wants to be treated, inspires positive change in people's lives, and is accountable for her actions and reactions."

"I believe a good service manager has the ability to run an operation with an eye towards profitability while servicing the customer in a fair and honest way."

"A successful travel marketing manager is able to listen to and act on behalf of the client to offer the high-end customer service expected from an airline."

CREATE AN EMAIL VERSION OF YOUR COVER LETTER

When you send out a printed version of your cover letter (along with your resume), you can make sure that it fits on one formatted, attractive page. If you email a full-page cover letter to a prospective employer, on the other hand, the text is likely to be too long to fit on one screen, and the employer might not take the time to scroll down to read the rest. Therefore, you should condense your cover letter to perhaps half the size of your original version when you send it out as an email message. You still can—*and should*—attach your "pretty," complete version in MS Word format or as a PDF for downloading.

SEND IT OUT!

If you've completed all the steps thoroughly and you are convinced that your cover letter is the best it can be in conveying your personal brand and making you shine, you are ready to send it out!

Apply to positions that are a match for your qualifications as well as those that may be above and below your professional level. You may be pleasantly surprised that the ones below your level may be more encompassing than they appeared and/or pay a similar salary, and the ones above may actually be suitable for your expertise level. Plus, the more interviews you go on, the better your interviewing skills will be for that "perfect" job opportunity.

Step 9

step 10

Review Complete Cover Letter Foundations and Samples

- Complete Personally Branded Cover Letters and Foundations
- Situational Cover Letter Foundations and Samples
- Profession-Specific Cover Letter Foundations
- Other Personally Branded Cover Letter Samples

COMPLETE PERSONALLY BRANDED COVER LETTERS AND FOUNDATIONS

In the pages that follow, you will find complete cover letter foundations as well as sample personally branded cover letters within which you will see many of the cover letter paragraph foundations from previous steps. Notice how the sample cover letters created by professional resume writers contain compelling value statements, state and back up the job seeker's personal brand, seamlessly flow from one paragraph to the next, and close with strong calls to action that compel hiring managers to want to reach out to the candidate. The following tables list what types of cover letter foundations are available in this step.

note The cover letter samples that follow were written by professional resume writers. The cover letter foundations were created from these professionally written letters so that you can use them as foundations to write your own. All cover letter foundations (full letters and paragraphs alike) are available as MS Word files on the CD at the back of the book, making it easier for you to draft your cover letter step by step, paragraph by paragraph.

TABLE 10.1: SITUATIONAL COVER LETTERS

Number	Cover Letter Foundation (by situation)	Sample Cover Letter (by job title)
1	An established professional or manager	Manufacturing executive
2	A candidate with professional experience and a degree	Corporate trainer
3	A candidate with some experience	Graphic designer
4	A professional candidate with solid experience	Electronic engineer
5	A high-level manager who revitalized an organization	Golf course superintendent
6	A change leader in any profession	Real estate professional
7	Any professional job candidate with experience	IT security solutions architect
8	An executive who is an industry change agent	Chief information officer
9	A subcontractor	Event manager
10	A candidate with a referral	Ground operations manager
11	A C-level executive	Racetrack chief executive officer
12	Someone with an exhilarating and rewarding career	Television show host/reporter
13	An industry achiever	Personal trainer
14	An executive in any profession	Chief executive officer
15	A candidate whose field has changed dramatically	Senior college administrator
16	An accomplished candidate with experience	Software application developer
17	Someone with specialized experience	Nanotechnologist
18	A talented professional with experience	Media writer/editor
19	A dually qualified candidate	Teacher/school psychologist
20	An executive who brings about change	Vice president
21	A consultant with solid experience	Management consultant
22	A candidate who received a referral	School program director
23	A manager applying to a recruiter	Health care operations executive
24	A change manager	Information technology director

Number	Cover Letter Foundation (by situation)	Sample Cover Letter (by job title)
25	A service provider with experience	Elementary education teacher
26	Any candidate with progressive responsibility	Corporate trainer
27	A manager in any profession	Retail manager
28	Any job candidate	Financial sales manager
29	A highly experienced candidate in any profession	Regional sales director
30	A qualified candidate in any profession	Program director
31	A manager in any profession	Sales and marketing manager

TABLE 10.2: PROFESSION-SPECIFIC COVER LETTERS

Number	Cover Letter Foundation (by industry)	Sample Cover Letter (by job title)
32	Human resources	Human resources director
33	Construction	Project manager
34	Marketing	Brand manager
35	Human resources	Training and development manager
36	Information technology	Website developer
37	Business/marketing	Business strategy innovator

Cover letter foundations and samples 32–36 are copyright of Creative Image Builders.com, from its product line, *Hybrid Resume and Cover Letter Foundations.*

After you see how the cover letter paragraph foundations from previous steps work within whole cover letters, determine whether you want to replace any paragraphs in your current cover letter draft. Or you may decide to develop your entire cover letter right within a single foundation by selecting options and filling in the blanks. Of course, you can mix and match paragraphs and sentences from any of the cover letter types. And just because the cover letter is recommended for a certain situation or profession does not mean you cannot use it for your own profession by completing it with information applicable to you. This book contains a nice, varied mix of professions and situations, so after going through all the steps and foundations, you will have an outstanding cover letter that works for you!

 tip Like *Step-by-Step Cover Letters*, the book *Step-by-Step Resumes: Build an Outstanding Resume in 10 Easy Steps!* (also by Evelyn U. Salvador and published by JIST Publishing) is filled with a plethora of foundations that make it easy to complete your resume.

Once you have completed your cover letter, be sure that your personal brand is conveyed throughout your resume through accomplishments that prove your value statement and return on investment to your current and past employers. Including achievement examples in your resume will convince hiring managers that your words are backed up with actions that demonstrate your expertise and that your stated personal brand is in fact what you say it is.

SITUATIONAL COVER LETTER FOUNDATIONS AND SAMPLES

The 32 foundations in this section can be adapted to many different types of job seekers. The full cover letter samples give you an idea of how your specific information can be incorporated into a polished final cover letter.

COVER LETTER FOUNDATION 1

This foundation works well for an established professional or manager with several years of experience.

Dear Hiring Manager:

As a successful _____ [type of] [executive/professional], I bring to your organization more than _____ [number] years of progressively responsible experience in _____, _____, and _____ [areas of expertise]. My expertise lies in _____ and _____ [benefits].

I have a proven track record of [increased sales/elevated profits/decreased costs/streamlining operations/ increased productivity/other: _____]. Notable achievements include _____, _____, and _____ [your most significant accomplishments]. Please see the attached resume for details.

Complementing my ability to _____ [do what?] and effectively _____ [do what?] are equally strong qualifications in _____, _____, and _____ [other significant targeted areas]. I am able to provide strategic direction with appropriate tactical action plans to meet these needs while responding to the constantly changing demands of the _____ [which?] industry. I lead by example and provide strong [decision-making/problem-solving/staff development/other: _____] skills.

I am confident that the [experience/drive/enthusiasm/strategic direction/other: _____] I can bring to _____ [company name] will prove to be an asset. I would appreciate hearing from you regarding any existing or future openings you might have and would welcome the opportunity to discuss a possible relationship that would prove to be mutually beneficial. I will call you next week to see whether you have time in your schedule so that we can meet and discuss a mutual return on investment.

Warm regards,

_____ [your signature]

_____ [your name]

Enclosure: Resume

Step 10

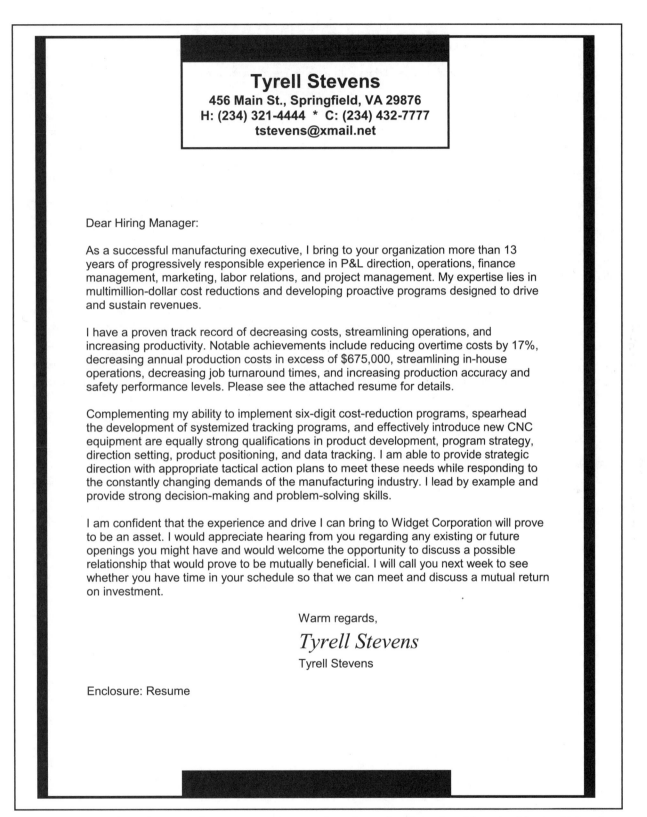

Tyrell Stevens
456 Main St., Springfield, VA 29876
H: (234) 321-4444 * C: (234) 432-7777
tstevens@xmail.net

Dear Hiring Manager:

As a successful manufacturing executive, I bring to your organization more than 13 years of progressively responsible experience in P&L direction, operations, finance management, marketing, labor relations, and project management. My expertise lies in multimillion-dollar cost reductions and developing proactive programs designed to drive and sustain revenues.

I have a proven track record of decreasing costs, streamlining operations, and increasing productivity. Notable achievements include reducing overtime costs by 17%, decreasing annual production costs in excess of $675,000, streamlining in-house operations, decreasing job turnaround times, and increasing production accuracy and safety performance levels. Please see the attached resume for details.

Complementing my ability to implement six-digit cost-reduction programs, spearhead the development of systemized tracking programs, and effectively introduce new CNC equipment are equally strong qualifications in product development, program strategy, direction setting, product positioning, and data tracking. I am able to provide strategic direction with appropriate tactical action plans to meet these needs while responding to the constantly changing demands of the manufacturing industry. I lead by example and provide strong decision-making and problem-solving skills.

I am confident that the experience and drive I can bring to Widget Corporation will prove to be an asset. I would appreciate hearing from you regarding any existing or future openings you might have and would welcome the opportunity to discuss a possible relationship that would prove to be mutually beneficial. I will call you next week to see whether you have time in your schedule so that we can meet and discuss a mutual return on investment.

Warm regards,

Tyrell Stevens

Tyrell Stevens

Enclosure: Resume

Figure 10.1: A cover letter for a manufacturing executive using Cover Letter Foundation 1 and Letterhead Design 10 (on the CD).

Step 10

COVER LETTER FOUNDATION 2

This foundation works well for a professional candidate with experience and a degree.

Dear Human Resources Manager:

I believe my broad experience in all phases of _____ [what?] coupled with my [master's/bachelor's/associate] degree in _____ [major] uniquely qualifies me for a _____ [title or type of] position in your firm. I am enclosing my resume for your consideration.

During my ____ [number] years of _____ [type of] experience, I have been involved in [just about every facet/nearly all aspects] of _____ [primary responsibility]—from _____ and _____ [primary functions] to _____ and _____ [primary functions]. I have utilized my _____ [type of] skills to [successfully/effectively] _____ [do what?].

My number one criteria is to _____ [mission]. I achieve that by _____, _____, and _____ [skills or competitive edge]. I always make it a practice to get to know _____ [whom?] so that _____ [benefit]. I also believe that _____ [another work goal], so _____ [skill] is essential.

My _____ [type of] expertise and ability to _____ [primary skill] are a perfect combination for the _____ [industry] field. For these reasons and more, I feel confident that I can apply my skills to work well within your firm.

I would very much like to discuss _____ [type of job] opportunities within your firm and would appreciate hearing from you regarding any existing or future openings you might have. Thank you for your time and consideration.

Best regards,

_____ [your signature]

_____ [your name]

Enclosure: Resume

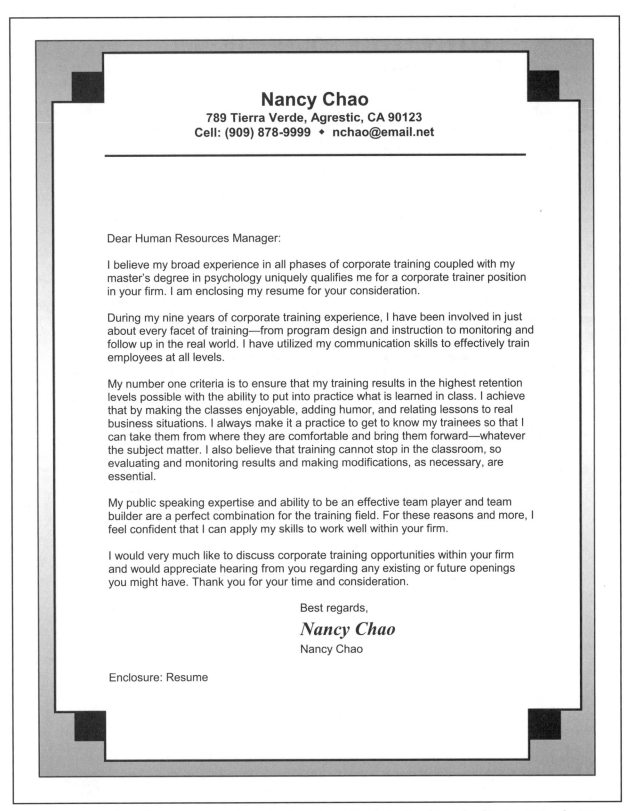

Nancy Chao
789 Tierra Verde, Agrestic, CA 90123
Cell: (909) 878-9999 ◆ nchao@email.net

Dear Human Resources Manager:

I believe my broad experience in all phases of corporate training coupled with my master's degree in psychology uniquely qualifies me for a corporate trainer position in your firm. I am enclosing my resume for your consideration.

During my nine years of corporate training experience, I have been involved in just about every facet of training—from program design and instruction to monitoring and follow up in the real world. I have utilized my communication skills to effectively train employees at all levels.

My number one criteria is to ensure that my training results in the highest retention levels possible with the ability to put into practice what is learned in class. I achieve that by making the classes enjoyable, adding humor, and relating lessons to real business situations. I always make it a practice to get to know my trainees so that I can take them from where they are comfortable and bring them forward—whatever the subject matter. I also believe that training cannot stop in the classroom, so evaluating and monitoring results and making modifications, as necessary, are essential.

My public speaking expertise and ability to be an effective team player and team builder are a perfect combination for the training field. For these reasons and more, I feel confident that I can apply my skills to work well within your firm.

I would very much like to discuss corporate training opportunities within your firm and would appreciate hearing from you regarding any existing or future openings you might have. Thank you for your time and consideration.

Best regards,

Nancy Chao
Nancy Chao

Enclosure: Resume

Figure 10.2: A cover letter for a corporate trainer using Cover Letter Foundation 2 and Letterhead Design 11 (on the CD).

Step 10

COVER LETTER FOUNDATION 3

This foundation can work for any job candidate with some experience.

Dear _____ [hiring manager name]:

I am interested in exploring _____ [type(s) of] opportunities within your firm and have enclosed my resume for your consideration. I believe my _____ and _____ [type of] experience coupled with my ability to _____ and _____ [do what?] could assist your firm in meeting its _____ [type of] needs. My solid experience in _____ and _____ [skill areas] would serve your [firm/clients/patrons/other: _____] well.

As _____ [job title] for _____ [most recent employer] for the past ____ [number] years, I _____ and _____ [primary functions]. Additionally, I have _____ [other skills or accomplishments]. Other areas of expertise include _____, _____, and _____ [what areas?]. I have a proven track record for [decreasing company costs/increasing sales and profits/streamlining operations/increasing productivity/other: _____] for my employers.

I believe my _____ [type of] expertise, _____ [type of] abilities, and _____ [type of] skills are a perfect combination for a _____ [type of] professional. I am confident that the enthusiasm and experience I can bring to your organization will prove to be assets in achieving your firm's goals as they have been for others.

Thank you in advance for your time and consideration. I look forward to hearing from you for a personal interview at your earliest convenience and would welcome the opportunity to meet with you. I will follow up next week to see whether we can set up a time to meet.

Regards,

_____ [your signature]

_____ [your name]

Enclosure: Resume

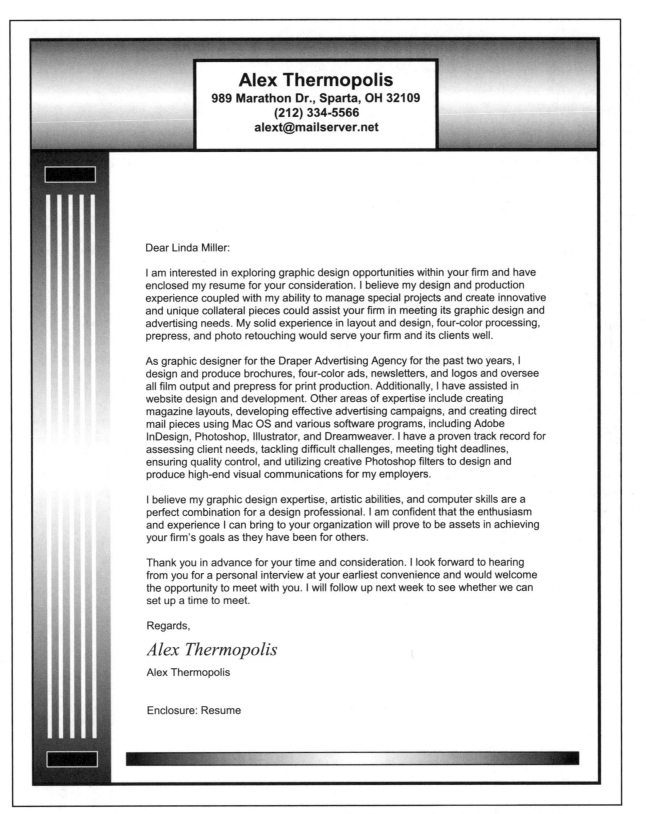

Alex Thermopolis
989 Marathon Dr., Sparta, OH 32109
(212) 334-5566
alext@mailserver.net

Dear Linda Miller:

I am interested in exploring graphic design opportunities within your firm and have enclosed my resume for your consideration. I believe my design and production experience coupled with my ability to manage special projects and create innovative and unique collateral pieces could assist your firm in meeting its graphic design and advertising needs. My solid experience in layout and design, four-color processing, prepress, and photo retouching would serve your firm and its clients well.

As graphic designer for the Draper Advertising Agency for the past two years, I design and produce brochures, four-color ads, newsletters, and logos and oversee all film output and prepress for print production. Additionally, I have assisted in website design and development. Other areas of expertise include creating magazine layouts, developing effective advertising campaigns, and creating direct mail pieces using Mac OS and various software programs, including Adobe InDesign, Photoshop, Illustrator, and Dreamweaver. I have a proven track record for assessing client needs, tackling difficult challenges, meeting tight deadlines, ensuring quality control, and utilizing creative Photoshop filters to design and produce high-end visual communications for my employers.

I believe my graphic design expertise, artistic abilities, and computer skills are a perfect combination for a design professional. I am confident that the enthusiasm and experience I can bring to your organization will prove to be assets in achieving your firm's goals as they have been for others.

Thank you in advance for your time and consideration. I look forward to hearing from you for a personal interview at your earliest convenience and would welcome the opportunity to meet with you. I will follow up next week to see whether we can set up a time to meet.

Regards,

Alex Thermopolis

Alex Thermopolis

Enclosure: Resume

Figure 10.3: A cover letter for a graphic designer using Cover Letter Foundation 3 and Letterhead Design 12 (on the CD).

COVER LETTER FOUNDATION 4

This foundation can work for any professional candidate with solid experience.

Dear _____ [hiring manager name]:

I believe my strong _____ and _____ [type of] expertise coupled with the ability to _____ [do or perform what?] makes me an excellent candidate for a(n) _____ [type of] position within your firm. With broad experience in all phases of _____ and _____ [areas of expertise], my forte is in _____ [what area?]. Based upon my _____ [type of] success, I am confident I can be of considerable value to your firm. I am enclosing my resume for your review.

Currently as _____ [job title] of _____ [employer name], I have _____ [list results of your primary achievements]. I also have _____ [other achievements].

My solid experience in _____ [what area(s)?] would serve your firm well in the areas of _____, _____, and _____ [areas of expertise]. I have a proven track record for _____ and _____ [state your achievement(s)].

Throughout my career, I have consistently demonstrated my ability to _____ [do or perform what?] by _____ [doing what?] to ensure attainment of goals. I have gained a solid reputation for _____ and _____ [attributes and skills], resulting in _____ [what benefit(s)?].

For all of these reasons, I feel I would be an asset to your firm. I would welcome the opportunity to discuss my background and accomplishments with you in greater detail and to learn more about your company and its goals. I will contact you next week to answer any questions you may have.

Sincerely,

_____ [your signature]

_____ [your name]

Enclosure: Resume

Step 10

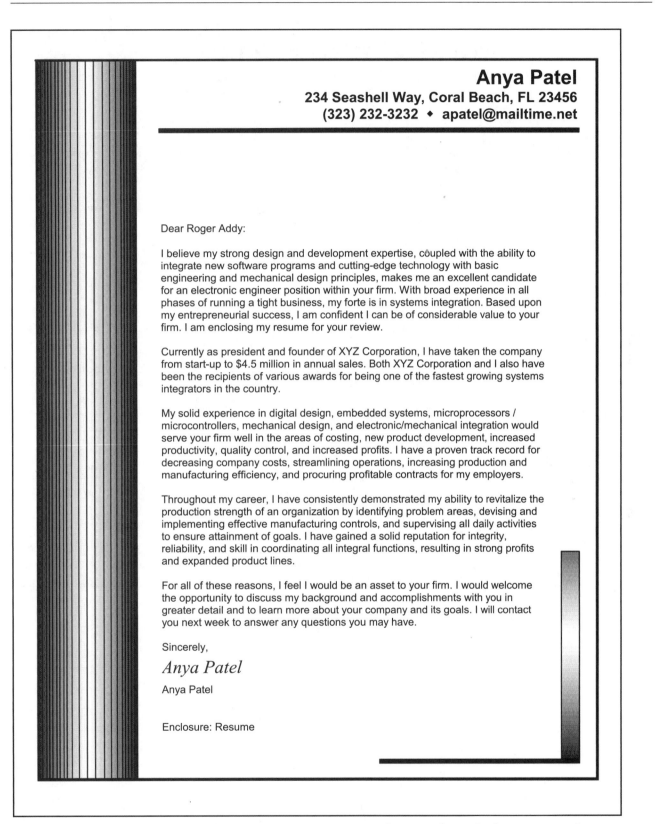

Anya Patel
234 Seashell Way, Coral Beach, FL 23456
(323) 232-3232 ◆ apatel@mailtime.net

Dear Roger Addy:

I believe my strong design and development expertise, coupled with the ability to integrate new software programs and cutting-edge technology with basic engineering and mechanical design principles, makes me an excellent candidate for an electronic engineer position within your firm. With broad experience in all phases of running a tight business, my forte is in systems integration. Based upon my entrepreneurial success, I am confident I can be of considerable value to your firm. I am enclosing my resume for your review.

Currently as president and founder of XYZ Corporation, I have taken the company from start-up to $4.5 million in annual sales. Both XYZ Corporation and I also have been the recipients of various awards for being one of the fastest growing systems integrators in the country.

My solid experience in digital design, embedded systems, microprocessors / microcontrollers, mechanical design, and electronic/mechanical integration would serve your firm well in the areas of costing, new product development, increased productivity, quality control, and increased profits. I have a proven track record for decreasing company costs, streamlining operations, increasing production and manufacturing efficiency, and procuring profitable contracts for my employers.

Throughout my career, I have consistently demonstrated my ability to revitalize the production strength of an organization by identifying problem areas, devising and implementing effective manufacturing controls, and supervising all daily activities to ensure attainment of goals. I have gained a solid reputation for integrity, reliability, and skill in coordinating all integral functions, resulting in strong profits and expanded product lines.

For all of these reasons, I feel I would be an asset to your firm. I would welcome the opportunity to discuss my background and accomplishments with you in greater detail and to learn more about your company and its goals. I will contact you next week to answer any questions you may have.

Sincerely,

Anya Patel

Anya Patel

Enclosure: Resume

Figure 10.4: A cover letter for an electronic engineer using Cover Letter Foundation 4 and Letterhead Design 13 (on the CD).

Step 10

COVER LETTER FOUNDATION 5

This foundation works for a high-level manager who has revitalized an organization.

Dear Hiring Manager:

Now that I have successfully revitalized _____ [most recent employer], overseeing a [multimillion-dollar/$_____] _____ [type of] project that _____ [accomplished what?], I am seeking my next challenge. Proudly dedicating my career to _____ [doing what?], I am pleased to submit my resume for the _____ [job title] position advertised [in/on] _____ [where?]. I am confident that I will lead _____ [prospective employer] in _____ [doing what?].

In addition to my expertise in _____, _____, and _____ [areas of expertise], I am actively involved with _____ [type or names of] organizations as well as _____ [other affiliation]. I am committed to _____ [doing what?].

A sample of my achievements in _____ [what areas?] include

- [Earning/Increasing/Elevating/Other: _____] _____ [type of] [revenues/profits/productivity/quality/other: _____] by way of _____ [doing what?].

- [Overseeing/Managing/Directing] _____ [what?] for _____ [purpose], benefiting the firm by way of _____ [doing what?].

- [Developing/Initiating/Championing/Spearheading] _____ [what?] for _____ [purpose], which resulted in _____ [company benefits].

- [Revitalizing/Invigorating/Rejuvenating] _____ [what?], resulting in _____ [benefits].

Please call me at your earliest convenience for the opportunity to discuss in person how my diverse experience will be an asset for _____ [prospective employer] in meeting its _____ [type of] challenges. I look forward to meeting with you.

Best regards,

_____ [your signature]

_____ [your name]

" _____ " _____ [testimonial]

WINSTON L. ROBERTS
⬧ C G C S ⬧
610 Shore Road ⬧ Hampstead, NY 12381 ⬧ 102.345.6789 ⬧ wlroberts@email.co

Dear Hiring Manager:

Now that I have successfully revitalized Eastbrook Country Club, overseeing a multimillion-dollar project that returned the club to its premier status, I am seeking my next challenge. Proudly ded career to executing significant restorations of classic golf courses and facilities, I am pleased to resume for the golf course superintendent position advertised on golf.net. I am confident that I will Cove Country Club in maintaining its rich history and rewarding playing conditions.

In addition to my expertise in turf management, long-range planning, and fiscal oversight, I a involved with several local golfing organizations as well as the Golf Course Superintendents Ass America. I am committed to embracing modern technological improvements for course manager preserving the character, tradition, and aesthetic of old courses with respect for their natural environ

A sample of my achievements in developing and maintaining Eastbrook Country Club include

➢ **Earning the "Top 50 Classic Courses" award** by *Golf World* magazine, honoring my improv

➢ **Overseeing the $5,000,000 renovation to the pool area and clubhouse.** Directed bidding pro supervised engineers, landscape designers, and utility staff. Modernized safety and security fea

➢ **Developing a long-range golf course improvement plan** that identified and resolved all issue regarding bunkers, tees, drainage, cart paths, and tree care. Installed a completely computerizec system.

➢ **Managing the successful refurbishment of 95 bunker complexes,** delivering project 30% un at $900,000. Greens were enlarged and restored back to original shape and size, and native gras introduced that cut down on maintenance and provided natural habitat.

➢ **Initiating programs to restore lost features of the course.** Reshaped and recountered ground original concept of designer. Selective removal of improperly planted trees allowed features of and mounds to be on full display.

Please call me at your earliest convenience for the opportunity to discuss in person how my diverse will be an asset for North Cove Country Club's prestigious renovation and enhancement. I look meeting with you.

Best regards,

Winston Roberts

Winston L. Roberts

"Golfers at the Eastbrook Country Club are calling Winston Roberts a miracle worker. The new superintendent's renovations are exceptional. Every tee, green, fairway, and trap has been improved." Greg Wilkes, golf editor, New Eastbrook Register.

Figure 10.5: A cover letter for a golf course superintendent using Cover Letter Foundation 5 (contributed by August Cohen, CARW, NCRW, CPRW).

COVER LETTER FOUNDATION 6

This foundation works well for a change leader in any profession.

Dear _____ [name of hiring manager]:

In today's tough economic climate, where change is constant, it can be difficult to _____ [industry challenge]. With expertise in _____, _____, _____, and _____ [areas of expertise], I can help _____ [prospective employer] avoid many of the pitfalls associated with _____ [challenge].

In reviewing my resume, you will find that I have more than _____ [number] years of experience _____, _____, _____, and _____ [doing what?] for _____ [whom or what?].

My expertise includes

- [Planning/Developing] _____ [what?].

- [Prospecting for/Seeking out] _____ [what?].

- [Preparing/Organizing] _____ [what?].

- [Acquiring/Obtaining] _____ [what?].

- [Managing/Supervising] _____ [what?].

- [Reviewing/Evaluating] _____ [what?].

If you feel that your company is in need of someone with my background, I would enjoy talking with you about opportunities. Please call me today at (___) ___-____ [phone number].

Best regards,

_____ [your signature]

_____ [your name]

Enclosure

GORDON B. BUCKLEY

456 Sheridan Drive ❑ Lincoln, NE 67890 ❑ (444) 333-2222 ❑ gordon.b.buckley@email.com

June 22, 20XX

Steven Oldman
Human Resources Manager
Stellar Investments
999 Corporate Drive
Lincoln, NE 67878

Dear Mr. Oldman:

In today's tough economic climate, where change is constant, it can be difficult to identify a property's future potential. With expertise in market trends, pricing, growth, and supply, I can help Stellar Investments avoid many of the pitfalls associated with the purchase of land or property.

In reviewing my resume, you will find that I have more than 15 years of experience identifying, sourcing, and acquiring land and residential, commercial, and hospitality properties for investors.

My expertise includes

- ❑ Planning, developing, and supervising the acquisition or divestiture of property and land rights.
- ❑ Prospecting for potential land/property acquisition opportunities.
- ❑ Preparing preliminary pro forma financial analysis for land and/or property opportunities.
- ❑ Acquiring property or land and entitling the land necessary to meet organizational goals and projections.
- ❑ Managing the preparation and approval of all entitlement documents required for new land purchases.
- ❑ Reviewing title reports and coordinating title objection letters to sellers.

If you feel that your company is in need of someone with my background, I would enjoy talking with you about opportunities. Please call me today at (444) 333-2222.

Best regards,

Gordon Buckley

Gordon B. Buckley

Enclosure

Figure 10.6: A cover letter for a real estate professional using Cover Letter Foundation 6 (contributed by Angie Jones, CPRW, CEIC).

COVER LETTER FOUNDATION 7

This foundation works well for any professional job candidate with some experience.

Dear _____ [contact name]:

Are you seeking a [certified/licensed/degreed/award-winning/other: _____] _____ [position title] with superior _____ and _____ [type of] skills? If so, we should talk.

For the past _____ [number] years, I have served as a _____ [position title] and _____ [position title] for _____ [most recent employer]. My expertise lies in _____ [what field or area?], including _____, _____, _____, and _____ [areas of expertise]. I offer extensive experience in _____ and _____ [specialization(s)]. I have established my reputation as a leader in _____ [what arena?] allowing for immediate solutions when needed to resolve _____ [type of] [situations/challenges/problems].

Prior to this, I served as a _____ [position title] for _____ [previous employer] for _____ [number] years. My roles included _____, _____, and _____ [primary job functions]. I know how to _____ and _____ [do what?]. I am able to work with _____ [whom or what?] to _____ [do what?] in order to effectively _____ [do what?].

Certifications include: _____, _____, and _____ [certification titles]. I hold a [master's/bachelor's/associate] degree in _____ [major] from _____ [name of school] in _____ [town and state].

Thank you for your time and professional consideration in reviewing the enclosed resume. I will call you next week to see whether we can talk further about how my expertise can meet the needs of _____ [prospective employer].

Sincerely,

_____ [your signature]

_____ [your name]

Enclosure: Resume

JASMINE KELLY, CISSP

| 8450 Fareway Road | Phone: (432) 890-3456 |
| Lincoln, NE 68502 | Email: jasminekelly@zmail.com |

September 7, 20XX

Paula Fletcher
Vice President, Human Resources
Compucorp
123 Technology Avenue
Lincoln, NE 67890

Dear Ms. Fletcher:

Are you seeking a certified IT security solutions architect with superior project management skills? If so, we should talk.

For the past 7 years, I have served as a security solutions architect and project leader for ABC Company. My expertise lies in data loss prevention (DLP), including solutions to protect data at rest, in motion, and in use. I offer extensive experience in network security monitoring and the development of network intrusion prevention solutions. I have established my reputation as a leader in rapid prototyping, allowing for near immediate solutions when needed to resolve business-critical situations.

Prior to this, I served as a senior solutions architect for XYZ Company for 8 years. My roles included both pre-sales support and customer delivery. I know how to drive solution development process maturity and clearly communicate goals, decisions, and recommendations to the appropriate parties. I am able to work with IT and business owners to understand business requirements and strategy related to my assigned line of business in order to effectively design solutions for that business.

Certifications include: Certified Information Systems Security Professional (CISSP), GIAC Information Security Professional (GISP), Information Technology Infrastructure Library Foundation (ITIL), and IT Services Management. I hold a Bachelor of Science degree in computer science from SUNY Potsdam in Potsdam, NY.

Thank you for your time and professional consideration in reviewing the enclosed resume. I will call you next week to see whether we can talk further about how my expertise can meet the needs of Compucorp.

Sincerely,

Jasmine Kelly

Jasmine Kelly

Enclosure: Resume

Figure 10.7: A cover letter for a IT Security Solution Architect using Cover Letter Foundation 7 (contributed by Angie Jones, CPRW, CEIC).

Step 10

COVER LETTER FOUNDATION 8

This foundation works well for an executive who is an industry change agent.

Dear _____ [hiring manager name]:

Are you seeking a hands-on _____ [job title] who believes in leading by example and is a change agent who earns respect by demonstrating _____ [what?] and by implementing _____ [what?] while collaborating with a broad cross section of leaders? If so, we should talk.

Currently, I am the _____ [current job title]. Throughout the past _____ [number] years, I have been heavily involved in _____ [what?]. I have built my reputation on _____ [type of] excellence through the delivery of [practical/cost-effective/logical/user-based/client-focused/other: _____] solutions that [increase efficiency/boost performance/elevate revenues/decrease costs/other: _____]. Prior to this, I spent many years working as a(n) _____ [previous job title].

With more than _____ [number] years of total _____ [type of] experience I know how to _____ [do what?] and clearly communicate [goals/decisions/recommendations/other: _____] to the appropriate parties. My expertise lies in _____, _____, _____, and _____ [what areas?]. I am recognized for my innate ability to coach, motivate, and inspire a staff to reach its full potential.

[Certifications/Licenses/Degrees/Awards/Other: _____] include: _____ and _____ [qualifications].

Thank you for your time and professional consideration in reviewing the enclosed resume. I look forward to speaking with you soon.

Sincerely,

_____ [your signature]

_____ [your name]

Enclosure

JEFF LOWENTHAL

1000 Pearl Road
Forks, NE 68358

Phone: (Cell) (404) 404-0404
Email: jlowenthal@zmail.net

July 31, 20XX

William Elliot
Human Resources Director
Conglomonet
787 Newsome Lane
Lincoln, NE 67890

Dear Mr. Elliot:

Are you seeking a hands-on chief information officer (CIO) who believes in leading by example and is a change agent who earns respect by demonstrating a sound understanding of business goals, objectives, and technology and by implementing key technology initiatives on-time and on-budget while collaborating with a broad cross section of leaders? If so, we should talk.

Currently, I am the manager of IT technical services for Workforce Development for the Department of Labor. Throughout the past 12+ years, I have been heavily involved in the strategic planning required to align technology initiatives with budget dollars in the support of mission-critical needs for the State of Nebraska. I have built my reputation on operational excellence through the delivery of practical, cost-effective solutions that increase efficiency and boost performance. Prior to this, I spent many years working as an application analyst.

With more than 17 years of total IT experience, I know how to drive the solution development process to maturity and clearly communicate goals, decisions, and recommendations to the appropriate parties. My expertise lies in network design, administration, security, application development, and integration. I am recognized for my innate ability to coach, motivate, and inspire a staff to reach its full potential.

Certifications include: Junior Level Linux Professional (LPIC-1)

Thank you for your time and professional consideration in reviewing the enclosed resume. I look forward to speaking with you soon.

Sincerely,

Jeff Lowenthal

Jeff Lowenthal

Enclosure

Figure 10.8: A cover letter for a chief information officer using Cover Letter Foundation 8 (contributed by Angie Jones, CPRW, CEIC).

Step 10

COVER LETTER FOUNDATION 9

This foundation works well for a subcontractor.

Dear _____ [hiring manager name]:

Understanding the _____ [type of] industry as intimately as I do, I appreciate the [seasonal changes/dramatic fluctuations/business ups and downs/other: _____] that can toss a company between _____ [what?] to _____ [what?]. During these times of _____ [what?], I offer to you my expert _____ [type of] services, confident in my ability to always hit the ground running to achieve outstanding results.

I offer a brief overview of my expertise and invite you to peruse my enclosed resume, which provides more in-depth information:

- *A history of undertaking challenging _____ [type of] assignments, including _____, _____, and _____ [challenges] where I _____ [did what?]. I have repeatedly been sought out to undertake numerous _____ [type of] challenges due to my _____, my _____, [skills] and my ability to _____ [benefit].*

- *An instinctive knowledge and ability to _____ [do what?] and to implement _____ [type of] changes. My excellent ability to _____ [do what?] combines with my skillful _____ [skill] to _____[do what?].*

- *A vital ability to communicate in an easy to understand and confident manner to _____ [what?]; to _____ [what?]; and to _____ [what?].*

- *Excellent academic qualifications include _____, _____ and _____ [related academic degrees or experience].*

I have found my niche in _____ [specialization], and I excel in this arena. If you are looking for a(n) [original/flexible/diverse/other: _____] professional able to _____ [do what?] within [time-critical goals/rigid budgets/other: _____], I would like to explore this opportunity with you. I look forward to hearing from you.

Yours sincerely,

_____ [your signature]

_____ [your name]

Enclosure: Resume

KAREN POPE

1445 Raceview Road
Mt. Waverley, WA 92345

kpope@zmail.com

Home: (978) 777-8888
Cell: (978) 334 4433

CORPORATE SPECIAL EVENT AND STAGE MANAGER WITH VERIFIABLE HISTORY OF OUTSTANDING ACHIEVEMENTS IN CHALLENGING ENVIRONMENTS

Audrey Marshall, Director
Excellent Events
989 Holly Lane
Seattle, WA 92310

Dear Ms. Marshall:

Understanding the event management industry as intimately as I do, I appreciate the seasonal changes and the dramatic fluctuations tossing a company between "a few jobs on" to "absolutely insanely busy." During these times of maximum capacity, I offer you my expert contractual services, confident in my ability to always hit the ground running to achieve outstanding results.

I offer a brief overview of my expertise and invite you to peruse my enclosed resume, which provides more in-depth information:

- *A history of undertaking challenging stage and event management assignments,* including two seven-day international family conferences consisting of 600 adults and 650 children/teens, an outdoor rock concert with six bands in a remote mining town, as well as a number of progressive dinners and unique venue special events. I have repeatedly been sought out to undertake these and numerous other events due to my methods of operation (which remove all stress from the client), my ability to guide and instruct in a fun environment, and my intrinsic ability to make the company look good.

- *An instinctive knowledge and ability to read the room and to implement rapid changes when required.* My excellent ability to prioritize and reprioritize combines with my skilful assessment of personalities to delegate and formulate the most effective teams and partnerships.

- *A vital ability to communicate in an easy to understand and confident manner* to brief all participants from actors, waitpersons, managing directors and others; to train personnel in all elements of the event industry; and to address, instruct, motivate, and inspire large groups.

- *Excellent academic qualifications* include a Bachelor of Arts in drama and design gained through the Victorian University of Technology, where I was accepted as one of only 33 students out of a total of 1,200 applicants and was chosen as joint lead set designer for the final year's productions, and certification in priority management, which I have found invaluable when combined with my natural organizational expertise and career experience.

I have found my niche in event and stage management, and I excel in this arena. If you are looking for an original, flexible, and diverse professional able to infuse creative and innovative ideas into cohesive strategies within time-critical goals and rigid budgets, I would like to explore this opportunity with you. I look forward to hearing from you.

Yours sincerely,

Karen Pope

Karen Pope

Enclosure: Resume

Figure 10.9: A cover letter for an event manager using Cover Letter Foundation 9 (contributed by Beverley Neil, CRW, CERW).

Step 10

COVER LETTER FOUNDATION 10

This foundation works well for a job candidate with a referral.

Dear _____ [hiring manager name]:

Recently I met with _____ [name of person who referred you] to discuss how my _____ [type of] background and my previous experience with _____, _____, and _____ [what related areas?] would benefit _____ [prospective employer]. With [Mr./Mrs./Ms.] _____' [referral last name] encouragement, I am forwarding you my resume in support of my application for the position of _____ [position title].

Due to my _____ [type of] experience, I offer the additional benefit of a firsthand understanding of _____ [type of] [culture/operations/other: _____], particularly in regard to _____ [what specialization or niche?]. As such, I am in a unique position to offer [additional insight in/an enhanced ability to] _____ [what?] in order to _____ [benefit].

Please consider these relevant achievements detailed further in my attached resume:

- [Championed/Spearheaded/Developed/Other: _____] _____ [what?] for _____ [purpose], which resulted in _____ [benefits].

- [Managed/Oversaw/Directed/Other: _____] _____ [what?] for _____ [purpose], benefiting the firm by way of _____ [doing what?].

- [Increased/Elevated/Maintained/Other: _____] _____ [type of] [revenues/profits/productivity/other: _____] by way of _____ [doing what?].

I have recently relocated to _____ [city or state] after completing a mutually successful contract with _____ [previous employer] and now seek a new and stimulating role within my sphere of expertise. My impression of _____ [prospective employer] is that of an industry leader in the area(s) of _____ [specialization].

Thank you for your time and consideration, _____ [hiring manager name]. I look forward to the possibility of discussing the opportunity of contributing my [own flair/unique talents] to your highly motivated and innovative team.

Sincerely,

_____ [your signature]

_____ [your name]

Enclosure: Resume

Step 10

CHARLES TURNBULL

49 Easterly Drive
Samford, CA 98765

909.111.2222
cturnbull@iserver.com

Carlos Martinez
Human Resources Director
West Coast Airlines
456 Airport Road
Santa Clara, CA 91326

COMMERCIAL MANAGER–GROUND OPERATIONS

Dear Mr. Martinez:

Recently I met with Tom Jeffries to discuss how my aviation background and my previous experience with pricing submissions, contract negotiations, and dealings with airport authorities and government regulators would benefit West Coast Airlines. With Mr. Jeffries' encouragement, I am forwarding you my resume in support of my application for the position of commercial manager–ground operations.

Due to my airport experience, I offer the additional benefit of a firsthand understanding of airport culture and operations, particularly in regard to their cost modeling to substantiate aeronautical and commercial lease pricing. As such, I am in a unique position to offer additional insight and an enhanced ability to communicate with the airports and government agencies in order to negotiate successful outcomes and form open, mutually beneficial relationships.

Please consider these relevant achievements detailed further in my attached resume:

- Designed, implemented, and managed performance platform used to produce critical corporate costing data in support of government applications for increases to aeronautical charges at both primary and secondary airports throughout the Midwest. Applications were successful in realizing additional revenues, projected to be $37 million (+13.8%) in 2008/09 and $110 million (+86%) in 2010/11.

- Undertook an extensive review of supplier contracts for a multibillion-dollar global corporation. Negotiated nationwide agreements for multiple services across a network of over 1500 retail outlets and recommended preferred suppliers for endorsement at board level.

- Reviewed domestic terminal infrastructure agreements to ensure maximum recovery of outgoings, return on infrastructure investment, and appropriate management of planned projects.

I have recently relocated to California after completing a mutually successful contract with Louisville International Airport and now seek a new and stimulating role within my sphere of expertise. My impression of West Coast Airlines is that of an unmistakable industry leader—vibrant, progressive, and going places fast.

Thank you for your time and consideration, Mr. Martinez. I look forward to the possibility of discussing the opportunity of contributing my own flair to your highly motivated and innovative team.

Sincerely,

Charles Turnbull

Charles Turnbull

Enclosure: Resume

Figure 10.10: A cover letter for an airline ground operations manager using Cover Letter Foundation 10 (contributed by Beverley Neil, CRW, CERW).

COVER LETTER FOUNDATION 11

This foundation works well for a C-level executive.

Dear _____ [hiring manager name]:

The position of _____ [position title] for _____ [prospective employer] combines my expertise, my experience, and my passion; therefore, it is with a high degree of confidence I forward to you my expression of interest and my attached resume for your perusal.

Here I draw to your attention my [past history/current involvement/strengths/experience/transferable skills/expertise/ knowledge/other: _____], which combine to position me as a strong candidate for this role:

- The challenge of [spearheading/championing/analyzing/formulating/executing/other: _____] _____ [what?], [growing/enhancing/elevating/increasing/other: _____] _____ [what?], and turning around struggling [companies/divisions/territories/markets/other: _____] has been my life. Inherent in all these challenges are the skills and experience required to increase the [firm's/organization's/other: _____] profitability and to _____ [do what?] while improving _____ [what?].

- I have _____ [specific experience or competitive edge]. Because of this, I have _____ [benefit]. I have a passion for _____ [relevant area], which would drive me further to _____ [benefit].

- I am well known for my outstanding _____ and _____ [which broad skill areas?] skills, including _____; _____, and _____ [specific skills]—_____ [benefit of skills], which invariably achieves outstanding results.

- I am experienced in _____ [area of expertise], _____ [specific achievements or skills in that area].

In applying for this position, I am not merely applying for a job that would involve me on a professional level only. I bring with me an extensive history and a total commitment to the growth and advancement of the industry.

I am eager to explore this new and challenging opportunity further, to advance my participation and commitment within the _____ [which?] industry, and to contribute in a strong and effective way. I believe a personal conversation and interview would reveal my suitability and passion for this role and hope we may speak soon. Thank you for your time and consideration.

Yours sincerely,

_____ [your signature]

_____ [your name]

Enclosure: Resume

ALAN STEWART

16 RUNAWAY BAY DRIVE, ROSEVALE **KY 45678**
404.444.4444 • astewart@internetplus.org

Edward Connor
President
Bluegrass Racing
789 Thoroughbred Way
Lexington, KY 40123

CHIEF EXECUTIVE OFFICER:
THE BLUE MILE RACETRACK

Dear Mr. Connor:

The position of chief executive officer for the Blue Mile Racetrack combines my expertise, my experience, and my passion; therefore, it is with a high degree of confidence I forward to you my expression of interest and my attached resume for your perusal.

Here I draw to your attention my past history, current involvement, strengths, experience, and transferable skills, which combine to position me as a strong candidate for this role:

- The challenge of **analyzing, formulating, and executing strong operational strategies** and sales and marketing initiatives; growing new enterprises; and turning around struggling companies and territories has been my life. Inherent in all these challenges are the skills and experience required to increase the racing club's profitability and to identify and secure outside sources of income while improving operations from within. Inherent in my nature is a depth of vision, creativity, and an exceptionally strong work ethic.

- I have been a **member of the Blue Mile Turf Club** for more than 20 years, in the past racing horses as an owner for 10 years. Because of this I have a thorough knowledge, grounding, and insider understanding of the racing industry. I have a passion for horses and a love of the industry, which would drive me further to ensure wide-ranging success.

- I am well known for my **outstanding communication and people skills**, including bringing out the best in my staff; healing rifts in client relations; and building exceptional rapport with peers, suppliers, clients, and others—taking relationships to a respectful, personal level that invariably achieves outstanding results.

- I am experienced in **organizing social corporate box events** on major race days for up to 40 guests, negotiating and overseeing all aspects (including food and beverage) and liaising with staff on each occasion.

In applying for this position, I am not merely applying for a job that would involve me on a professional level only. I bring with me an extensive history and a total commitment to the growth and advancement of the industry.

I am eager to explore this new and challenging opportunity further, to advance my participation and commitment within the racing industry, and to contribute in a strong and effective way. I believe a personal conversation and interview would reveal my suitability and passion for this role and hope we may speak soon. Thank you for your time and consideration.

Yours sincerely,

Alan Stewart

Alan Stewart

Enclosure: Resume

Figure 10.11: A cover letter for a racetrack chief executive officer using Cover Letter Foundation 11 (contributed by Beverley Neil, CRW, CERW).

Step 10

COVER LETTER FOUNDATION 12

This foundation works well for someone with an exhilarating and rewarding career.

Dear _____ [hiring manager name]:

It was [illuminating/energizing/other: _____] speaking with you on _____ [date] regarding the currently available position as _____ [job title] at _____ [prospective employer]. As we discussed, please find my resume attached.

_____ [Doing what?] to me is an [exhilarating/rewarding/other: _____] experience. However, my particular passion is _____ and _____ [what specialization(s) or niche market(s)?].

I have an innate ability to _____ and _____ [do what?], which _____ [does what?] for _____ [whom?].

My love of _____ and _____ [what?] is long-standing. As a member of _____ [which?] [organization(s)/foundation(s)/association(s)/club(s)/other: _____], I have undertaken _____ [what venture or challenge?] and have a real joy in [participating in/contributing to/observing/other: _____] _____ [what arena or functions?]. I have _____ [provide example(s)].

When studying at _____ [name of school you attended], my special interest was in _____ [which?] studies, especially concerning _____, _____, and _____ [which?] topics.

I am excited by the possibility of contributing to _____ [prospective employer] and truly believe my _____, _____, and _____ [which attributes or benefits?] will _____ [do what?] and deliver _____ [what results?]. I appreciate the time you have already taken discussing this role with me and look forward to speaking with you again soon.

Yours sincerely,

_____ [your signature]

_____ [your name]

Enclosure: Resume

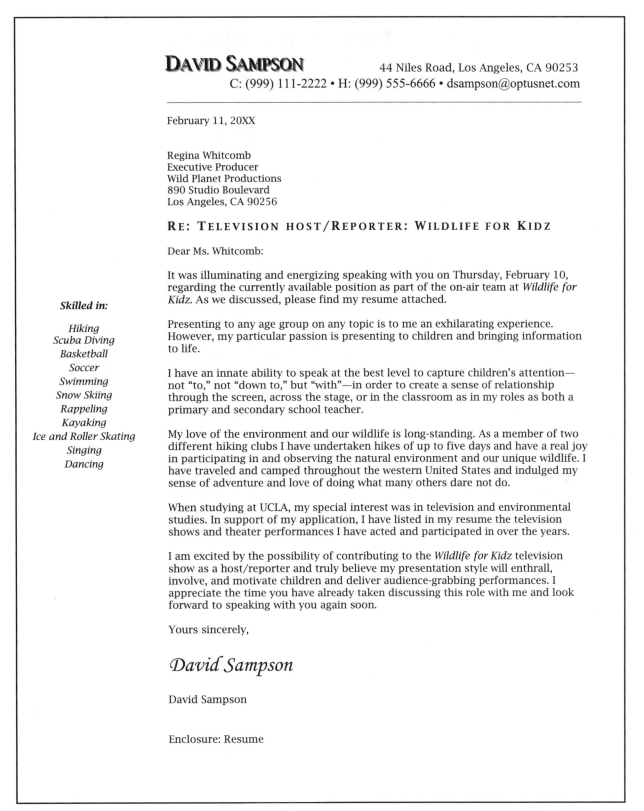

DAVID SAMPSON   44 Niles Road, Los Angeles, CA 90253
C: (999) 111-2222 • H: (999) 555-6666 • dsampson@optusnet.com

February 11, 20XX

Regina Whitcomb
Executive Producer
Wild Planet Productions
890 Studio Boulevard
Los Angeles, CA 90256

RE: TELEVISION HOST/REPORTER: WILDLIFE FOR KIDZ

Dear Ms. Whitcomb:

It was illuminating and energizing speaking with you on Thursday, February 10, regarding the currently available position as part of the on-air team at *Wildlife for Kidz.* As we discussed, please find my resume attached.

Presenting to any age group on any topic is to me an exhilarating experience. However, my particular passion is presenting to children and bringing information to life.

I have an innate ability to speak at the best level to capture children's attention—not "to," not "down to," but "with"—in order to create a sense of relationship through the screen, across the stage, or in the classroom as in my roles as both a primary and secondary school teacher.

My love of the environment and our wildlife is long-standing. As a member of two different hiking clubs I have undertaken hikes of up to five days and have a real joy in participating in and observing the natural environment and our unique wildlife. I have traveled and camped throughout the western United States and indulged my sense of adventure and love of doing what many others dare not do.

When studying at UCLA, my special interest was in television and environmental studies. In support of my application, I have listed in my resume the television shows and theater performances I have acted and participated in over the years.

I am excited by the possibility of contributing to the *Wildlife for Kidz* television show as a host/reporter and truly believe my presentation style will enthrall, involve, and motivate children and deliver audience-grabbing performances. I appreciate the time you have already taken discussing this role with me and look forward to speaking with you again soon.

Yours sincerely,

David Sampson

David Sampson

Enclosure: Resume

Skilled in:

Hiking
Scuba Diving
Basketball
Soccer
Swimming
Snow Skiing
Rappeling
Kayaking
Ice and Roller Skating
Singing
Dancing

Figure 10.12: A cover letter for a television show host/reporter using Cover Letter Foundation 12 (contributed by Beverley Neil, CRW, CERW).

Step 10

COVER LETTER FOUNDATION 13

This foundation works well for an industry achiever.

Dear _____ [hiring manager name]:

Consistently Achieve _____ [type of results]

_____ [Award or Nomination]

To achieve these results there can only be one reason—a consuming passion for _____ [what area?]! Working within the _____ [which?] industry and with _____ [whom?] to _____ [do what?] has been my lifeblood.

Throughout my career, _____ and _____ [doing what?] have been major sources of [challenge/achievement/reward/other: _____] for me. My enclosed resume details my career thus far, but I would like to draw your attention to the following highlights that meet with your criteria:

- _____ [achievement or skills] _____ [results or benefits].

- _____ [achievement or skills] _____ [results or benefits].

- _____ [achievement or skills] _____ [results or benefits].

I believe in _____ [doing what?], finding that this always brings its own rewards in _____, _____, and _____ [what areas?]. I have also always believed in [hard work/loyalty/other: _____] and have consistently worked to the highest standard of professionalism. I am confident that these innate belief systems, in conjunction with my ability to _____ [do what?], position me as an ideal candidate for your role of _____ [job title].

Thank you for your time and consideration. I earnestly hope we meet soon to discuss this exciting opportunity.

Yours sincerely,

_____ [your signature]

_____ [your name]

Enclosure: Resume

BRIE MCALLISTER

42 Southbury Road, Sandgate, FL 20678
Cell: (333) 777-0000   Email: bmca@intercon.com

June 19, 20XX

Alan Sattison
Manager
Advanced Fitness
111 Workout Way
Miami, FL 20677

RE: OPPORTUNITY AS PERSONAL TRAINER

Dear Mr. Sattison:

Consistently Achieve Top 10 Out Of 350 Nationwide
2010 Training Coach of the Year Nominee

To achieve these results, there can only be one reason—a consuming passion for personal training! Working within the health industry and with individuals to sell, promote, and educate on a product or program that is beneficial has been my lifeblood.

Throughout my career, building outstanding customer rapport and securing the sale have been major sources of challenge and achievement for me. My enclosed resume details my career thus far, but I would like to draw your attention to the following highlights that meet with your criteria:

☆ **Have built my own territory within a club from zero to 170 clients within 12 months.** As you know, this is regarded as an outstanding achievement in our challenging, competitive industry.

☆ **Approach rejection with a proactive attitude,** reassessing, asking for feedback, and formulating a new angle of approach. This philosophy, combined with my ability to interact with individuals on all levels within a team environment or autonomously and the adrenalin I draw from challenging environments, has ensured my ongoing success and the club's bottom line.

☆ **Utilize motivational and management aptitude** to work with new trainers to advance their communication and selling skills and build a strong client base. When one succeeds, we all succeed!

I believe in really listening and showing the customer respect, finding that this always brings its own rewards in trust, open communication, and increased sales. I have also always believed in hard work and loyalty and have consistently worked to the highest standard of professionalism. I am confident that these innate belief systems, in conjunction with my ability to rapidly assimilate new information and techniques, position me as an ideal candidate for your advertised role of personal trainer.

Thank you for your time and consideration. I earnestly hope we meet soon to discuss this exciting opportunity.

Yours sincerely,

Brie McAllister

Brie McAllister

Enclosure: Resume

Figure 10.13: A cover letter for a personal trainer using Cover Letter Foundation 13 (contributed by Beverley Neil, CRW, CERW).

Step 10

COVER LETTER FOUNDATION 14

This foundation works well for an executive.

Dear _____ [hiring manager name]:

My search for companies who share my passion for _____ [type of] success put _____ [prospective employer] at the top of my list. Here's why: As the _____ [job title] of a _____ [type of] company, I took it as my number one priority to _____ [do what?] and made it happen.

Now that my mission at _____ [current employer] has been fulfilled, I would like that dream to be fulfilled again in a partnership with _____ [prospective employer]. I offer a strong return on investment for both of us.

Throughout my _____ [number] years of _____ [type of] experience, I have been guided by this professional code:

- **Being passionate about my business isn't good enough.** I must _____ [do what?] that results in _____ [benefits/ROI].

- **Being productive isn't good enough.** I must _____ [do what?].

- **Being _____ [relevant personal attribute] isn't good enough.** What I must deliver is _____ [benefit] by way of _____ [skill].

- **Being _____ [relevant personal attribute] isn't good enough.** I want to _____ [ROI] by _____ [skills].

Proof of that kind of performance is contained in my enclosed resume.

In the end, however, words on paper are no substitute for people speaking with people. Because your company has the culture in which I thrive, I would like to explore how I might serve the _____ [prospective employer] team. May I call in a few days to get on your calendar for that purpose?

Sincerely,

_____ [your signature]

_____ [your name]

Enclosure: Resume

Carter Morris

2114 Ranchlands Drive, Dallas, Texas 75201 ✉cmorris@knology.net ☎ 214.555.5555 – 214.666.6666

Donald Yamata
President
ABC Company
777 Parkview Way
Dallas, TX 75201

Dear Mr. Yamata:

Toward a mutually satisfying ROI

Let me put the bottom line right at the top: My search for companies who share my passion for success put ABC Company at the top of my list. Here's why: As the CEO of an aggressively successful company, I took it as job number one to replicate my passion in every member of my team. And since nobody told me it couldn't be done, I made it happen.

Now that my company has been sold to a public entity, I want that dream to come true again, this time in a partnership with ABC Company. But I would never make such a bold suggestion if I couldn't offer a strong return on investment for both of us.

For now, I want to concentrate on what years of experience have equipped me to offer you, your team, and your customers. What I do isn't magic; this professional code guides me:

- ❑ **Being passionate about my business isn't good enough.** I must instill systemic passion, helping every team member trace his or her daily efforts to our profitability. In short, I must align every team member's personal goals with our corporate aims.

- ❑ **Being productive isn't good enough.** I must have every employee, every vendor, and every customer see his or her personal growth tied to ABC Company's corporate growth.

- ❑ **Being compassionate isn't good enough.** What I must deliver is courageous compassion. That irresistible force for good comes from my relentless search for excellence in others so that I can reward them publicly.

- ❑ **Being sales driven isn't good enough.** I want our customers to see us as their success partner, believing that using ABC Company's per-seat, on-demand services is their own good idea.

Proof of that kind of performance is too important to be diluted by the usual resume format. So I've included a leadership addendum on the next page. I chose those examples of my passion in action because I am confident they are transferable to your industry.

In the end, however, words on paper are no substitute for people speaking with people. Because your company has the culture in which I thrive, I would like to explore how I might serve the ABC Company team. May I call in a few days to get on your calendar for that purpose?

Sincerely,

Carter Morris

Carter Morris

Enclosure: Leadership addendum

Figure 10.14: A cover letter for a chief executive officer using Cover Letter Foundation 14 (contributed by Don Orlando, MBA, CPRW, JCTC, CCM, CCMC, CJSS).

Step 10

COVER LETTER FOUNDATION 15

This foundation works well for a job candidate whose field has changed dramatically.

Dear _____ [hiring manager name]:

The _____ [type of] needs of _____ [type of] employers have changed dramatically over the [years/past decades/other: _____]. For more than _____ [number] years, as a _____ [job title] at _____ [employer name], I have embraced change and _____ [done what?]. My passion for _____ [what?] and my expertise in _____ [area of expertise] have contributed to my successes in _____, _____, _____, and _____ [areas of expertise].

Here is a partial listing of my key accomplishments:

_____ [Area of expertise]

- [Launched/Introduced/Other: _____] _____'s [previous employer] first _____ [type of] program, which _____ [benefits and ROI].

- [Accelerated/Expedited/Increased/Other: _____] [revenues/productivity/sales/quality/other: _____] by _____ [dollar amount or percentage] for _____ [previous employer] by _____ [doing what?].

- Improved _____ [what?] at _____ [previous employer] and _____ [did what?] by _____ [doing what?].

_____ [Area of expertise]

- [Instituted/Initiated/Other: _____] _____ [type of] opportunities that provided _____ [what?].

- [Created/Developed/Other: _____] a unique _____ [type of] program for _____ [whom or what?] that resulted in _____ [benefits and ROI].

_____ [Area of expertise]

- [Preserved/Maintained/Other: _____] a _____ [type of] environment during _____'s [previous employer] transition from _____ [what?] to _____ [what?].

- [Realigned/Adjusted/Other: _____] _____ [type of] programs at _____ [previous employer], which increased _____ [what?] by _____ [dollar amount or percentage].

I am excited by the prospect of an opportunity with _____ [prospective employer]. I would like to meet with you to discuss my qualifications in more detail and look forward to a personal interview.

Sincerely,

_____ [your signature]

_____ [your name]

Attachment

JEREMY HANOVER, Ph.D.

250 Round Ridge Road ▪ Lincroft, NJ 07738 ▪ C: 732-399-7780 ▪ jeremyhanover@optonline.net

David Poland
Chancellor
XYZ College
222 University Parkway
Trenton, NJ 01234

Dear Mr. Poland:

The higher education needs of students, parents, and employers have changed dramatically over the past decade. For more than 10 years, as a higher education senior administrator at ABC University and DEF College, I have embraced change and introduced creative and more flexible curriculums that cater to the needs of the 21st-century student. My passion for education and my expertise in analyzing processes and people have contributed to my successes in program development; curriculum redesign; blended, virtual, and experiential learning; and administrative process reengineering.

Here is a partial listing of my key accomplishments:

Innovation

- Launched ABC University's first master's degree program and introduced novel business administration and human services curriculum and MBA in the first year. On track to incorporate new programs in educational leadership, nursing, and public administration in 2011 and a total of 12 programs over a 3-year period.

- Accelerated revenues by millions of dollars for both ABC University and DEF College by utilizing Six Sigma quality methodologies to analyze program ROI, spearhead flexible curriculum delivery formats, expand online and brick-and-mortar facilities, improve student performance and retention, and create faculty accountability.

- Improved admissions strategy at ABC University and recruited students with higher academic success rates by shifting from traditional school success predictors, SAT and high school ranking, to more creative and cognitive-based assessments.

Strategic Partnerships

- Instituted co-op and experiential learning opportunities across all ABC undergraduate programs.

- Created a unique Capstone program for the ABC graduate business school that matched student teams working on business solutions with potential investors.

Change Management

- Preserved a cohesive and collaborative environment during ABC University's transition from a not-for-profit to a for-profit institution.

- Realigned curriculums of numerous poorly performing programs at ABC University and DEF College and increased enrollment numbers by as much as 300%.

I am excited by the prospect of an opportunity with XYZ College. I would like to meet with you to discuss my qualifications in more detail and look forward to a personal interview.

Sincerely,

Jeremy Hanover, Ph.D.

Jeremy Hanover, Ph.D.

Attachment

Figure 10.15: A cover letter for a senior college administrator using Cover Letter Foundation 15 (contributed by Barbara Safani, MA, CERW, NCRW, CPRW, CCM).

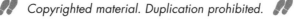

Step 10

COVER LETTER FOUNDATION 16

This foundation works well for an accomplished candidate with experience.

Dear _____ [hiring manager name]:

All _____ [type of] companies want _____s [occupation name] who not only exhibit _____ [type of] expertise, but who also save time and money while increasing [client satisfaction/customer service levels/productivity/revenues/other: _____]. Few _____s [occupation name] can deliver all of these results. I can, and I would like to deliver them for _____ [prospective employer] as your new _____ [job title].

As an accomplished _____ [job title], I excel at _____ and _____ [doing what?]. I am proficient in _____, _____, _____, and _____ [areas of expertise], and I am certified in _____ [what?]. Throughout my attached resume, you will find descriptions of my _____ [type of] accomplishments.

In addition, I am passionate about _____ [doing what?] to meet the needs of _____ [whom?]. I achieve this by _____ [your action(s) or method(s)]. In this way, I avoid the costly _____ [what expenses?] that result from _____ [what problems?].

Satisfied companies have testified:

"_____ _____ ____ [endorsement]." —_____ [person's name], _____ [title]

"_____ _____ ____ [endorsement]." —_____ [person's name], _____ [title]

I would love the opportunity to find out how I can satisfy _____'s [prospective employer] needs, too. I will call you in a week to see whether we can arrange an interview.

Sincerely,

_____ [your signature]

_____ [your name]

Attachment: resume

Eileen Gaffney

34 Holly Lane, Darien, CT 06820
egaffney@email.com • 203.555.5555

 CERTIFIED PROFESSIONAL
Adobe® Flex™ Developer

Delivering Impeccably Designed Applications That Fulfill Client Needs

James Gladwell
Vice President of Human Resources
Excellent Software
101 Technology Road
Hartford, CT 06820

Dear Mr. Gladwell:

All technology companies want software developers who not only exhibit technical expertise, but who also save time and money while increasing client satisfaction. Few developers can deliver all of these results. I can, and I would like to deliver them for Excellent Software as your new Flex developer.

As an accomplished application developer, I excel at building rugged frameworks and writing clear, maintainable code. I am proficient in all of the languages, architecture, platforms, and tools that you require, and I am Adobe-certified in Flex. Throughout my attached resume, you will find links to some of my online code, articles, and demonstrations.

In addition, I am passionate about ensuring that my applications meet my clients' needs. I achieve this by asking key questions and using an "active listening" process at the outset of a project. In this way, I avoid the costly mid- or end-project disruptions that result from unclear initial communications.

Satisfied companies have testified:

 We work with a lot of talented professionals, but Eileen Gaffney's performance was exceptional. She saw to it that we exceeded our goals, on schedule and under budget.
—Cherise Anderson, Innovations in Math Education

Eileen's work for Tower combined true customer service with excellent technical skills to create a positive outcome from a difficult starting point.
—Matthew George, former CEO, Tower Teaching and Development, Inc.

I would love the opportunity to find out how I can satisfy Excellent Software's needs, too. I will call you in a week to see whether we can arrange an interview.

Sincerely,

Eileen Gaffney

Eileen Gaffney

Attachment: resume

Figure 10.16: A cover letter for a application developer using Cover Letter Foundation 16 (contributed by Reya Stevens, MA, MRW).

Step 10

COVER LETTER FOUNDATION 17

This foundation works well for someone with specialized experience.

Dear _____ [hiring manager name]:

[Global competition/Cost containment/Changing market conditions/Economic stability/Other: _____]— these are the critical issues facing _____ [type of] firms. With my expertise in _____, _____, _____, and _____ [areas of expertise], I can lead _____ [prospective employer] in successfully confronting these tough challenges. As your _____ [job title], I will...

- Provide _____ [what?] to _____ [do what?] in the _____ [type of] business climate.

- Contain costs by _____ [doing what], resulting in _____ [what benefits and ROI?].

- Swiftly correct course to adapt to fluctuation in the _____ [type of] business landscape, navigating change that results in _____ [ROI].

More than _____ [number] years in top-tier roles of multimillion-dollar [firms/organizations/other: _____] as well _____ [what area(s)?] have afforded me the opportunity to continuously sharpen my talent for [driving revenue/catalyzing aggressive growth/other: _____]. I can...

- _____ [asset]—_____ [achievement].

- _____ [asset]—_____ [achievement].

- _____ [asset]—_____ [achievement].

The enclosed resume sheds more light on my abilities to _____ [do what?]. I look forward to discussing some ideas I have on accelerating _____'s [prospective employer name] trajectory to the top and will contact you early next week to schedule an introductory meeting.

Sincerely,

_____ [your signature]

_____ [your name]

Enclosure: resume

GERARD J. LADIEU, PH.D.

6 Lancaster Road | Belmont, MA 02478
H 617.444.5555 | **C** 617.555.4444 | **gladieu@email.com**

Gail Redmond
Vice President of Human Resources
Next Generation
676 Oak Drive
Boston, MA 02134

Dear Ms. Redmond:

Global competition, cost containment, and changing market conditions—these are the critical issues facing cutting-edge technology firms. With my expertise in nanotechnology, semiconductors, solar energy, and photonics, I can lead Next Generation in successfully confronting these tough challenges. I will…

- **Provide global perspective** to identify opportunistic industry trends in the international business climate.
- **Contain costs** by continuously revisiting the value proposition of a business.
- **Swiftly correct course** to adapt to fluctuation in the business landscape, navigating change that determines the winner in today's business environment.

More than 20 years in top-tier roles of multimillion-dollar organizations as well as emerging start-ups have afforded me the opportunity to continuously sharpen my talent for driving revenue and catalyzing aggressive growth. I can…

- **Build business opportunities**—I led negotiations that made Lacymer the preferred supplier of EUV scanners for the #1 provider of lithography systems in the semiconductor industry.
- **Breathe life into new organizations**—I built and propelled a sales organization to strategic partnerships and profitable growth throughout countries in Europe, the Middle East, and Asia.
- **Communicate across cultural boundaries**—I held leadership roles in operations, sales, and product development for major firms in Europe as well as the United States. I am fluent in German and Dutch.

The enclosed resume sheds more light on my abilities to penetrate new markets and develop business opportunities. I look forward to discussing some ideas I have on accelerating Next Generation's trajectory to the top and will contact you early next week to schedule an introductory meeting.

Sincerely,

Gerard Ladieu

Gerard J. Ladieu

Enclosure: resume

Figure 10.17: A cover letter for a nanotechnologist using Cover Letter Foundation 17 (contributed by Marjorie Sussman, MRW, ACRW, CPRW).

Step 10

COVER LETTER FOUNDATION 18

This foundation works well for a talented professional with experience and a referral.

Dear _____ [hiring manager name]:

A mutual friend, _____ [name of friend], suggested I answer your confidential opening for a _____ [job title]. As a _____ [job title or function] with _____ [number] years of _____ [type of] experience, I fully understand _____ [what industry issues or goals?]. I have successfully _____ [accomplishment], drawing upon my considerable _____ [type of] training (_____ [degree or certification]), on current _____ [type of] [thinking/strategies/research/other: _____], on feedback from _____ [whom?], and, of course, on my own experiences as a(n) _____ [job title or function].

I honed my gift in _____ [which?] field while serving as a _____, _____, _____, and _____ [functions] [on/at] _____ [which firms, panels, colleges, or associations?].

Excellent _____ and _____ [type of] skills have resulted in _____ [type of] positions, including the current one at _____ [firm name] where I _____ [do what?].

As a dedicated _____ [type of] professional, I [have an in-home office/telecommute/other: _____]; however, [relocation/telecommuting/traveling/other: _____] [is/are] a definite "yes."

I look forward to discussing how we can _____ [return on investment] while _____ [doing what?]. I will call to see whether we can arrange an appointment. Thank you for your consideration.

Warmly,

_____ [your signature]

_____ [your name]

Enclosure: Resume

LAWRENCE "LARRY" ELROD
5555 Channel Islands Parkway, Ventura, California 93004
Cell: (805) 555 1234 / Email: lelrod999@heavensent.com

Gerald Davis
Program Director
Disciple Network
778 Sunlight Way
Memphis, TN 45678

Dear Mr. Davis:

A mutual friend, Mr. Andrew Simpson, suggested I answer your confidential opening for a **Christian broadcast media personality/writer/editor.** As a minister with 20-plus years at the pulpit, I fully understand broadcast media's power for reaching the world with the Gospel and compassionate life solutions. I have fielded just about every question imaginable, responding authoritatively, gracefully, and humorously regarding religion and its role in modern life, morality, sexuality, politics, business, education, and law. My views draw upon considerable biblical training (a doctorate in theology/divinity); on current theological thinking; on live feedback from my audiences; and, of course, on my own experiences as a husband, father, and human being.

I honed my gift in live broadcasting while serving as a guest theologian, expert, and panelist on several well-known radio and television syndicated broadcasts, including those hosted by Daniel Pastor (Hartford Communications), James Stuart, and the Church Television Network (CTN). In fact, I have appeared on several airings of CTN's *Spread the Word.*

Excellent written communications skills have resulted in senior editorial positions, including the current one at CTN Media Group, where I write and produce newsletters and other marketing projects. The glowing e-mails we received on a recent article entitled, "Surviving Terrorism: Faith Heals," swamped our website for several days.

As a dedicated broadcast media professional, I have an in-home broadcast studio with live simulcast capability; however, relocation and/or telecommuting are a definite "yes."

I look forward to discussing how we can increase your subscriber audiences while helping them cope with the new millennium's daily challenges. I will call you to see whether we can arrange an appointment. Thank you for your consideration.

Warmly,

Larry Elrod

Lawrence "Larry" Elrod

Enclosures:
(1) Resume
(2) Live track (CD/MP3) from *Spread the Word* radio broadcast

Figure 10.18: A cover letter for a media writer/editor using Cover Letter Foundation 18 (contributed by Roleta Fowler Vasquez, CPRW, CEIP).

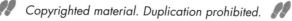

Step 10

COVER LETTER FOUNDATION 19

This foundation works well for a dually qualified candidate.

Dear _____ [hiring manager name]:

Dual qualifications as a _____ [title or function] and _____ [title or function] allow me to deliver excellent _____ [type of] and _____ [type of] services [even in times of dwindling budgets/other: _____]. As a _____ [subject] major, I have special interest and success in _____ [doing what?]. Along this theme, I welcome any _____ [type of] opportunities that will allow me to _____ [do what?] for your [institution/firm/organization/other: _____].

My well-rounded _____ [field] portfolio includes the following:

_____ [Type of] **Credentials**

- A recently completed [master's/bachelor's/associate] degree in _____ [major]

- _____ [number] years of _____ [type of] experience _____ [in what field or area?]

- _____ [name of] [certification/license] with emphasis on _____ [area]

_____ [Type of] **Successes**

- [Introduced/Executed/Produced/Other: _____] _____ [what?] to _____ [benefit or result].

- [Spearheaded/Championed/Other: _____] _____ [what?] to _____ [benefit or result].

- [Developed and implemented/Managed and oversaw/Other: _____] _____ [what?] to _____ [benefit or result].

I look forward to meeting with you to discuss how I can help you achieve your _____ [which?] goals. Please call or email me at the contact information above.

Sincerely yours,

_____ [your signature]

_____ [your name]

Enclosure: Resume

ARTHUR M. BAKER

555 North Peninsula Road – Apt. #55, Ventura, CA 93004
(760) 555-1212 • abaker@earthmail.com

Alma Montez
Principal
Fairview Academy
454 Via Rosa
Ventura, CA 93004

Dear Ms. Montez:

As our state cuts more budgets, one thing I know is that educational quality must prevail—where education fails, a community fails. Dual qualifications as a teacher and school psychologist allow me to deliver excellent educational and socio-psychological services, even in times of dwindling budgets. As a school psychology major, I have special interest and success in reprogramming and mainstreaming difficult students. Along this theme, I welcome any school counselor or teacher opportunities that will allow me to protect and serve the students, the community, and your educational institution.

My well-rounded teaching portfolio includes the following:

Current & Socially Relevant Teaching Credentials

- A recently completed Master of Science degree in school psychology, preceded by a B.A. in liberal studies
- Ten years of teaching experience at K–12, adult, and special needs levels, with an additional 5 semesters as a school psychologist/intern
- School psychology and multiple subject teaching credentials, with emphasis on Cross-cultural Language and Development (CLAD)
- Certifications including Highly Qualified Teacher, Language Arts/Reading First, and Math Matters

Teaching Successes

- Introduced an after-school counseling program—Best Step—to teach violence prevention and conflict negotiation and resolution.
- Spearheaded a Student Study Team (SST) for students with behavioral and academic problems.
- Worked with students and parents from multicultural backgrounds during my early teaching positions in the Los Angeles Inner City School System. I rose to the challenge of developing and teaching courses that blend literacy, problem solving, and social skills.
- Developed and implemented curriculum to raise student learning and performance benchmarks 92–100%.

I look forward to meeting with you to discuss how I can help you achieve your educational and community service goals. Please call or email me at the contact information above.

Sincerely yours,

Arthur Baker

Arthur M. Baker

Enclosure: Resume

Figure 10.19: A cover letter for a teacher/school psychologist using Cover Letter Foundation 19 (contributed by Roleta Fowler Vasquez, CPRW, CEIP).

Step 10

COVER LETTER FOUNDATION 20

This foundation works well for an executive who brings about change.

Dear _____ [hiring manager name]:

A true leader brings about positive change in alignment with strategic business objectives without organizational disruption. I am reputed for [spearheading/championing/producing/other: _____] _____ [what benefit(s)?] by _____ [doing what?] and devising win-win solutions for _____ [whom?] and _____ [whom?]. This is the value and strength that I bring to the position of _____ [job title].

Core to my experience are

- _____ [asset]. _____ [benefits].

- _____ [asset]. _____ [benefits].

- _____ [asset]. _____ [benefits].

Throughout my career, I have provided _____ [what?], created _____ [what?], and _____ [did what?] while [winning/providing/other: _____] _____ [what benefits and ROI?].

I believe _____ [prospective employer] will benefit from my _____ [type of] approach to _____ [type of] excellence and _____ [value proposition]. I look forward to speaking with you soon to discuss how my expertise can bring immediate results to your company. I will contact you soon to set up an interview, or you may contact me via the information above.

Sincerely,

_____ [your signature]

_____ [your name]

Enclosure: Resume

JOHN A. SMITH

123 Hopeful Hills Drive · Cary, NC 27519 · 919-123-4567 · jsmith1274@email.com

November 4, 20XX

Michael Andrews
Chief Executive Officer
Ginormous Sports
323 Mountain Drive
Charlotte, NC 27520

Re: Vice President, Learning and Organizational Development Opportunity

Dear Mr. Andrews,

A true leader brings about positive change in alignment with strategic business objectives without organizational disruption. I am reputed for producing cost and operational efficiencies by building local and global relationships and devising win-win solutions. This is the value and strength that I bring to the position of vice president of learning and development at Ginormous Sports.

Core to my experience are

- **Building relationships.** My in-depth knowledge of training and development occurred early on as a SCUBA instructor, where I developed a following of students and colleagues who still consult with me to this day. **–Built a reputation as a sought-after presenter, author, training consultant, and confidante.–**
- **Driving the business.** Today, I exercise these principles in developing best practices and creating and streamlining training organizations with a $16 million budget for a prominent recreational training and safety organization with over 3,500 instructors worldwide. **–Led membership levels to groundbreaking new heights.–**
- **Communicating clearly.** I thrive on maintaining positive press for my company inside and out while leveraging relationships to create new initiatives, which strengthen the brand of the organization. **–Named Department of the Year.–**

Throughout my career, I have provided turnaround leadership, created alliances and partnerships, and reengineered organizations while **winning greater profitability, providing best-in-class learning strategies and curricula, and motivating teams to perform their best.**

I believe Ginormous Sports will benefit from my ethical, relationship-based approach to operational excellence and increased profitability. I look forward to speaking with you soon to discuss how my expertise can bring immediate results to your company. I will contact you soon to set up an interview, or you may contact me via the information above.

Sincerely,

John Smith

John Smith

Enclosure: Resume

Figure 10.20: A cover letter for a vice president using Cover Letter Foundation 20 (contributed by Kelly Welch, CPRW, MA, GPHR).

COVER LETTER FOUNDATION 21

This foundation works well for a consultant with solid experience.

Dear _____ [hiring manager name]:

_____..._____..._____ [assets]

I have a passion for _____ [doing what?]. I analyze _____ [type of] challenges, identify [issues/problems/other:_____], and partner to offer solutions that result in _____ [benefit(s)].

With my expertise in _____ and _____ [what areas?], I am able to _____ [do what?] and _____ [do what?]. I approach each [challenge/situation/problem/other: _____] with a holistic understanding of business challenges, drawing upon a combination of winning experiences as _____ [job title] at _____ [employer], _____ [job title] at _____ [employer], and _____ [job title] at _____ [employer].

In the role of _____ [job title], I look forward to making an immediate contribution to the needs of _____ [prospective employer] by offering

- _____ [asset]. _____ [related achievement].

- _____ [asset]. _____ [related achievement].

- _____ [asset]. _____ [related achievement].

I am certain that my experiences and competencies would be immediately transferable to the _____ [job title] role and would add to the continued success of _____ [prospective employer] and its [clients/customers/patrons/other: _____]. I look forward to the opportunity to speak with you soon to discuss my qualifications and the organization's objectives in further detail.

Sincerely,

_____ [your signature]

_____ [your name]

Enclosure: Resume

JEFF MILLER, MBA

–Strategic Change Through Collaborative Leadership–

223 Waterton Avenue, Apt. #1201 ▪ Richardson, TX 77382 ▪ 781.338.9882 ▪ jmillermba@email.com

May 29, 20XX

Edward Nguyen, Chief Executive Officer
YourCo
134 Cowboy Highway
San Antonio,TX 77888

Dear Mr. Nguyen,

Collaborative leadership…strategic change and transformation…buy in and sustainability

I have a passion for opening new business avenues using strategic collaboration. I analyze client challenges, identify issues, and partner to offer solutions that complement and expand existing offerings. **This model delivers high performance and lasting results within client service lines.**

With my **expertise in organization and talent performance,** I am able to conceptualize change strategies and modeling to accompany existing service offerings and/or to differentiate conventional service lines or projects. I approach each engagement with a holistic understanding of business challenges, drawing upon a combination of winning experiences as senior human capital consultant at FGH, human capital planning consultant at Q&R Consulting, and HR strategist and entrepreneur with technology startup PersonTech.com.

In the role of organization and talent consultant, I look forward to making an immediate contribution to the needs of YourCo by offering

- **Collaboration.** My **unparalleled collaborative nature and demonstrated results** enabled me to mobilize a 200-person multidisciplinary project team to launch a change management program for a $50 million worldwide ERP/SAP implementation.

- **Creative problem solving.** At PersonTech.com, I led the conception and launch of client-validated technology with a business model that will **transform online recruitment models and reduce time-to-hire by 75%.**

- **Change leadership.** I led the transformation of cross-company HR processes from a noncollaborative culture to successful implementation, **raising client satisfaction with the initiative from 30% to 100%,** and gained **recognition as key collaboration expert**.

I am certain that my experiences and competencies would be immediately transferable to the organization and talent consultant role and would add to the continued success of YourCo and its clients. I look forward to the opportunity to speak with you soon to discuss my qualifications and the organization's objectives in further detail.

Sincerely,

Jeff Miller

Jeff Miller

Enclosure: Resume

Figure 10.21: A cover letter for a management consultant using Cover Letter Foundation 21 (contributed by Kelly Welch, CPRW, MA, GPHR).

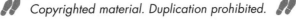

Step 10

COVER LETTER FOUNDATION 22

This foundation works well for a candidate who has received a referral.

Re: _____ [position title]

Dear _____ [hiring manager name]:

Your advertisement for the above referenced position was forwarded to me by my colleague, _____ [colleague's name], who recognized that my blend of experience in _____, _____, and _____ [areas of expertise] would be an ideal fit. Please consider me as an applicant for this role. My qualifications include _____ and _____ [qualifications] along with the ability to _____ [do what?]. This background is enhanced by a [master's/bachelor's/associate] degree in _____ [major].

Though secure in my current position, I am seeking an opportunity with a progressive organization such as _____ [prospective employer]. I can add value to your organization in multiple ways, including the following:

- _____ [area of expertise]: _____ [achievement].

- _____ [area of expertise]: _____ [achievement].

- _____ [area of expertise]: _____ [achievement].

These proven abilities, detailed in the attached resume, can contribute to _____'s [prospective employer] continued growth. I look forward to speaking with you further and will call next week to arrange a mutually convenient time. Should you wish to contact me earlier, my telephone number and email address are provided above. Thank you for your consideration, and I look forward to speaking with you.

Sincerely,

_____ [your signature]

_____ [your name]

Enclosure: Resume

Brandy McCarthy

9227 E. 15th St. • Chicago, IL 60112 • 312-555-5148 • brandy.mccarthy@email.com

August 5, 20XX

Jill Reeves
Human Resources Director
Barkley Education Development Corporation
343 Roosevelt Rd.
Chicago, IL 60110

Re: School Program Director

Dear Ms. Reeves:

Your advertisement for the above referenced position was forwarded to me by my colleague Michael Thomas, who recognized that my blend of experience in adult education, high school instruction, and business training would be an ideal fit. Please consider me as an applicant for this role. My qualifications include practical use of school best practices along with the ability to educate other teachers. This background is enhanced by a master's degree in English.

Though secure in my current position, I am seeking an opportunity with a progressive organization such as Barkley Education Development Corporation. I can add value to your organization in multiple ways, including the following:

- **Training teachers and staff**: I have facilitated multiple training sessions for educators in public and private schools, as well as professionals in business environments.

- **Developing and implementing successful programs**: After assessing the unique needs of the audience, I have created customized programs for both teachers and students.

- **Presenting to school leaders**: I have successfully persuaded administrators and department leaders to purchase educational materials.

These proven abilities, detailed in the attached resume, can contribute to Barkley's continued growth. I look forward to speaking with you further and will call next week to arrange a mutually convenient time. Should you wish to contact me earlier, my telephone number and e-mail address are provided above. Thank you for your consideration, and I look forward to speaking with you.

Sincerely,

Brandy McCarthy

Brandy McCarthy

Enclosure: Resume

Figure 10.22: A cover letter for a school program director using Cover Letter Foundation 22 (contributed by Charlotte Weeks, CCMC, CPRW).

Step 10

COVER LETTER FOUNDATION 23

This foundation works well for a manager applying to a recruiter.

Dear _____ [recruiter name]:

With more than _____ [number] years of experience and a stunning track record of increasing [profitability/sales/income/revenues/other: _____] and improving _____ [what?], I am confident that I can do the same for your clients seeking a _____ [job title]. A successful change leader, I have dramatically improved _____ [what?] in a relatively short amount of time.

Currently, I serve as _____ [job title] of _____ [current employer]. I was brought in to turn around an underperforming department and went well beyond expectations by spearheading the creation of _____ [what?], improving _____ [what area?] through _____ [type of] initiatives, and _____ [achieving what?].

The ability to see the big picture and strategically plan is one of my strongest skills. Detailed in the attached resume, you will see examples of the multiple successes that I have implemented at my former employers. In addition, I have greatly improved _____ [what?]. By _____ [doing what?], I have also reduced expenditures without compromising [quality/service/productivity/other: _____].

Though secure in my current position, I am seeking a new challenge in _____ [field]. I am open to relocation and am particularly interested in opportunities _____ [where?]. Should you wish to contact me, I can be reached at the telephone number and email address listed above. Thank you for your time and consideration.

Sincerely,

_____ [your signature]

_____ [your name]

Enclosure: Resume

CASEY MILLER, MPA

44 N. Monroe Avenue, New York, NY 12364
Cellular: 212.555.6498 • Work: 947.222.6738
casey.miller@email.com

HEALTH CARE OPERATIONS EXECUTIVE

January 17, 20XX

Helen Miyagi
WX Health Recruiting
545 Wellness Avenue
San Francisco, CA 97865

Dear Ms. Miyagi,

With more than 15 years of experience and a stunning track record of increasing profitability and improving service for medical facilities, I am confident that I can do the same for your clients seeking a health care operations executive. A successful change leader, I have dramatically improved faltering programs in a relatively short amount of time.

Currently, I serve as department administrator of the emergency department at ABC Foundation and University. I was brought in to turn around an underperforming department and went well beyond expectations by spearheading the creation of a standardized revenue cycle, improving staff morale through team-building initiatives, and leading this former division to acquire departmental status.

The ability to see the big picture and strategically plan is one of my strongest skills. Detailed in the attached resume, you will see examples of the multiple successes that I have implemented while at ABC. In addition, I have greatly improved the financial situation of an area not typically profitable for hospitals. By tightly managing finances, I have also reduced expenditures without compromising quality.

Though secure in my current position, I am seeking a new challenge in health care operations. I am open to relocation and am particularly interested in opportunities on the West Coast. Should you wish to contact me, I can be reached at the telephone number and email address listed above. Thank you for your time and consideration.

Sincerely,

Casey Miller

Casey Miller, MPA

Enclosure

Figure 10.23: A cover letter for a health care operations executive using Cover Letter Foundation 23 (contributed by Charlotte Weeks, CCMC, CPRW).

COVER LETTER FOUNDATION 24

This foundation works well for a change manager.

Dear _____ [hiring manager name]:

After successfully directing and operating the _____ [which?] department of a(n) $_____ [number] million corporation, I am seeking new challenges with a cutting-edge organization such as _____ [prospective employer]. My _____ [number]-year leadership career encompasses multiple promotions in which I used my [strategic planning/organizational leadership/change management/other: _____] skills to drive business development.

My passion for bringing _____ [type of] leadership to business situations is what drives me to create innovative solutions. For example, when promoted to _____ [job title] at _____ [past employer], I _____ [achieved what?]. To turn around _____ [what?], I set about _____ and _____ [doing what?] and quickly brought about _____ [type of] changes. In a short time, the _____ [which?] department was [recognized/respected/other: _____] by the executive committee.

While _____ [job title] of _____ [past employer] and _____ [job title] at _____ [past employer], I utilized my _____, _____, and _____ [type of] abilities to _____ [do what?]. For example, I

- _____ [achievement].

- _____ [achievement].

- _____ [achievement].

Detailed in the attached resume, you will find additional examples of ways I have benefited former employers. If _____ [prospective employer] could benefit from a visionary [executive/manager/professional/other: _____], I would welcome the opportunity to speak with you in more detail. I will call next week to schedule a meeting. If you would like to contact me earlier, I can be reached at the telephone number and email address listed above. Thank you for your time and consideration.

Sincerely,

_____ [your signature]

_____ [your name]

Enclosure

COLLIN JACOB

319 Louise Drive ■ Chicago, Illinois 60224
H: 312.555.2714 ■ collin.jacob@email.com ■ M: 312.555.3475

July 12, 20XX

Duke Bradford
Human Resources Director
The Copper Company
667 Polk Avenue
Chicago, IL 60225

Dear Mr. Bradford,

After successfully directing and operating the information systems department of an $800 million corporation, I am seeking new challenges with a cutting-edge organization such as The Copper Company. My 15+-year leadership career encompasses multiple promotions in which I used my strategic planning, organizational leadership, and change management skills to drive business development.

My passion for bringing technology leadership to business situations is what drives me to create innovative solutions. For example, when promoted to director of IT at Brandy Restaurants, I took on an underperforming division. To turn around the area's negative image, I set about analyzing the staff and level of customer service and quickly brought about changes. In a short time, the IT department was recognized and respected by the executive committee.

While vice president of information technology and vice president of interactive services at Brandy Restaurants, I utilized my leadership and financial abilities to initiate and develop cost-savings activities. For example, I

■ Restructured staff and reorganized electronic systems for an anticipated 287% ROI.
■ Saved $420,000 in overhead and training expenses by developing internal solutions.
■ Strategically planned and directed technology projects of up to 5 years in scope.

Detailed in the attached resume, you will find additional examples of ways I have benefited former employers. If The Copper Company could benefit from a visionary executive, I would welcome the opportunity to speak with you in more detail. I will call next week to schedule a meeting. If you would like to contact me earlier, I can be reached at the telephone number and email address listed above. Thank you for your time and consideration.

Sincerely,

Collin Jacob

Collin Jacob

Enclosure

Figure 10.24: A cover letter for a information technology director using Cover Letter Foundation 24 (contributed by Charlotte Weeks, CCMC, CPRW).

COVER LETTER FOUNDATION 25

This foundation works well for a service provider with experience.

Dear _____ [hiring manager name]:

Throughout my _____ [number] years of _____ [job function], I have consistently _____ [done what?], and I am confident that I can do the same for the [clients/customers/patrons/other: _____] at _____ [prospective employer]. A winner of multiple awards, I have been recognized by _____ [whom?] for my dedication to _____ [what field?]. In addition to _____ [area of responsibility], I have _____ [achievement].

My most recent position was at _____ [most recent employer], a _____ [type of] [firm/organization/facility/other: _____]. While there, I repeatedly _____ [performed or achieved what?] and _____ [did what?]. Along with _____ [characteristic], I proved that I could _____ [do what?] by _____ [achievement].

The passion I bring to _____ [field] is one of my greatest strengths. My commitment to _____ [what arena?] is evident in the attached resume, as I have not only attained my [master's/bachelor's] degree in _____ [major], but also am currently pursuing _____ [what degree or certification?] from _____ [name of school or training organization]. In addition, I have contributed to the success of _____ [what?] by _____ _____ [doing what?].

This distinctive blend of [practical knowledge/formal education/other: _____] and [enthusiasm/passion/other: _____] for _____ [field] is an ideal match for a _____ [type of organization] such as _____ [prospective employer]. I would welcome the opportunity to speak with you and will call to follow up. If you would like to contact me sooner, I can be reached at the telephone number and email address listed above. Thank you for your time and consideration.

Regards,

_____ [your signature]

_____ [your name]

Enclosure: Resume

Kenneth Chase

4499 N. Marshall Street Chicago, Illinois 60113
kenneth.chase@email.com
Home: (312) 555-3180
Cell: (773) 555-9245

Elementary Education Teacher

March 23, 20XX

Mr. Grant Lasky, Principal
Gap Academy
443 Carter Way
Chicago, IL 60115

Dear Mr. Lasky,

Throughout my 12 years of teaching, I have consistently improved student achievement in math, reading, and writing, and I am confident that I can do the same for the children at Gap Academy. A winner of multiple awards, I have been recognized by students and their parents for my dedication to teaching. In addition to instructing students in core academic subjects, I have led them to improve their behavior through strong classroom management.

My most recent position was at Brandywine Language and Math Elementary, a Chicago public school. While there, I repeatedly raised student test scores and mentored teachers to do the same with their classes. Along with interacting well with coworkers, I proved that I could lead by overseeing teachers involved in an after-school program that was designed to provide student enrichment and individual instruction in math.

The passion I bring to teaching is one of my greatest strengths. My commitment to continuing education is evident in the attached resume, as I have not only attained my master's degree in education, but also am pursuing math and science endorsements from Chicago University. In addition, I have contributed to the success of a probationary school by implementing teaching methods based on each student's learning style.

This distinctive blend of practical knowledge, formal education, and enthusiasm for teaching is an ideal match for a high-ranking school such as Gap Academy. I would welcome the opportunity to speak with you and will call to follow up. If you would like to contact me sooner, I can be reached at the telephone number and email address listed above. Thank you for your time and consideration.

Regards,

Kenneth Chase

Kenneth Chase

Enclosure

Figure 10.25: A cover letter for an elementary education teacher using Cover Letter Foundation 25 (contributed by Charlotte Weeks, CCMC, CPRW).

Step 10

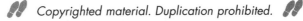

COVER LETTER FOUNDATION 26

This foundation works well for any candidate with progressive responsibility.

Dear _____ [hiring manager name]:

The posted opportunity for a _____ [job title] is an excellent match with my experience. My career includes more than _____ [number] years of progressive responsibility in _____, _____, and _____ [areas of expertise].

Highlights of my strengths include

- _____ [matching requirement]. _____ _____
  _____ [relevant achievement].

- _____ [matching requirement]. _____ _____
  _____ [relevant achievement].

- _____ [matching requirement]. _____ _____
  _____ [relevant achievement].

Currently exploring new opportunities, I am confident in my ability to make an immediate and lasting contribution to your organization and would welcome an interview at your earliest convenience. I look forward to speaking with you soon.

Sincerely,

_____ [your signature]

_____ [your name]

Enclosure

DAVID COLLARI

249 Appleburn Drive, Buffalo, NY 14201
(716) 888-4444 ▪ david_collari@mco.com

Iris Weinstein
Human Resources Manager
QRS Incorporated
778 Industry Avenue
Buffalo, NY 14201

Dear Ms. Weinstein,

The posted opportunity for a corporate trainer is an excellent match with my experience. My career includes more than eight years of progressive responsibility in training, marketing, and customer service.

Highlights of my strengths include

- **Program development.** Designed and delivered training materials for technical and business skill development, including a creative—and successful—plan to increase training opportunities for customer service representatives in a call center environment without taking away from their phone time.

- **Skills assessment.** Analyzed and interpreted quality-monitoring data to best enhance workplace productivity, office functionality, and employee peak performance. Proposed and facilitated new peer feedback sessions in which employees were grouped with varying strengths so that participants benefited by learning from each other.

- **Coaching techniques.** Developed and utilized effective one-on-one coaching methods. Co-created a thriving in-house model for coaching customer service representatives based on results of their monitoring. Created easily remembered acronym that identifies the stages of a session in which the coach guides the employee in identifying his/her own strengths and areas for further development. Created related training module and employed technique in actual coaching sessions.

Currently exploring new opportunities, I am confident in my ability to make an immediate and lasting contribution to your organization and would welcome an interview at your earliest convenience. I look forward to speaking with you soon.

Sincerely,

David Collari

David Collari

Enclosure

Figure 10.26: A cover letter for a corporate trainer using Cover Letter Foundation 26 (contributed by Laurie Berenson, CPRW).

Step 10

COVER LETTER FOUNDATION 27

This foundation works well for a manager in any profession.

Dear _____ [hiring manager name]:

Improving the cost-effectiveness of _____ [what?] is critical in today's business environment. My _____ [type of] management experience utilizing _____ [what?] and _____ [what?] would add measurable value to your _____ [which?] function(s). I am enclosing my resume for your consideration.

Highlights of my [achievements/qualifications] include

- _____ [skill]: _____ [related achievement summary].
- _____ [skill]: _____ [related achievement summary].
- _____ [skill]: _____ [related achievement summary].

I am confident my experience in _____ [doing what?] would be valuable to your firm's _____, _____, and _____ [functions/mission/objectives/goals]. I bring to the table a record of achieving _____ [what?] and _____ [what?] by _____ [doing what?].

Thank you in advance for your time and consideration. I look forward to hearing from you for a personal interview at your earliest convenience.

Sincerely,

_____ [your signature]

_____ [your name]

Enclosure: Resume

BARBARA SANDERS

145 West 67th Street, Apt 21C, New York, NY 10023
Cell (212) 446-8286 • barbara_sanders@msn.com

May 20, 20XX

David Roth
Director of Human Resources
JKL Department Stores
123 Madison Ave.
New York, NY 10023

Dear Mr. Roth,

Improving the cost-effectiveness of store operations is critical in today's business environment. My departmental management experience utilizing disciplined analysis and cross-functional coordination would add measurable value to your store development function. I am enclosing my resume for your consideration.

Highlights of my qualifications include

- **Handling global, large-scale, complex situations:** Supported 15 presidents, 25+ brands, and 75 business units worldwide relative to corporate store design, architecture, and construction and to retail, wholesale, and franchisee growth.

- **Implementing new ideas and processes with an eye toward operating results:** Reduced operating costs for 600+ stores with new Web-based store facilities systems and significantly improved forecasting accuracy by establishing comprehensive budgeting systems.

- **Supervising large groups and budgets to achieve company objectives:** Successfully managed more than 50 employees, 250 projects annually, and a $200 million budget while reorganizing to improve organizational efficiency and monitoring key metrics through a newly developed executive-level tracking report.

I am confident my experience in developing and executing new store and shop designs would be valuable to your store design, architecture, and construction functions. I bring to the table a record of achieving greater department productivity and shortening project cycle times by leveraging resources, knowledge base, and vendors.

Thank you in advance for your time and consideration. I look forward to hearing from you for a personal interview at your earliest convenience.

Sincerely,

Barbara Sanders

Barbara Sanders

Enclosure

Figure 10.27: A cover letter for a retail manager using Cover Letter Foundation 27 (contributed by Laurie Berenson, CPRW).

Step 10

COVER LETTER FOUNDATION 28

This foundation works well for any job candidate.

Dear _____ [hiring manager name]:

I believe my experience in successfully _____ [doing what?] coupled with my ability to _____ [do what?] qualifies me for a _____ [position title] position with your _____ [type of] firm.

My enclosed resume shows that I am a

- _____ [professional attribute]. _____ [related achievement and benefit].

- _____ [professional attribute]. _____ [related achievement and benefit].

- _____ [professional attribute]. _____ [related achievement and benefit].

I am confident that the dedication and experience I can bring to your firm will prove to be assets in _____ [doing what?]. Thank you in advance for your time and consideration. I look forward to hearing from you for a personal interview at your earliest convenience.

Sincerely,

_____ [your signature]

_____ [your name]

Enclosure

FRED COWAN

53 Highbow Lane, Worcester, MA 01601

Home (508) 667-1111 • Cell (508) 999-9999
fred_cowan@email.com

October 15, 20XX

Kyle Stewart
President
HIJ Investments
444 Stockton Boulevard
Boston, MA 02134

Dear Mr. Stewart,

I believe my experience in successfully building and managing client relationships coupled with my ability to provide ongoing, value-added client service qualifies me for a senior financial sales position with your investment firm.

My enclosed resume shows that I am a

- **Top-notch client service provider.** I successfully built a strong client base and retained client relationships over time by providing *accurate service and attention to detail* at every point.

- **Calm, effective multitasker.** As a Fed funds trader, I remained levelheaded in extremely tense situations, *reacting quickly to new information to add value* for clients.

- **Valued team player.** I am respected by colleagues for my *long-standing commitment to improve the team's performance*—whether training new hires, mentoring a junior associate, or taking on additional projects outside the scope of my responsibilities—in addition to meeting and exceeding individual sales goals.

I am confident that the dedication and experience I can bring to your firm will prove to be assets in **increasing sales and market share**. Thank you in advance for your time and consideration. I look forward to hearing from you for a personal interview at your earliest convenience.

Sincerely,

Fred Cowan

Fred Cowan

Enclosure

Figure 10.28: A cover letter for a financial sales manager using Cover Letter Foundation 28 (contributed by Laurie Berenson, CPRW).

Step 10

COVER LETTER FOUNDATION 29

This foundation works well for a highly experienced candidate in any profession.

Dear _____ [hiring manager name]:

With broad experience in all [aspects/phases/nuances/other: _____] of _____ [what area(s)?] and strong knowledge of _____ [what?], I am uniquely qualified for the _____ [position title] position at _____ [prospective employer].

As the attached resume shows, I have the key skills that this position requires:

- Ability to _____ [do what?]. Recognized for consistently _____ [doing what?] and successfully _____ [achieving what?], I can _____ [benefit] by _____ [doing what?].

- Strong _____ [type of] experience. I have been involved in nearly every facet of _____ [what area?] during a progressive _____ [type of] career—from _____ [what?] to _____ [what?], including _____ [achieving what?] and _____ [achieving what?].

- Attention to _____ [what?]. I am known for always exceeding [goals/objectives/client expectations/other: _____] and the ability to effectively solve _____ [type of] [problems/challenges] with the [firm's/client's/patron's/other: _____] best interests in mind. I am also skilled at _____ [doing what?] with a _____ [type of] approach. My _____ [type of] skills have successfully _____ [accomplished what?].

I would welcome the opportunity to meet with you to discuss how my [dedication/enthusiasm/passion/strategic leadership/other: _____] could prove to be an asset in achieving your firm's goals. I will call next week to check when this meeting might be possible. Thank you for your time and consideration. I look forward to speaking with you.

Best regards,

_____ [your signature]

_____ [your name]

Enclosure

ALEX P. GARNER

94 Forest Court, Easton, CT 06612
Phone (200) 888-9999 • Alex.Garner@ymail.net

June 22, 20XX

Eliza Sanchez
Vice President, Sales
Triplax Incorporated
778 Widget Way
Hartford, CT 06677

Dear Ms. Sanchez,

With broad experience in all aspects of sales and sales management and strong knowledge of luxury goods, I believe that I am uniquely qualified for the regional director of sales position at Triplax Incorporated.

As the attached resume shows, I have the key skills that this position requires:

- **Ability to penetrate accounts and develop territories.** Recognized for consistently increasing accounts' share of business year-over-year and successfully converting previously resistant key national accounts and independents, I can expand territory sales by gaining proper placement and space.

- **Strong sales management experience.** I have been involved in nearly every facet of sales management during a progressive sales career—from developing sales strategies to managing new product promotions, including developing national sales and marketing programs for specialty chains and independents and managing account advertising, promotions, and budgeting functions.

- **Attention to customer service.** I am known for always exceeding client expectations with quick follow-up and the ability to effectively solve problems with the client's best interests in mind. I am also skilled at establishing immediate bonds with a personable approach. My hands-on relationship skills have successfully converted declining accounts into growth accounts.

I would welcome the opportunity to meet with you to discuss how my enthusiasm and experience could prove to be assets in achieving your firm's goals. I will call next week to check when this meeting might be possible. Thank you for your time and consideration. I look forward to speaking with you.

Best regards,

Alex Garner

Alex P. Garner

Enclosure

Figure 10.29: A cover letter for a regional sales director using Cover Letter Foundation 29 (contributed by Laurie Berenson, CPRW).

Step 10

COVER LETTER FOUNDATION 30

This foundation works well for a qualified candidate in any profession.

Dear _____ [hiring manager name]:

I believe my [professional skill set/other: _____] combined with my _____ [type of] experience qualifies me to serve as your _____ [position title]. I am enclosing my resume for your consideration.

My qualifications include these highlights:

- Day-to-day _____ [type of] experience, including more than _____ [number] years of _____ [type of] experience at _____ [type of firm] providing _____ [what?] to _____ [whom?].

- Significant experience with _____ [what area?]. Well-versed in _____, _____, and _____ [what niche areas?] from _____ [what?] to _____ [what?].

- Strong background in _____ [what area or functions?]. Provided _____, _____, _____, and _____ [functions], covering _____, _____, and _____ [areas]. I also hold [a/dual] [master's/bachelor's/associate] degree in _____ [what major?].

I am certain that the enthusiasm and experience I can bring to your company will prove to be assets in managing _____ [what?].

Thank you in advance for your time and consideration. I look forward to hearing from you for a personal interview at your earliest convenience.

Sincerely,

_____ [your signature]

_____ [your name]

Enclosure

SUSAN TREVOR, LCSW, CASAC

26 Greenbriar Court, Livingston, NJ 07039
Home (973) 444-1111 • Cell (973) 888-2222 • STrevor@email.net

April 15, 20XX

Belinda Worthington
President
Forest Grove Outreach
212 Service Street
Trenton, NJ 07890

Dear Ms. Worthington,

I believe my professional skill set combined with my clinical experience qualifies me to serve as your director of programs. I am enclosing my resume for your consideration.

My qualifications include these highlights:

❖ **Day-to-day senior management experience,** including more than 10 years of administrative and staff management experience at a satellite clinic providing outpatient care to more than 400 lower income patients and families.

❖ **Significant experience with family dynamics.** Well-versed in family interactions from multiple clinical perspectives—general mental health, MICA, and substance abuse—and across a variety of cultures.

❖ **Strong background, both clinically and academically.** Provided individual, couple, and family psychotherapy, diagnosing and treating a variety of diagnoses, including depression, anxiety, and substance abuse. I also hold dual master's degrees in public affairs and social work.

I am certain that the enthusiasm and experience I can bring to your company will prove to be assets in managing your direct service agencies.

Thank you in advance for your time and consideration. I look forward to hearing from you for a personal interview at your earliest convenience.

Sincerely,

Susan Trevor

Susan Trevor

Enclosure

Figure 10.30: A cover letter for a program director using Cover Letter Foundation 30 (contributed by Laurie Berenson, CPRW).

Step 10

COVER LETTER FOUNDATION 31

This foundation works well for someone seeking a management position.

Dear _____ [hiring manager name]:

With progressive responsibility in _____, _____, _____ [areas of expertise] in the _____ [which?] industry, my [background/experience/hands-on knowledge/education/other: _____] makes me a strong [match/candidate] for a _____ [type of] position within your organization.

Highlights of my strengths include the following:

- _____ [area of expertise from first sentence]. Established _____ [what?]. Experienced in day-to-day _____ [job function], including full _____ [type of] responsibilities and _____ [other area]. Recognized for successful _____ [which initiatives?].

- _____ [area of expertise from first sentence]. Contributed to increased [market share/revenues/productivity/return on investment/profits/sales/other: _____] with a successful record of _____ [doing what?]. Effectively developed and lead _____ [what area(s)] and provided _____ [type of] service to _____ [whom?].

- _____ [area of expertise from first sentence]. Known for providing _____ [what?] and _____ [what?]. Experienced in _____ and _____ [what functions?] that result in increased [productivity/revenues/sales/other: _____] through _____ [method(s)].

I am confident in my ability to make an immediate and lasting contribution to your organization and would welcome an interview at your earliest convenience. My resume is enclosed for your review.

I look forward to speaking with you soon.

Sincerely,

_____ [your signature]

_____ [your name]

GARY WESTON

1345 Court Street, Apt. #29 • Fairfax, VA 22031

(703) 333-2663 • GWeston@email.net

September 23, 20XX

Jamilla Eastman, President
PQR Travel
899 Midway Circle
Richmond, VA 22035

Dear Ms. Eastman,

With progressive responsibility in management, marketing, and sales in the tourism industry, my background and hands-on knowledge make me a strong match for a management position within your organization.

Highlights of my strengths include the following:

✓ **Sales Management.** Established *strong relationships with wholesale tour operators and airlines* to heighten awareness and increase revenues. Experienced in day-to-day sales office management, including full budget responsibilities and employee hiring and training. Recognized for successful training programs.

✓ **Marketing and Promotions.** Contributed to increased market share, revenues, and return on investment with a successful record of *introducing new profitable market segments and niche markets* to the destination. Effectively developed and lead marketing plans and provided customized service to clients.

✓ **Office Management.** Known for *providing clear direction and recognition for good work* and consistent feedback and coaching. Motivated others across all levels to achieve individual and company goals. Experienced in office relocation and in increasing productivity through process automation.

I am confident in my ability to make an immediate and lasting contribution to your organization and would welcome an interview at your earliest convenience. My resume is enclosed for your review.

I look forward to speaking with you soon.

Sincerely,

Gary Weston

Gary Weston

Figure 10.31: A cover letter for a sales and marketing manager using Cover Letter Foundation 31 (contributed by Laurie Berenson, CPRW).

Step 10

PROFESSION-SPECIFIC COVER LETTER FOUNDATIONS

The cover letter foundations and samples contained in this section show how you can take the generic foundations from the prior situational cover letter foundations and plug in qualifications and areas of expertise specific to your own profession and still have many options available to you.

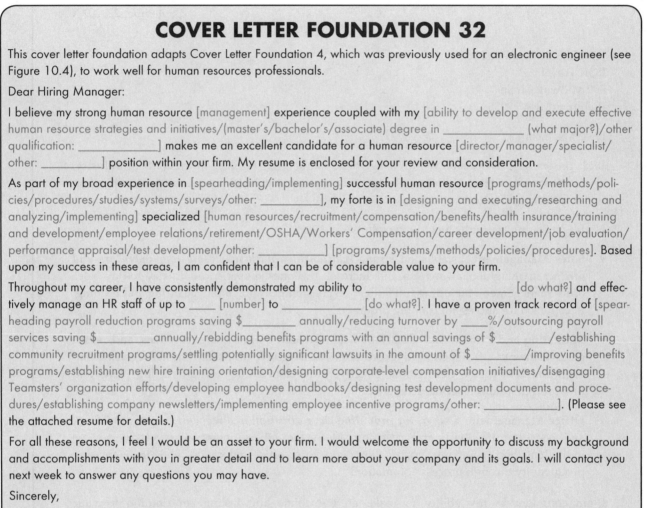

COVER LETTER FOUNDATION 32

This cover letter foundation adapts Cover Letter Foundation 4, which was previously used for an electronic engineer (see Figure 10.4), to work well for human resources professionals.

Dear Hiring Manager:

I believe my strong human resource [management] experience coupled with my [ability to develop and execute effective human resource strategies and initiatives/(master's/bachelor's/associate) degree in _____ (what major?)/other qualification: _____] makes me an excellent candidate for a human resource [director/manager/specialist/ other: _____] position within your firm. My resume is enclosed for your review and consideration.

As part of my broad experience in [spearheading/implementing] successful human resource [programs/methods/poli- cies/procedures/studies/systems/surveys/other: _____], my forte is in [designing and executing/researching and analyzing/implementing] specialized [human resources/recruitment/compensation/benefits/health insurance/training and development/employee relations/retirement/OSHA/Workers' Compensation/career development/job evaluation/ performance appraisal/test development/other: _____] [programs/systems/methods/policies/procedures]. Based upon my success in these areas, I am confident that I can be of considerable value to your firm.

Throughout my career, I have consistently demonstrated my ability to _____ [do what?] and effec- tively manage an HR staff of up to _____ [number] to _____ [do what?]. I have a proven track record of [spear- heading payroll reduction programs saving $_____ annually/reducing turnover by _____%/outsourcing payroll services saving $_____ annually/rebidding benefits programs with an annual savings of $_____/establishing community recruitment programs/settling potentially significant lawsuits in the amount of $_____/improving benefits programs/establishing new hire training orientation/designing corporate-level compensation initiatives/disengaging Teamsters' organization efforts/developing employee handbooks/designing test development documents and proce- dures/establishing company newsletters/implementing employee incentive programs/other: _____]. (Please see the attached resume for details.)

For all these reasons, I feel I would be an asset to your firm. I would welcome the opportunity to discuss my background and accomplishments with you in greater detail and to learn more about your company and its goals. I will contact you next week to answer any questions you may have.

Sincerely,

_____ [your signature]

_____ [your name]

Enclosure: Resume

Aisha Taylor

655 Summer Drive, Kansas City, MO 44555 ▪ 432.109.8765 ▪ ataylor1@email.net

Dear Hiring Manager:

I believe my strong human resource management experience coupled with my ability to develop and execute effective human resource strategies and initiatives makes me an excellent candidate for a human resource director position within your firm. My resume is enclosed for your review and consideration.

As part of my broad experience in spearheading successful human resource programs, systems, and procedures, my forte is in designing and executing specialized recruitment, training and development, employee relations, career development, performance appraisal, and test development programs. Based upon my success in these areas, I am confident that I can be of considerable value to your firm.

Throughout my career, I have consistently demonstrated my ability to revitalize my employer's workforce and effectively manage an HR staff of up to 15 to recruit winning candidates and train and develop productive employees. I have a proven track record of spearheading payroll reduction programs, saving $225,000 annually; reducing turnover by 34%; outsourcing payroll services, saving $150,000 annually; and establishing new hire training orientation.

In addition, I have championed the development and execution of corporate-level compensation initiatives, community recruitment programs, employee handbooks, test development documents and procedures, and employee incentive programs. (Please see the attached resume for details.)

For all these reasons, I feel I would be an asset to your firm. I would welcome the opportunity to discuss my background and accomplishments with you in greater detail and to learn more about your company and its goals. I will contact you next week to answer any questions you may have.

Sincerely,

Aisha Taylor

Aisha Taylor

Enclosure: Resume

Figure 10.32: A cover letter for a human resources director using Cover Letter Foundation 32 and Letterhead Design 7 (on the CD).

Step 10

COVER LETTER FOUNDATION 33

This cover letter foundation changes the original Cover Letter Foundation 4 even further by adding bullet points and a slogan. The keyword examples given in this foundation are appropriate for construction management professionals.

Dear Hiring Manager:

I believe my strong project management experience combined with my ability to [direct and oversee all aspects of construction/coordinate and schedule trades/lead and motivate teams/estimate projects/negotiate contracts/purchase materials/other: _____] and my [master's/bachelor's] degree in [architecture/other: _____] makes me an excellent candidate for a construction project manager position within your firm. My resume is enclosed for your review and consideration.

As part of my broad experience in managing all phases of construction from project start through completion, my specialty is in supervising [commercial/residential/public works/civil/other: _____] projects, including [commercial buildings/shopping malls/stores/restaurants/manufacturing plants/schools/colleges and universities/corporate offices/state or government agencies/hospitals/laboratories/clean rooms/landmark restorations/roads and highways/houses/condominiums/apartment buildings/other: _____]. Based upon my success in these areas, I am confident I can be of considerable value to your firm.

Throughout my career, I have consistently demonstrated my ability to coordinate the [demolition/construction/remodeling/renovation/restoration/other: _____] of construction projects ranging from $_____ [number] to $_____ [number] million and to effectively manage, coordinate, and schedule a trades team of up to _____ [number] to bring projects in on time and within budget. Examples include

- Spearheading the construction of a [$_____/____(number)-square foot/____(number)-story/_____(number)-room/ other: _____] _____ [type of] project for _____ [previous employer].

- Simultaneously managing _____ [number] construction projects averaging $_____ [number], with property values totaling $_____[number] to $_____[number] million annually.

- Receiving commendations from [clients/employers] for [professional expertise/dedication to job/a job well done/ other: _____].

I have a proven track record of [developing job estimates and budgets/securing competitive bids/handling contract negotiations/maintaining client relationships/scheduling and coordinating trades/performing on-site construction supervision/reviewing and modifying plans/negotiating and processing change orders/other: _____]. (Please see attached resume for details.)

For all these reasons, I feel I would be an asset to your firm. I would welcome the opportunity to discuss my background and accomplishments with you in greater detail and to learn more about your company and its goals. I will contact you next week to answer any questions you may have.

Regards,

_____ [your signature]

_____ [your name]

Enclosure: Resume

_____ [slogan]

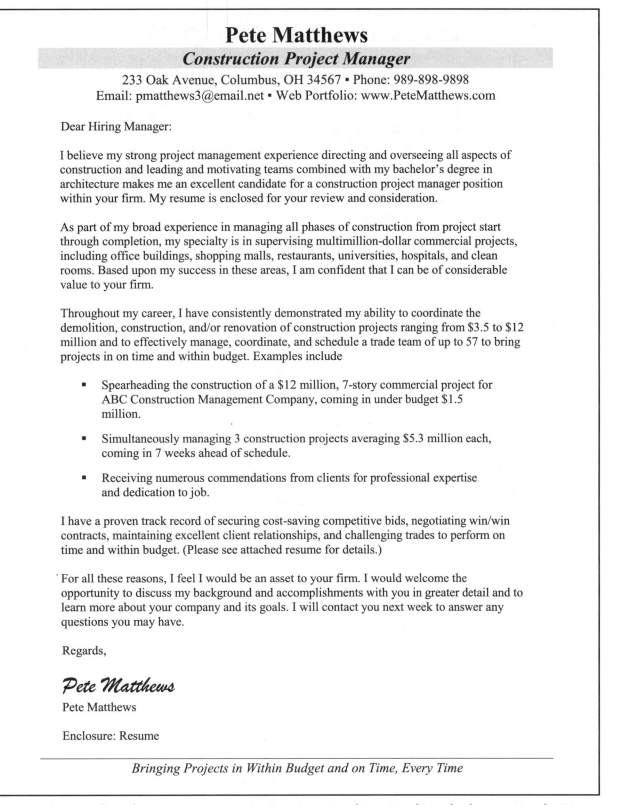

Pete Matthews

Construction Project Manager

233 Oak Avenue, Columbus, OH 34567 ▪ Phone: 989-898-9898
Email: pmatthews3@email.net ▪ Web Portfolio: www.PeteMatthews.com

Dear Hiring Manager:

I believe my strong project management experience directing and overseeing all aspects of construction and leading and motivating teams combined with my bachelor's degree in architecture makes me an excellent candidate for a construction project manager position within your firm. My resume is enclosed for your review and consideration.

As part of my broad experience in managing all phases of construction from project start through completion, my specialty is in supervising multimillion-dollar commercial projects, including office buildings, shopping malls, restaurants, universities, hospitals, and clean rooms. Based upon my success in these areas, I am confident that I can be of considerable value to your firm.

Throughout my career, I have consistently demonstrated my ability to coordinate the demolition, construction, and/or renovation of construction projects ranging from $3.5 to $12 million and to effectively manage, coordinate, and schedule a trade team of up to 57 to bring projects in on time and within budget. Examples include

- Spearheading the construction of a $12 million, 7-story commercial project for ABC Construction Management Company, coming in under budget $1.5 million.

- Simultaneously managing 3 construction projects averaging $5.3 million each, coming in 7 weeks ahead of schedule.

- Receiving numerous commendations from clients for professional expertise and dedication to job.

I have a proven track record of securing cost-saving competitive bids, negotiating win/win contracts, maintaining excellent client relationships, and challenging trades to perform on time and within budget. (Please see attached resume for details.)

For all these reasons, I feel I would be an asset to your firm. I would welcome the opportunity to discuss my background and accomplishments with you in greater detail and to learn more about your company and its goals. I will contact you next week to answer any questions you may have.

Regards,

Pete Matthews

Pete Matthews

Enclosure: Resume

Bringing Projects in Within Budget and on Time, Every Time

Figure 10.33: A cover letter for a project manager using Cover Letter Foundation 33 and Letterhead Design 4 (on the CD).

COVER LETTER FOUNDATION 34

This cover letter foundation adapts Cover Letter Foundation 1, which was previously used for a manufacturing executive (see Figure 10.1), to work well for marketing professionals specializing in brand management.

Dear Human Resources Professional:

As a successful brand management [executive/professional], I bring to your organization more than ___ [number] years of progressively responsible experience in brand [strategizing/development/positioning/advertising/marketing/management/execution/other: _____] in the _____ [which?] industry. My expertise lies in developing and launching successful [(new/remerchandised) products/private label brands/consumer packaged goods/marketing plans/advertising campaigns/promotional events/other: _____] and proactive programs designed to drive and sustain revenues. My resume is enclosed for your consideration.

I have a proven track record of expanding [product visibility/market share/advertising sales/service levels/revenues/other: _____] and [decreasing costs/streamlining operations/increasing productivity/other: _____]. Notable achievements include [expanding product visibility by ____%/increasing market share by (____%/$_____)/growing untapped markets in _____ (what area?)/elevating advertising sales by $_____/increasing service levels by ____%/spearheading my firm's entrance into _____ (which?) market(s)/increasing profits by $_____/other: _____]. (Please see attached resume for details.)

Complementing my ability to develop and execute successful product marketing [initiatives/research/plans/strategies/campaigns/programs/other: _____] and effectively manage a creative staff of ____ [number] to create and implement those plans are equally strong qualifications in [competitive analysis/new market identification/consumer brand discovery/forecasting/pricing strategies/market segmentation/position tracking/strategic relationship management/distribution channels support/licensing requirements and relationships/promotional event planning/presentation development/product life cycle management/sales materials creation/packaged goods marketing/new packaging innovation/vendor relations/safety assurance process management/budget development/classic brand marketing/variance analyses and projections/other: _____].

I am able to provide strategic product and staff direction in all areas of brand development and management with appropriate tactical action plans to meet consumer needs. I lead by example and provide strong [decision-making/problem-solving/creative direction/staff development/other: _____] skills.

I am confident that the experience and drive I can bring to your organization will prove to be assets. I would appreciate hearing from you regarding any existing or future openings you might have and would welcome the opportunity to discuss a possible relationship that would prove to be mutually beneficial! Thank you for your time and consideration.

Best regards,

_____ [your signature]

_____ [your name]

Enclosure: Resume

ISAAC WILLIAMS

654 Clamstock Road, Providence, RI 01234
Email: iwilliams2@email.net

Home phone: (101) 111-1111
Cellular: (101) 222-2222

Dear Human Resources Professional:

As a successful brand manager, I bring to your organization more than 10 years of progressively responsible experience in brand strategizing, development, positioning, and marketing in the food industry. My expertise lies in developing and launching successful new products and proactive programs designed to drive and sustain revenues. My resume is enclosed for your consideration.

I have a proven track record of expanding product visibility, market share, and service levels. Notable achievements include expanding product visibility by 38.5%, increasing market share by $1.5 million, growing untapped markets in the recreation field, and increasing service levels by 12%. (Please see the attached resume for details.)

Complementing my ability to develop and execute successful product marketing initiatives, strategies, and campaigns and effectively manage a creative staff of seven to create and implement those plans are equally strong qualifications in competitive analysis, new market identification, consumer brand discovery, forecasting, pricing strategies, and market segmentation. In addition, I have hands-on knowledge in the areas of position tracking, strategic relationship management, distribution channels support, presentation development, product life cycle management, and sales materials creation.

I am able to provide strategic product and staff direction in all areas of brand development and management with appropriate tactical action plans to meet consumer needs. I lead by example and provide strong decision-making, creative direction, and staff development skills.

I am confident that the experience and drive I can bring to your organization will prove to be assets. I would appreciate hearing from you regarding any existing or future openings you might have and would welcome the opportunity to discuss a possible relationship that would prove to be mutually beneficial! Thank you for your time and consideration.

Best regards,

Isaac Williams

Isaac Williams

Enclosure: Resume

Figure 10.34: A cover letter for a brand manager using Cover Letter Foundation 34 and Letterhead Design 1 (on the CD).

Step 10

COVER LETTER FOUNDATION 35

This cover letter foundation also adapts Cover Letter Foundation 1, this time for human resources professionals specializing in training and development.

Dear Hiring Manager:

As a successful training and development [manager/specialist/professional], I bring to your organization more than _____ [number] years of progressively responsible experience in the training field. My expertise lies in [planning/organizing/coordinating/developing/conducting/integrating/other: _____] training [programs/methods/guides/procedures/lessons/classes/workshops/other: _____] designed to [develop knowledge/enhance productivity/increase skills base/promote quality work/build loyalty to the firm/improve employee morale/develop future leaders/increase sales/meet your firm's needs/other: _____]. My resume is enclosed for your consideration.

I have a proven track record of delivering effective training and development programs that keep up with [new products/organizational changes/technological advances/corporate restructuring/company transitions/learning theories and practices/mergers and acquisitions/new _____ (type of) knowledge/other: _____]. Notable achievements include _____, _____, _____, and _____ [your most significant accomplishments]. (Please see attached resume for details.)

Complementing my ability to [lead/facilitate/develop/implement/other: _____] training programs are equally strong qualifications in [identifying and assessing a firm's training and development needs/translating business requirements into successful training programs/determining implementation strategy and methodology/evaluating current training effectiveness/developing user-friendly technical procedures/other: _____] and incorporating various training methods and modalities into [on-the-job/simulation/apprenticeship/orientation/classroom/distance learning/computer/satellite/video/interactive/Internet-based/computer-aided instructional/conference/workshop/multimedia/self-paced/instructor-led/other: _____] training.

I am confident that the [experience/drive/enthusiasm/strategic direction/other: _____] I can bring to your organization will prove to be an asset. I would appreciate hearing from you regarding any existing or future openings you might have and would welcome the opportunity to discuss a possible relationship that would prove to be mutually beneficial. I will call you next week to see whether you have time in your schedule to meet with me.

Warm regards,

_____ [your signature]

_____ [your name]

Enclousre: Resume

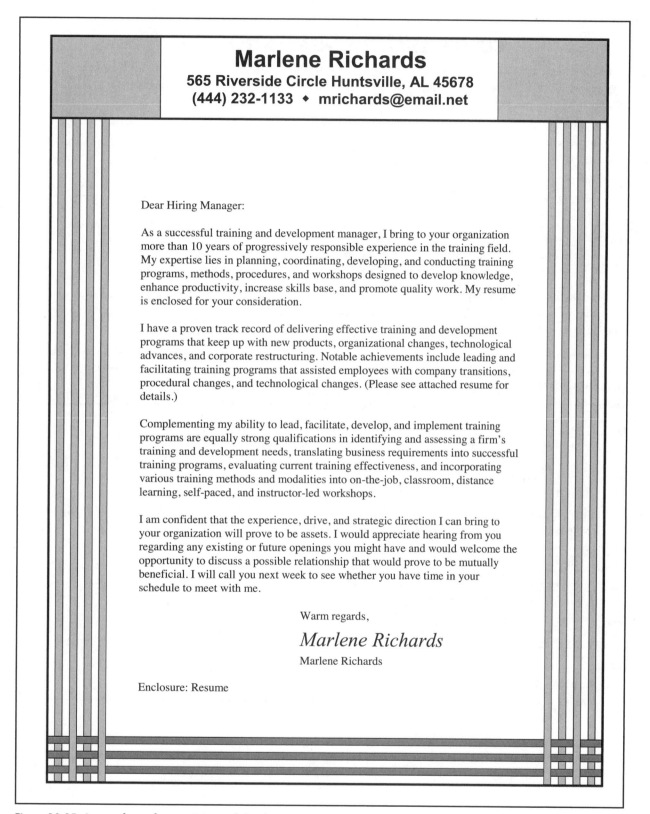

Marlene Richards
565 Riverside Circle Huntsville, AL 45678
(444) 232-1133 ◆ mrichards@email.net

Dear Hiring Manager:

As a successful training and development manager, I bring to your organization more than 10 years of progressively responsible experience in the training field. My expertise lies in planning, coordinating, developing, and conducting training programs, methods, procedures, and workshops designed to develop knowledge, enhance productivity, increase skills base, and promote quality work. My resume is enclosed for your consideration.

I have a proven track record of delivering effective training and development programs that keep up with new products, organizational changes, technological advances, and corporate restructuring. Notable achievements include leading and facilitating training programs that assisted employees with company transitions, procedural changes, and technological changes. (Please see attached resume for details.)

Complementing my ability to lead, facilitate, develop, and implement training programs are equally strong qualifications in identifying and assessing a firm's training and development needs, translating business requirements into successful training programs, evaluating current training effectiveness, and incorporating various training methods and modalities into on-the-job, classroom, distance learning, self-paced, and instructor-led workshops.

I am confident that the experience, drive, and strategic direction I can bring to your organization will prove to be assets. I would appreciate hearing from you regarding any existing or future openings you might have and would welcome the opportunity to discuss a possible relationship that would prove to be mutually beneficial. I will call you next week to see whether you have time in your schedule to meet with me.

Warm regards,

Marlene Richards

Marlene Richards

Enclosure: Resume

Figure 10.35: A cover letter for a training and development manager using Cover Letter Foundation 35 and Letterhead Design 14 (on the CD).

Step 10

COVER LETTER FOUNDATION 36

This cover letter foundation adapts Cover Letter Foundation 11, which is based on the cover letter for a racetrack chief executive officer that was written by Beverley Neil (see Figure 10.11), to work for information technology professionals specializing in website development.

Dear Hiring Manager:

The position of website [developer/designer] for _____ [prospective employer] combines my [experience/creativity/passion/skills/education/other: _____]. Therefore, it is with a high degree of confidence that I forward you my expression of interest and my resume for your review and consideration.

I draw to your attention my website innovation, knowledge, and skills, which combine to position me as a strong [candidate/match] for this role:

- The challenge of designing and developing creative websites that meet my employers' [and their clients'] satisfaction is my life. Inherent in all these challenges are the skills and experience required to position my [clients as experts in their fields/employers as high-end, cost-effective website developers/other: _____].

- I am known for my outstanding web [design/layout/coding/other: _____] skills, including website [setups/configuration/implementation/maintenance/troubleshooting/support/monitoring/other: _____] that provides visibility to the largest possible audience, thereby increasing leads generation.

- My proven [web design/logo design/photo retouching/animation/other: _____] skills coupled with my ability to develop and facilitate all technical aspects of web pages are surpassed only by my thorough knowledge of web applications, including [Adobe Dreamweaver/Adobe InDesign/Microsoft Expression Web/other: _____] as well as [Flash/Fireworks/Freeway/Photoshop/other: _____]—providing versatility to all of your clients.

- In addition, I am skilled in writing web pages in a combination of codes, including [HTML/JavaScript/ColdFusion/Perl/Flash/Visual Basic/other: _____]. And—unlike most web developers—I am also _____ [competitive edge], which allows me to _____ [benefit].

In applying for this position, I am not merely applying for a job that would involve me on a professional level only. In applying for the position of website [developer/designer], I also bring with me my [passion/creativity/versatility/technical skills/commitment/other: _____].

I am interested in exploring this challenging opportunity further and contributing in creative and effective ways. I believe a personal conversation and interview would reveal my suitability and passion for this role and hope we may speak soon. Thank you for your time and consideration.

Sincerely,

_____ [your signature]

_____ [your name]

Enclosure: Resume

Henry Lyon
Website Developer
887 Cyber Highway, Seattle, WA 90876
(988) 777-6666
hlyon@email.net

There isn't a website I can't write, design, code, and develop.

Dear Hiring Manager:

The position of website developer for ABC Agency combines my experience, my creativity, and my passion. Therefore, it is with a high degree of confidence that I forward you my expression of interest and my resume for your review and consideration.

I draw to your attention my website innovation, knowledge, and skills, which combine to position me as a strong candidate for this role:

- The challenge of designing and developing creative websites that meet my employers' and their clients' satisfaction is my life. Inherent in all these challenges are the skills and experience required to position clients as experts in their fields and drive revenues.

- I am known for my outstanding web design, layout, and coding skills, including website setups, configuration, implementation, maintenance, troubleshooting, and support that provide visibility to the largest possible audience, thereby increasing leads generation.

- My proven web design, logo design, photo retouching, and animation skills coupled with my ability to develop and facilitate all technical aspects of web pages are surpassed only by my thorough knowledge of many web applications, including Dreamweaver—*providing versatility to all of your clients.*

- In addition, I am skilled in writing web pages in a combination of codes, including HTML, JavaScript, ColdFusion, and Flash. And—*unlike most web developers*—I am also an excellent content writer, which allows me to write and design sites simultaneously.

In applying for this position, I am not merely applying for a job that would involve me on a professional level only. In applying for the position of website developer, I also bring with me my passion, creativity, and commitment.

I am interested in exploring this challenging opportunity further and contributing in creative and effective ways. I believe a personal conversation and interview would reveal my suitability and passion for this role and hope we may speak soon. Thank you for your time and consideration.

Sincerely,

Henry Lyon

Henry Lyon

Enclosure: Resume

Figure 10.36: A cover letter for a website developer using Cover Letter Foundation 36 and Letterhead Design 15 (on the CD).

Step 10

COVER LETTER FOUNDATION 37

This cover letter foundation works well for business professionals specializing in marketing strategy.

Dear _____ [hiring manager name]:

Developing the strategic roadmaps that help businesses [define their market differentiators/optimize brand reach/maximize customer acquisition and retention/other: _____] is my expertise and my passion. My strengths in [e-business transformation/brand unification/new market penetration/product innovation/other: _____] have been leveraged across multiple industries including _____, _____, and _____ [which industries?] and span [Fortune (50s/100s/500s)/start-ups/consulting practices/other: _____]. Toward that end, I am enclosing my resume for a _____ [job title] position in your firm.

My accomplishments include:

_____ [Area of Expertise]

- For _____ [previous employer], _____
  _____ [accomplishment, benefit, ROI].

_____ [Area of Expertise]

- For _____ [previous employer], _____
  _____ [accomplishment, benefit, ROI].

_____ [Area of Expertise]

- For _____ [previous employer], _____
  _____ [accomplishment, benefit, ROI].

Excited by the prospect of an opportunity with your company and impressed by the strength of your brand, I would welcome the chance to meet with you to discuss your company's business needs and my qualifications in more detail. I am confident that I can deliver results similar to those described above for your organization and look forward to a personal interview.

Sincerely,

_____ [your signature]

_____ [your name]

Attachment

Rhonda Lucas

H: 314-222-5555 ▪ C: 314-333-5555 ▪ rlucas@email.net
75 Sunset Avenue ▪ St. Louis, MO 63101

BUSINESS STRATEGY INNOVATOR

Bradley Davidson
Marketing Director
WXY Incorporated
787 Corporation Avenue
St. Louis, MO 63122

Dear Mr. Davidson:

Developing the strategic roadmaps that help businesses define their market differentiators, optimize brand reach, and maximize customer acquisition and retention is my expertise and my passion. My strengths in e-business transformation, brand unification, new market penetration, and product innovation have been leveraged across multiple industries including consumer goods, technology, telecommunications, financial services, and advertising and span Fortune 50s, start-ups, and consulting practices. Toward that end, I am enclosing my resume for a marketing strategist position in your firm.

My accomplishments include the following:

E-Business Reengineering

- For CredDirect, accelerated online credit card applications by 60% in one year by repositioning the way the card product was marketed online, optimizing the user experience, and targeting an untapped segment of customers.

- For Yummy Foods, created the blueprint for an enterprise-wide initiative to align disparate lines of business within a more unified user experience to improve site usability and consistency of brand messaging.

Innovation

- For X&Y Tech, a boutique software firm, redefined the value proposition and brand reach for the world's first proprietary software and 3D visualization technology used to create on-demand, made-to-measure apparel to target new and nontraditional markets.

Strategic Business Roadmapping

- For YXW Consulting, simplified complexities of sophisticated project processes for multitiered implementation plans to deliver on business goals, unify branding initiatives, and ensure a superlative customer experience.

Excited by the prospect of an opportunity with your company and impressed by the strength of your brand, I would welcome the chance to meet with you to discuss your company's business needs and my qualifications in more detail. I am confident that I can deliver results similar to those described above for your organization and look forward to a personal interview.

Sincerely,

Rhonda Lucas

Rhonda Lucas

Attachment

"Rhonda is an exceptional strategist I truly admire. She drives strategic visions, influences team members, and achieves success with strong leadership and project management skills. She has in-depth knowledge of web analytic tools, their strengths and limitations, and gleans insights to improve customer experience out of complex web user behavior data. She constantly comes up with actionable solutions and brings them to completion." **Colleague, CredDirect**

"Diligent, motivated, knowledgeable, and a great deal of pleasure to work with. We work well together, and she seems to always be considering the needs of the project from various viewpoints, something I find rare in this industry." **Colleague, CredDirect**

"Rhonda quickly assesses what is needed for the business, contributes new insights, and brings everyone to the table, eliciting the best from each team member. She develops effective plans to reduce costs and increase business results." **Manager, Yummy Foods**

Figure 10.37: A cover letter for a business strategy innovator using Cover Letter Foundation 37 (contributed by Barbara Safani, MA, CERW, NCRW, CPRW, CCM).

Step 10

OTHER PERSONALLY BRANDED COVER LETTER SAMPLES

Use these five bonus cover letter samples from professional resume writers to inspire you to create your own compelling cover letter:

- ✔ A cover letter for a sales professional (Figure 10.38)
- ✔ A cover letter for a sales and marketing professional (Figure 10.39)
- ✔ A cover letter for a senior executive (Figure 10.40)
- ✔ A cover letter for a special assistant (Figure 10.41)
- ✔ A cover letter for a plant maintenance supervisor (Figure 10.42)

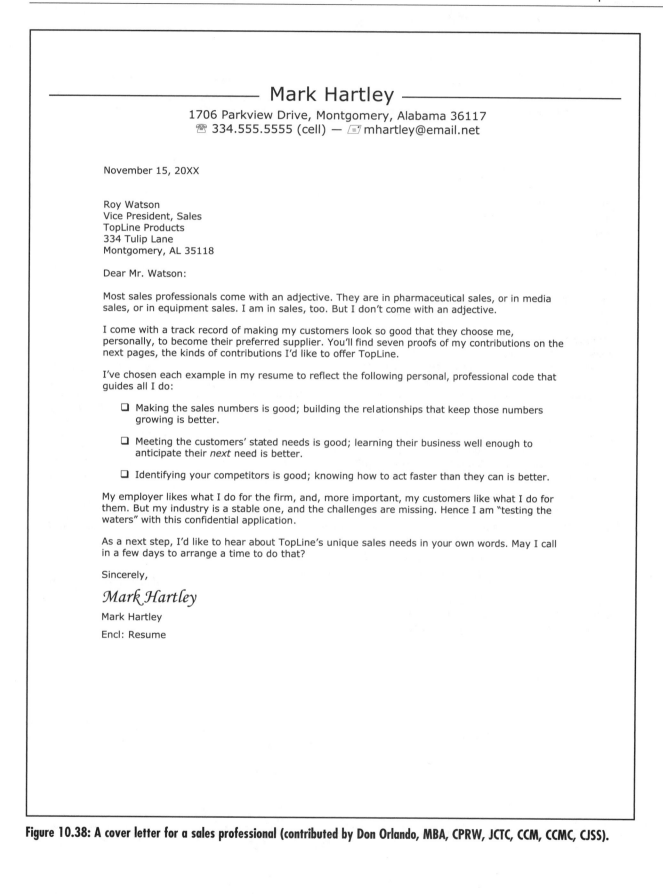

Mark Hartley

1706 Parkview Drive, Montgomery, Alabama 36117
☎ 334.555.5555 (cell) — ✉ mhartley@email.net

November 15, 20XX

Roy Watson
Vice President, Sales
TopLine Products
334 Tulip Lane
Montgomery, AL 35118

Dear Mr. Watson:

Most sales professionals come with an adjective. They are in pharmaceutical sales, or in media sales, or in equipment sales. I am in sales, too. But I don't come with an adjective.

I come with a track record of making my customers look so good that they choose me, personally, to become their preferred supplier. You'll find seven proofs of my contributions on the next pages, the kinds of contributions I'd like to offer TopLine.

I've chosen each example in my resume to reflect the following personal, professional code that guides all I do:

❑ Making the sales numbers is good; building the relationships that keep those numbers growing is better.

❑ Meeting the customers' stated needs is good; learning their business well enough to anticipate their *next* need is better.

❑ Identifying your competitors is good; knowing how to act faster than they can is better.

My employer likes what I do for the firm, and, more important, my customers like what I do for them. But my industry is a stable one, and the challenges are missing. Hence I am "testing the waters" with this confidential application.

As a next step, I'd like to hear about TopLine's unique sales needs in your own words. May I call in a few days to arrange a time to do that?

Sincerely,

Mark Hartley

Mark Hartley

Encl: Resume

Figure 10.38: A cover letter for a sales professional (contributed by Don Orlando, MBA, CPRW, JCTC, CCM, CCMC, CJSS).

Step 10

MATT LENNOX

630-444-4550 ~ mlennox@email.net
456 Cycle Street ~ Bolingbrook, IL 60902

Sonya Ivanovich
Human Resources Manager
Nuplace Inc.
656 Wilson Street
Chicago, IL 60999

Dear Ms. Ivanovich:

Leadership by example … Maintained high personal sales results as I progressed through increasingly responsible workforce management roles.

Creativity and vision … Initiated major staff development programs and repaired damaged relations with district leaders to transform a sales team's attitude from indifference to high performance and productivity.

Motivator … Established clear goals and effectively kept the team focused on achieving annual performance objectives.

Although my resume reflects my more notable accomplishments, it does not accurately reflect my passion for bringing out the best in others. Causing transformation in business strategy, staff performance, and financial results is what I do best. I have consistently succeeded by …

► Pioneering big ideas and inspiring teams to go above and beyond pre-conceived limits for the greater good.

► Redesigning and executing organizational initiatives to improve performance and increase productivity.

► Managing meaningful relationships with internal and external clients.

► Developing effective products and programs that attract new business.

Let me convince you that I have the ability to expedite realizing your organizational goals. Please permit me to present some ideas I have formulated at your earliest convenience.

Sincerely,

Matt Lennox

Matt Lennox

Enclosure: Resume

Six years of experience with Fortune 50 Wells Fargo and the American Red Cross

Additional background in professional services and management consulting

MBA with focus in Organizational Development and Sales Leadership from DePaul University

BBA in Marketing and Finance from Augustan College

Figure 10.39: A cover letter for a sales and marketing professional (contributed by Marjorie Sussman, MRW, ACRW, CPRW).

Step 10

Jerry Levine

(440) 347-5263 • jlevine@email.net • 5482 Meadow Wood Blvd., Lyndhurst, OH 44124

Senior executive delivering double- and triple-digit growth by attaining strategic goals, developing win-win business partnerships, and providing skillful, proactive leadership.

March 22, 20xx

Andrea Drake
Vice President, Human Resources
American Conglomerate Technologies
888 Smithville Road
Toledo, OH 44456

Dear Ms. Drake:

Building sustainable growth and profitability is what I do best. I would like to build value now for American Conglomerate Technologies as its next vice president of operations.

Please consider the following examples of my past achievements as harbingers of what I could do for American Conglomerate Technologies:

- **Converted a start-up R&D organization bearing a 65% sales loss into a profitable and growing manufacturing and marketing company, with gross margins at 50+%.** How? By expanding sales to existing customers; creating new, high-margin products for other markets; zealously seeking out inefficiencies; and streamlining operations.

- Grew a division of a midsized company by cultivating strategic relationships with large customers and suppliers, negotiating long-term agreements, developing innovative solutions to reduce costs for all involved, and **increasing sales by nearly 500%**.

- **Turned around a failing business unit of a Fortune 500 company** by modernizing operations, expanding product offerings, revamping supplier networks, and **growing sales by an average of 23% annually**.

You will find more details of these and other accomplishments on my enclosed resume.

In closing, I would be delighted to learn more about the opportunities and challenges that you currently face and to explore how I could best help you define, meet, and exceed your goals. I will call in a week from your receipt of this letter to arrange an interview.

Sincerely,

Jerry Levine

Jerry Levine

Enclosure

Figure 10.40: A cover letter for a senior executive (contributed by Reya Stevens, MA, MRW).

Step 10

Edward Eric Martin

1440 Dahlia Lane Denver, Colorado 80002
✆ eem@martin.net ☎ 720.339.5555 (home) – 720.855.5556 (office) – 720.360.5557 (cell)

May 6, 20XX

Robert Wendal
Director
Universal Services Foundation
433 Mountain Pass
Denver, CO 80003

Dear Mr. Wendal:

As soon as I saw your call for applications to be your **special assistant**, I made putting this package together my first priority. What drives me is the lifelong conviction that strategic connections between cultures must bolster real world globalization. That was the underlying theme of my work as a Rockefeller Foundation Humanities Fellow earlier in my career. It drives my efforts on the Board of the Professional Educational Organization International, delivering classes in English and computer skills that prepare learners in the developing world to benefit from globalization faster.

Many application packages that I've reviewed have not given me clear and compelling evidence that the authors understand the problems I would ask them to solve. In addition, I rarely have seen transferable examples of the ability to think critically, remove obstacles effectively, and do both in a "real world" tempo. I have tried to avoid those distractions in the documents you are about to read. That's why my resume may not look like others you have seen.

Right at the top is my pledge of value to you and the foundation. You should see me demonstrating those six elements on the job from day one. Further evidence of this value are eight, very brief, selected outcomes made to constituencies I've served. Finally, I've included a leadership addendum: four extended examples to illustrate not just my performance, but also my critical thinking and communication skills. As you read, I hope a central thought stands out clearly: I am very comfortable connecting social institutions with private entities to produce synergies that overcome formidable obstacles.

Of course, I've followed the directions to apply online. But if my track record, philosophy, and background appeal to you, I'd like to hear about the foundation's special needs in your own words. May I call in a few days to arrange time for that purpose?

Sincerely,

Edward Martin

Edward E. Martin

Encl.: Resume and Leadership Addendum

Figure 10.41: A cover letter for a special assistant (contributed by Don Orlando, MBA, CPRW, JCTC, CCM, CCMC, CJSS).

Step 10

Charles W. Moran

3061 Saguaro Loop Mesa, Arizona 85201
✉ charlesmoran001@email.net ☎480.285.6733

September 12, 20XX

Arthur Hayes
Vice President, Manufacturing
TopLine Products
987 Mesa Avenue
Phoenix, AZ 85233

Dear Mr. Hayes:

> *Payoffs:* Put an **end to unscheduled shutdowns** and **saved thousands** in expensive repairs… Cut a **30 percent reject rate to 1.5 percent in 5 days**, 2 days early—without disturbing production… **Fixed an environmental problem** in just 5 weeks that once cost my employer thousands in EPA fines.

You have just read the 47-word version of my resume. I've sent this package to you because I want to help you make the production numbers you want for TopLine.

I love what I do. And the reason this is the first real resume I've ever had is because companies always sought me out. So when my recent employer downsized me a few days ago, I took responsibility for matching what I do with what companies need.

That's why the next pages don't look like a typical resume. I thought you deserved to see 6 profit-building capabilities I want to put at TopLine's disposal at once as your newest plant maintenance supervisor. Backing them up are 9 examples with payoffs like the ones you just read.

I'm a lot better at listening to people than I am writing to them. So I'd like to call in a few days to see how I can help you.

Sincerely,

Charles Moran

Charles W. Moran

Encl: Resume

Figure 10.42: A cover letter for a plant maintenance supervisor (contributed by Don Orlando, MBA, CPRW, JCTC, CCM, CCMC, CJSS).

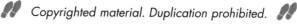

Index of Contributors

Laurie Berenson, CPRW
Sterling Career Concepts LLC
P.O. Box 142
Park Ridge, NJ 07656
Phone: (201) 573-8282
Fax: (201) 255-0137
Website: www.sterlingcareerconcepts.com
Email: laurie@sterlingcareerconcepts.com

August Cohen, CARW, NCRW, CPRW
Get Hired Stay Hired LLC
Phone: (919) 816-7878
Website: GetHiredStayHired.com

Angie Jones, CPRW, CEIC
Haute Résumé & Career Services LLC
9900 Nicholas Street, Suite 390
Omaha, NE 68114
Phone: (866) 695-9318
Fax: (866) 596-0153
Website: www.ANewResume.com
Email: angie@anewresume.com

Beverley Neil, CRW, CERW
d'Scriptive Words
P.O. Box 3281
Victoria Point West, QLD 4165, Australia
Website: d-scriptivewords.com
Email: beverley@d-scriptivewords.com

Don Orlando, MBA, CPRW, JCTC, CCM, CCMC, CJSS
The McLean Group
3001 Zelda Road, Suite 400
Montgomery, AL 36106
Phone: (334) 264-2020
Website: www.linkedin.com/in/donorlandocareercoach
Email: yourcareercoach@charterinternet.com

Barbara Safani, MA, CERW, NCRW, CRPW, CCM, COIS
Career Solvers
470 Park Avenue South, 10th Floor
New York, NY 10016
Phone: (866) 333-1800
Website: www.careersolvers.com
Email: info@careersolvers.com

Reya Stevens, MA, MRW
StandOut Résumés
29 Driscoll Avenue
Maynard, MA 01754
Phone: (978) 897-1574
Website: www.StandoutResumes.com
Email: reya@standoutresumes.com

Marjorie Sussman, MRW, ACRW, CPRW
Dover Productions
148 Undercliff Avenue #3
Edgewater, NJ 07020
Phone: (201) 941-8237
Website: www.linkedin.com/in/marjoriesussmanmrw
Email: marjorie1130@aol.com

Roleta Fowler Vasquez, CPRW, CEIP
Wordbusters Résumé and Writing Services
433 Quail Court
Fillmore, CA 93015-1137
Phone: (805) 524-3493
Website: www.WordBusters.com
Email: wbresumes@yahoo.com

Charlotte Weeks, CCMC, NCRW, CPRW
Weeks Career Services, Inc.
703 S. Dearborn
Chicago, IL 60605
Phone: (312) 662-1410
Website: www.weekscareerservices.com
Email: charlotte@weekscareerservices.com

Kelly Welch, MHRM, GPHR, CPBS, CPRW, COID
YES Career Services
P.O. Box 38003
Raleigh, NC 27627
Phone: (919) 744-8866
Website: www.YesCareerServices.com
Email: kelly@yescareerservices.com

Index

A

accomplishments, 30–31, 43
  skill statements, 86
  summarizing, 87
  third paragraph finalization, 98
  third paragraph foundations,
    87–98
Accomplishments That Support Your
  Brand worksheet, 43
achievements. *See* accomplishments
acquired knowledge, 25
administrative and general business
  keywords, 122
airline ground operations manager,
  161
application developer, 59, 173
areas of expertise
  first paragraph, 53
  personal branding, 23–24
Areas of Expertise worksheet, 24
assets/features, 7, 16, 20–25, 34–35,
  51, 67, 121

B

benefits, 4, 7, 16, 51, 67, 121
Benefits of Your Qualifications
worksheet, 70
Berenson, Laurie, 223
brand identification, 136–137
business branding, 2
business consultant, 60
business keywords, 122
business strategy innovator, 215

C

call to action, 110–111
career branding. *See* personal
  branding

certifications, 25
characteristics, 20
chief executive officer, 57, 93, 98,
  163, 169
chief information officer, 57, 77, 157
children's television show host, 81
civil engineer, 37
closing, 117–118
Closing Paragraph Foundation
  worksheets, 111–116
Cohen, August, 223
columns, 132
competitive edge, 7, 16, 36–37, 51,
  67, 73, 121
Complete Cover Letter Draft
  worksheet, 120
compliance keywords, 122–123
compliance officer, 40
condensing, 129
contact information, 132
corporate trainer, 54, 74, 97, 145,
  193
Cover Letter Purpose worksheet, 20
Create a Tagline worksheet, 44
customer service manager, 40

D

degrees, 25
Degrees, Licenses, and Certifications
  worksheet, 25
department administrator, 78
Dream Job Description worksheet, 19

E

electronic engineer, 55, 75, 88, 149
email versions, 138
Employer Challenges and Possible
  Solutions worksheet, 33
employers' challenges, 32–33

employers' needs, 7–11, 32–33,
  102–103
employers' requirements, 25–29, 68
employers' vulnerabilities, 11–12
esteem needs, 10
EvelynSalvador.com, 4
event planner, 91, 159

F

features. *See* assets/features
Final Draft of Your Brand Message
  worksheet, 46
finance keywords, 123
first draft, 120–129
first paragraph
  areas of expertise, 53
  draw in readers, 52
  finalize, 63
  foundations, 54–62
  personal brand message, 48–51
  position particulars, 53
  purpose, 48
First Paragraph Foundation
  worksheets, 54–62
The Five Critical Components of
  Personal Branding worksheet, 17
fonts, 132
formatting, 132
foundations
  closing paragraph, 111–116
  first paragraph, 54–62
  second paragraph, 74–81
  fourth paragraph, 104–106
  profession-specific letters, 204–215
  situational letters, 140–203
Fourth Paragraph Foundation
  worksheets, 105–106
freelance event manager, 62

G–H

goals, assessment, 19–20
golf course superintendent, 56, 75, 89, 151
grammar, 129
graphic designer, 36, 55, 74, 88, 147
graphology. *See* handwriting analysis
ground operations manager, 56
handwriting analysis, 117–118
health care executive, 62, 94, 187
higher education senior administrator, 58
human resources professional, 90, 205

I

Ideas to Draw in Your Reader worksheet, 52
industry issues/needs, 102–103
information systems director, 61, 189
inventory control keywords, 123–124
irrelevant information, 129
IT executive, 30, 80, 101
IT (information technology) keywords, 124–125
IT security solutions architect, 76, 155
italic, 132

J–K

Job Requirements and Qualifications worksheet, 69
Jones, Angie, 223
keywords, 23, 121–128
    administrative and general business, 122
    compliance, 122–123
    finance, 123
    information technology, 124–125
    inventory control, 123–124
    purchasing, 125
    research, 125–126
    training and development, 127
Keywords for Your Specific Profession worksheet, 127

L

land acquisition professional, 57
letterhead designs, 133–135
licenses, 25

M

management consultant, 78, 103, 183
manufacturing executive, 55, 75, 87, 143
Maslow, Abraham, 7–10
Maslow's hierarchy of needs, 7–10
masthead, 132
marketing or brand manager, 56, 62, 203, 209
marketing specialist, 40, 102, 218
Match Your Assets to Employer Requirements worksheet, 29
media writer/editor, 177
message, 40–46, 48–51
    employer's needs, 102–103
    fourth paragraph, 100, 104–106
    industry issues/needs, 102–103
    passion statement, 100–101
    story, compelling, 104
misdirected information, 129
mission statements, 137

N–O

nanotechnologist, 175
Neil, Beverley, 223
new business development director, 59
Ogilvy, David, 2
operations manager, 92
Orlando, Don, 223
Other Acquired Knowledge or Related Skills worksheet, 25

P

The Particulars You Need to Convey worksheet, 53
passion statement, 100–101
perceived value, 3
personal attributes, 20
Personal Attributes and Characteristics worksheet, 21–22
Personal Brand Exercise worksheet, 6
Personal Brand Message First Draft worksheet, 6
personal branding
    accomplishments, 30–31, 43
    acquired knowledge, 25
    areas of expertise, 23–24
    assets/features, 7, 16, 20–25, 34–35

benefits, 4, 7, 16
    building, 13–14
    business branding, 2
    campaign, 12–13
    certifications, 25
    characteristics, 20
    competitive edge, 7, 16, 36–37
    critical components, 7, 16–18
    defined, 3
    degrees, 25
    developing, 12–13
    employers' challenges, 32–33
    employers' needs, 7–11, 32–33
    employers' requirements, 25–29
    employers' vulnerabilities, 11–12
    esteem needs, 10
    goals, assessment, 19–20
    identifying, 5–7
    keywords, 23
    licenses, 25
    Maslow's hierarchy of needs, 7–10
    message, 40–46
    perceived value, 3
    personal attributes, 20
    physiological/survival needs, 9
    promoting, 7
    related skills, 25
    return on investment, 7, 12, 16, 39
    safety needs, 9
    sample cover letter, 51
    self-actualization needs, 10
    slogans, 43
    social/belonging needs, 9
    strategy, 42
    taglines, 43–44
    talents, multiple, 4–5
    transferable skills, 23–24
    value proposition, 7, 16, 37–38
    worksheets, 6, 17–22, 24–25, 27, 29, 31, 33, 37–38, 41–42, 44, 45
personal trainer, 58, 167
Personally Branded Cover Letter Paragraph Foundation worksheets, 49–50
personally branded letters, 216–221
Peters, Tom, 3
pharmaceutical executive, 30
physiological/survival needs, 9
plant maintenance supervisor, 221
position particulars, first paragraph, 53

profession-specific letters, 141
   Foundation worksheets, 204–215
program director, 201
project manager, 207
proofreading, 129
Prospective Employer's Requirements
   worksheet, 27
purchasing agent, 40
purchasing keywords, 125

Q–R

qualifications, 68–70
real estate professional, 90, 153
redundant information, 129
regional director of sales, 54
registered nurse, 30
research keywords, 125–126
resume writers, 37
retail manager, 62, 91, 195
return on investment, personal
   branding, 7, 12, 16, 39, 51, 67, 72,
   121
Revised Draft of Your Brand Message
   worksheet, 41
ROI on Your Value Proposition
   worksheet, 72

S

Safani, Barbara, 223
safety needs, 9
sales associate, 30, 103, 217–218
sales manager, 36, 62, 93, 97, 197,
   199, 203
salutation, 117
school program director, 61, 96, 185
school psychologist, 96, 102, 179
second paragraph
   assets, 67
   benefits, 67
   competitive edge, 67, 73
   developing, 66–67
   employer's requirements, 68
   features, 67
   finalizing, 82–84
   foundations, 74–81
   qualifications, 68–70
   return on investment, 67, 72
   value proposition, 71
Second Paragraph Development
   worksheet, 82–84

Second Paragraph Foundation
   worksheets, 74–81
secretary, 36
self-actualization needs, 10
self-branding. *See* personal branding
senior college administrator,
   101–102, 171
senior executive, 219
senior financial sales manager, 54
signature, 117–118
situational letters, Foundation
   worksheets, 140–203
skill statements, 86
slogans, personal branding, 43, 136
social/belonging needs, 9
social worker, employers'
   requirements
special assistant, 58, 102, 220
spelling, 129
State Your Passion worksheet, 101
statement of interest, 110
Stevens, Reya, 224
store manager, 79
story, compelling, 104
strategy, personal branding, 42
Sussman, Marjorie, 224

T

taglines, 43–44, 136
talents, multiple, 4–5
teacher, 61, 79–80, 96, 102, 179, 191
television host/reporter, 101, 165
testimonials, 136
third paragraph Foundation
   worksheets, 87–98
tone, 129
training and development keywords,
   127
training and development manager,
   211
transferable skills, 23–24
Transferable Skills worksheet, 24
typewritten name, 118

U–V

value proposition, 7, 16, 37–38, 51,
   71, 121
Value Proposition of Your Benefits
   worksheet, 71
Vasquez, Roleta Fowler, 224

vice president, 77, 81, 95, 181
vice president of new business
   development, 40
vice president of research, 60

W

Ways Your Features Help Employers
   worksheet, 35
website developer, 36, 213
Weeks, Charlotte, 224
Welch, Kelly, 224
white space, 132
winning formula, 66
word processor, 36
worksheets
   Accomplishments That Support
      Your Brand, 43
   Areas of Expertise, 24
   Benefits of Your Qualifications, 70
   Closing Paragraph Foundation
      1–31, 111–116
   Complete Cover Letter Draft, 120
   Cover Letter Purpose, 20
   Create a Tagline, 44
   Degrees, Licenses, and
      Certifications, 25
   Dream Job Description, 19
   Employer Challenges and Possible
      Solutions, 33
   Final Draft of Your Brand
      Message, 46
   First Paragraph foundations,
      54–62
   The Five Critical Components of
      Personal Branding, 17
   Fourth Paragraph foundations,
      105–106
   Ideas to Draw in Your Reader, 52
   Job Requirements and
      Qualifications, 69
   Keywords for Your Specific
      Profession, 127
   Match Your Assets to Employer
      Requirements, 29
   Other Acquired Knowledge or
      Related Skills, 25
   The Particulars You Need to
      Convey, 53
   Personal Attributes and
      Characteristics, 21–22
   Personal Brand Exercise, 6

Personal Brand Message First Draft, 6

Personally Branded Cover Letter Paragraph foundations, 49–50

profession-specific letters, foundations, 204–215

Prospective Employer's Requirements, 27

Revised Draft of Your Brand Message, 41

ROI on Your Value Proposition, 72

Second Paragraph Development, 82–84

Second Paragraph foundations, 74–81

situational letters, foundations, 140–203

State Your Passion, 101

Third Paragraph foundations, 87–97

Transferable Skills, 24

Value Proposition of Your Benefits, 71

Ways Your Features Help Employers, 35

Your Approach to Meeting an Organization's Needs, 103

Your Brand Strategy, 42

Your Closing Paragraph, 116

Your Competitive Edge, 37

Your First Paragraph, 63

Your Fourth Paragraph, 107

Your Interesting Story, 104

Your Key Accomplishments, 31

Your Key Competitive Edge Components, 73

Your Matching Accomplishments, 86

Your Own Personal Branding Components, 18, 45

Your Primary Areas of Expertise, 53

Your ROI to Prospective Employers, 39

Your Statement of Interest, 110

Your Third Paragraph, 98

Your Value Proposition, 38

X–Z

Your Approach to Meeting an Organization's Needs worksheet, 103

Your Brand Strategy worksheet, 42

Your Closing Paragraph worksheet, 116

Your Competitive Edge worksheet, 37

Your First Paragraph worksheet, 63

Your Fourth Paragraph worksheet, 107

Your Interesting Story worksheet, 104

Your Key Accomplishments worksheet, 31

Your Key Competitive Edge Components worksheet, 73

Your Matching Accomplishments worksheet, 86

Your Own Personal Branding Components worksheet, 18, 45

Your Primary Areas of Expertise worksheet, 53

Your ROI to Prospective Employers worksheet, 39

Your Statement of Interest worksheet, 110

Your Third Paragraph worksheet, 98

Your Value Proposition worksheet, 38